Language in Ernst Bloch's
Speculative Materialism

Historical Materialism Book Series

Editorial Board

Loren Balhorn (*Berlin*)
David Broder (*Rome*)
Sebastian Budgen (*Paris*)
Steve Edwards (*London*)
Juan Grigera (*London*)
Marcel van der Linden (*Amsterdam*)
Peter Thomas (*London*)
Gavin Walker (*Montréal*)

VOLUME 299

Bloch Bibliothek

Series Editors

Johan Siebers (*University of London*)
Catherine Moir (*University of Sheffield*)
Peter Thompson (*University of Sheffield*)

VOLUME 2

The titles published in this series are listed at *brill.com/blb*

Language in Ernst Bloch's Speculative Materialism

Nathaniel J. P. Barron

Haymarket Books
Chicago, IL

First published in 2023 by Brill Academic Publishers, The Netherlands
© 2023 Koninklijke Brill NV, Leiden, The Netherlands

Published in paperback in 2024 by
Haymarket Books
P.O. Box 180165
Chicago, IL 60618
773-583-7884
www.haymarketbooks.org

ISBN: 979-8-88890-326-1

Distributed to the trade in the US through Consortium Book Sales and
Distribution (www.cbsd.com) and internationally through Ingram
Publisher Services International (www.ingramcontent.com).

This book was published with the generous support of Lannan
Foundation, Wallace Action Fund, and the Marguerite Casey Foundation.

Special discounts are available for bulk purchases by organizations and
institutions. Please call 773-583-7884 or email info@haymarketbooks.org
for more information.

Cover art and design by David Mabb. Cover art is an adaption
developed from *Luibov Popova Untitled Textile Design on William Morris
Wallpaper for Historical Materialism*, edition of 100, screen print on
wallpaper (2010).

Printed in the United States.

Library of Congress Cataloging-in-Publication data is available.

In loving memory of Robina Walker (1932–2012)
& Bridget Coyle (1923–2013)

∴

Contents

Acknowledgements

This book has been a long time in the making. My journey with it certainly has not been straight and narrow. It was produced in stays in London, Glasgow, Bochum, Berlin, Mannheim, Rugeley, Birmingham, and Liège. It has seen me transition into fatherhood and marriage, and the book itself, perhaps like me, has undergone changes which render it almost unrecognisable from its earlier form. Bloch's adage that hope can be disappointed certainly came to define the original PhD thesis from which this book emerged. And, if I were to be honest with myself, the present work, while better approximating the original idea, still carries with it undertones of 'something's missing'.

And yet, the journey I've gone on with this book has been one that has enriched my life. I have met people, all of whose insight, support, and friendship has made the work better than it would have been without them. Although naturally I am solely responsible for its shortcomings, David Bowie's line that 'I never thought I'd need so many people' rings true here too.

For instance, Johan Siebers's generosity of spirit was matched by his deep knowledge of the philosophical tradition; I could not have had a better guide. Volker Schneider first taught me to understand Bloch in the German – I still greatly appreciate his and Gordana's hospitality during my first forays into the Hegel Archive. Ifor Duncan, Jessica Feely, and Daniel Neofetou all acted as excellent partners in discussion. In their own ways, knowingly or not, they helped clarify Bloch for me. And I am indebted to Rainer Zimmermann, who was also very helpful in casting a critical eye on an earlier version of the text.

Thanks should also be given to those involved in this book at Historical Materialism: Cat Moir and Sam Dolbear's respective reviews helped me to rethink my aims, and Danny Hayward and Simon Mussell helped me to get the work over what often appeared to be an ever receding line.

But most of all I would like to thank Justine and Rauree. They have taught me what it truly means to move with an invariant of direction. *Incipit vita nova.*

Introduction

The sentence which [Bloch] often quotes from Isaac Babel, 'Banality is counter-revolution', is valid in the first instance for language itself ...

OSKAR NEGT[1]

∴

The overriding claim of this book is straightforward. Just as Jean-Jacques Lecercle has found in *A Thousand Plateaus* 'the outline of ... a Marxist philosophy of language',[2] so I take it that Ernst Bloch's corpus similarly provides us categories with which to achieve the same ends. Bloch, I will argue, equally develops 'alternative principles and determinations for a concept of language', as Lecercle discovers in Deleuze and Guattari.[3] Utopia, I argue, stands at the centre of these principles and determinations. Indeed, a banal conception of language for Ernst Bloch would consist of an absence of utopia, just as a concept of being or of culture more broadly, without utopia, forgets that future tense which was so vital to Bloch's philosophy. The question of where Bloch can be positioned within Marxism's engagement with the language question, and so then what Bloch offers up to a Marxist interrogation of language, is the key concern for this book.

What use is Bloch to a Marxist philosophy of language? Reminding ourselves of Valentin Nikolaevich Voloshinov's work, composed during the Russian Revolution and constituting a clear starting point for Marxist philosophy of language, will initially help to shed light on how, in fact, relating Bloch and the question of language is not so straightforward. Voloshinov was of course one of the first, if not the first, Marxists to seriously develop a philosophy of language: 'Problems in the philosophy of language have acquired exceptional topicality and importance for Marxism at the present time'[4] writes Voloshinov, in an early plan composed in 1927/28, of what would later become his notable work *Marx-*

---

1 Negt 1975, p. 15.
2 Lecercle 2006, p. 118. The same operation is evident in Peter Ives's (2004) work on Antonio Gramsci and Philip Hogh's (2017) on Adorno.
3 Lecercle 2008, p. 476.
4 Voloshinov 2004, p. 228, see also p. 232.

ism and the Philosophy of Language. In the aftermath of the Russian Revolution, Voloshinov's sense was that a novel philosophical approach to language was taking hold, granting language a growing importance in culture and in cultural study. Marxism needed to keep up with these shifts and Voloshinov set to work.

The context which sharpened Voloshinov's mind on this issue was a growing imperative for Marxism to develop a comprehensive 'science' of the 'ideological refraction of socio-economic being', with which a philosophy of culture centring on the word was synonymous.[5] As I show in a later chapter, 'refraction' is a concept of Voloshinov's that seeks to grasp culture (and one might say, other superstructural functions of society) not merely as reflecting in a simplistic manner the economic conditions of existence, but instead in some sense helping to shape those conditions as a real material force. In a departure from orthodox economism, for Voloshinov a concept of language had to grow in stature as a serious topic of concern for Marxism because, as he contended, 'the word [*slovo*] is the ideological phenomenon *par excellence*', indeed it is 'the most faithful refractive ideological medium'; 'all ideological content in general' passes through and is accompanied by the word.[6] Language took on a far from banal role in the still young revolution.

So far, Bloch and Voloshinov – this key initiator of Marxist philosophy of language – have much to share. Bloch too is famous for lending more credence to culture in understanding and changing class society. However, if philosophy was 'beginning to develop beneath the sign of the word', Voloshinov then sought to develop a Marxian account by struggling against a specific adversary: what Voloshinov termed the 'cult of the word' that was to his mind in full-swing as a counter-project to what he saw as his own vocation.[7] This 'cult' stood for a general tendency to detach language from 'the surrounding social actuality' of which, for Voloshinov, language was a part and from which language arose and always returned to; as such, the wider 'conditions of discursive intercourse' were not taken into account in the ongoing attempts in linguistics to grasp the core essence of language.[8] Clearly, however novel, the concept of 'refraction' did not imply a simple and crude reversal of economism, such that language becomes a severed force independent of wider social being. Voloshinov singles out Stéphane Mallarmé, Stefan George's Symbolism, and the Futurists as representatives of this 'new' and (for Voloshinov) petty bourgeois 'perception

---

5   Voloshinov 2004, p. 229.
6   Ibid.
7   Voloshinov 2004, p. 232.
8   Voloshinov 2004, p. 230.

of the word'.[9] But the German Expressionists are held up as the key protagonists in this new concept of language – their 'verbal radicalism' was 'alien' to the classical vision of the word in which the word 'piously' conformed to something higher than itself, to 'the *realia* standing behind the word'.[10] The German Expressionists epitomised, then, the worst of this 'cult' attitude. The 'self-sufficient word' of these aesthetic movements, Voloshinov claimed, would also come to influence the theory of literariness developed by the Russian Formalists, which, interestingly, Voloshinov worked both with and against.[11]

What Voloshinov found so problematic about this 'cult of the word' was that it contained 'a two-fold estrangement of the word from actuality'; that the word was viewed as detached from its social context merely reflected the word's lack of political freedom in a socio-historical period of authoritarian suppression, a clear detachment 'of the word from the deed' was baked into this new perception of language.[12] And in a philosophical iteration of the same point, the word contained an estrangement from 'an actuality external to it', which the word, in the bourgeoisie's 'middle period' – in this class's realism and its naturalism of an earlier phase – was meant to depict as its foremost function; and so this 'separation of the word from the concrete thing, from the real' is said to have 'reached its extreme in Expressionism'.[13] For Voloshinov this new-found 'independent force of the word' was a tendency which gave rise to the 'utopian radicalism' and 'mystical anarchism' of German Expressionism.[14] The word detached from its real conditions of existence only spawns abstractions.

All of this only then seems to diminish the importance of any contribution that Bloch might make to a Marxist philosophy of language. For Bloch's utopian philosophy is said to be the foremost philosophical-linguistic representative of German Expressionism.[15] Should one follow Voloshinov's position on Expressionism to its logical conclusion, it becomes apparent that Bloch remains redundant when the ambition is to contribute to a Marxist philosophy of language: will not any contribution he offers render language utopian in the pejorative sense of that term; that is, will it not only produce a notion that sees language as disjoined from the real conditions of language's existence, thus rendering language politically ineffective? The argument of this book, however, is

---

9   Voloshinov 2004, p. 241.
10 Voloshinov 2004, pp. 238–9.
11 See Voloshinov 2004, p. 240.
12 Voloshinov 2004, pp. 241–2.
13 Voloshinov 2004, p. 241.
14 Voloshinov 2004, p. 242.
15 See Moir 2019b, p. 303.

that when one digs into Bloch's works (one does not have to descend too far) a nascent theory of language is there to be discovered, one that is constructed in the vein of Bloch's 'warm stream' of Marxism, and thus one that is useful to Marxism itself. As I show later on, engaging with Bloch on the question of language even allows us to scrutinise the notion of the 'real' in Voloshinov's own work. Bloch lends to us the idea that transcending real conditions of existence is itself a real process of material being. The drawback with Expressionism was how it understood this process and how it related it to a radical collective politics.

Recent scholarship has in fact already shown this claim to stand steady: Bloch's work can be deployed for a materialist philosophy of language. Cat Moir's research into Bloch's 'materialist philosophy of language' focuses precisely on Bloch's Expressionist inheritance,[16] which Moir explores via Bloch's Nietzsche-reception, and which she argues, was 'at least as productive as Bloch's engagement with Marx'.[17] I will return to the problem with this separation that Moir establishes between what Bloch draws from the legacies of Marx and Nietzsche. It is a problem and a separation, admittedly, which emerges from the very tradition of German Expressionism itself. Moir's work can be drawn on, however, to provide an initial sense of why Voloshinov's assessment of Expressionism is not cause to abandon the ambitions of this book.

Moir relies on two texts, *The Spirit of Utopia* and *Experimentum Mundi*, that is, the first and last of Bloch's works, to analyse Bloch's Nietzscheanism and its impact on his materialist philosophy of language. Moir demonstrates how the influence of Nietzschean positions – those concerning the incompleteness of reality, the value-generating power of art and culture, and more besides – were assimilated by the German Expressionist movement and indeed impacted and helped shape Bloch's implicit philosophy of language.[18] Particularly important here for Bloch, according to Moir, was Nietzsche's claim that language does not refer to or represent 'a given or immutable truth'.[19] Instead, in the vein of a post-Kantian perspectivism, Nietzsche saw language as socially constructed and as hinging on the creativity of social valuation, as opposed to the certainty of truth.[20] Language, according to this position, does not re-present the reality of an established order or of an immutable truth, but creatively shapes reality – or what is deemed real – with its own emotional intentionality. Moir

---

16   Moir 2019b, pp. 306 and 318.
17   Moir 2019b, p. 318.
18   See Moir 2019b, pp. 304–6.
19   Moir 2019b, p. 305.
20   See Moir 2019b, p. 309.

argues that this non-objective, non-rational, creative philosophy of language, which viewed language as being capable of conjuring up new realities – 'language as essentially a creative medium'[21] – was an inspirational impulse for much of the Expressionist movement,[22] Bloch included. It certainly echoes precisely what Voloshinov found so problematic with the 'cult of the word', which, as Moir says of Expressionism, intended to transform society by constructing 'a new language', or at least a new ordering of old language.[23] Indeed a recurrent drawback of its philosophical vision of language was that Expressionism either lacked a clear idea or was ambiguous on its purported aim of societal transformation.[24] And yet however much Voloshinov sought to create a concept of language that could contest Expressionism, undoubtedly his notion of 'refraction' shares this active role that Nietzsche, and later the Expressionists, attributed to language.

However, Nietzsche's influence on Bloch's incipient philosophy of language is not said to be total, without qualifications. Nietzsche's irrationalism[25] and his concomitant rejection of 'verbal realism' were features of his linguistic philosophy that Bloch was less willing to embrace, as Moir's work shows.[26] While purportedly assimilating many features of Nietzsche's project, Bloch could not accept the radical disjunction which Nietzsche's linguistic nominalism posited between language and reality. Even if the creative notion of language Nietzsche had developed was appealing to Bloch and was clearly taken up by him, Bloch developed instead a realist epistemology behind this creativity, indeed he 'ascrib[ed] a certain logic to the world which ... language is able to access'.[27] Bloch's more rational Nietzscheanism, Moir suggests, is tied to a greater concern on Bloch's part with the goal of practically transforming society in the form of a radical collective politics.[28] Expression, yes, but an Expressionism of the real and of a 'we'. And indeed, the Hegelian influence on Bloch in this respect is articulated by Moir very much along lines similar to Voloshinov's realist concept of refraction (see Chapter 3).[29] Already,

---

21   Moir 2019b, p. 312.
22   See Moir 2019b, p. 311.
23   See Moir 2019b, pp. 311–13.
24   See Taylor 1990.
25   See Moir 2019b, p. 329.
26   Emden 2005, p. 40.
27   Moir 2019b, p. 324.
28   See Moir 2019b, pp. 305 and 329.
29   See Moir 2019b, p. 325. Moir suggests that, for Bloch, the access that language has with reality comes via the word's relation to concepts. Conceptual structures can, and do in fact, accurately reflect real world logic, and language sensuously expresses this accurate

then, there is a possibility that despite Bloch's Expressionism, or because of its peculiar inheritance or reception, Bloch does not seek to fully detach the word from its conditions of existence. As I show below in a later chapter, a Blochian concept of 'refraction' nevertheless departs from Voloshinov's own in key respects.

In sum, Moir's work gives rise to the question of how an incipient materialist philosophy of language in Bloch's corpus could be pressed further. Moir's useful research reveals a number of areas for further inquiry, and, in fact, does so due to its own drawbacks and omissions. Firstly, despite the evident merits of Moir's account there is a strong tendency to position Bloch's philosophy of language from the departure point of aesthetic composition, focusing as Moir does, quite rightly and insightfully, on the 'aesthetic and subjectivist spirit' of Expressionism.[30] The problem of Expressionism with respect to its ambiguity concerning societal transformation, then, is somewhat mirrored in Moir's own treatment. Moir's suggestion that Bloch's philosophy of language contained rationalist and collectivist-transformative intentions can therefore be unpacked further and given more weight. Admittedly this limitation is somewhat immanent to Bloch's work itself. As I will show later on in Chapter 2, Bloch's anacoluthon essay, key for my reading in this book, runs along these aesthetic lines. Reconstructive work is therefore required to extend an understanding of how the Expressionism which underlies Bloch's philosophy of language points not merely to a transformation of aesthetic concern but to a collective, social transformation. Despite some of his own tendencies, Bloch in fact intimates this need, and does so in relation to the anacoluthon, the key linguistic figure for my reading below. For instance, the context of the following passage is one where Bloch is attempting to distinguish an authentic 'speech-act irrationalism' from its artificial (*Kunstgriff*) use for reactionary ends (read: by Nazism):

reflection – words therefore relate to concepts just as much as they relate to one another (see Moir 2019b, p. 327). The issue of *refraction* arises here when Moir discusses Bloch's use of the musicological word '*umspielen*' to describe this linguistic articulation of real world logic via its relation to concepts – a German verb which 'means to paraphrase, or to express in a different way', such that the word and concept bear a non-identical relation (Moir 2019b, p. 326). As we will see in Chapter 3, if correct, this means that Bloch has an interesting account of *linguistic refraction* which, as such, draws him into the orbit of Voloshinov's work.

30   Moir 2019b, p. 330. Seth Taylor (1990, p. 5) will describe German Expressionism as deriving from classical 'philosophies of individualism', but will also note the movement's political, although not class-based, tendency (see Taylor 1990, pp. 37 and 48–53).

Of course, it is not just a matter of separating a darkly irrational tone from the speech act itself. Another, equally inverted, misconception of the *viva vox* must be avoided as well, wherein the living voice is categorized and understood entirely in terms of its literary form.[31]

The point here is that while Moir shows well that 'Bloch locates language at the front of the world process, transcending the limits of the merely empirical',[32] Moir's account of this process of transcending often refers only to artistic style and thereby gets caught up in the Nietzschean view of language as a creative action assigned to an individual artist (say the *meinen* of an *Übermensch*). This tendency is clearly observable in German Expressionism. Though this is not an explicit claim in Moir's account, the danger here is that linguistic creativity becomes theorised in the purview of an elitist contempt of mass society and the linguistic forms one finds there.[33] Instead, my claim, and one that pervades Bloch's work as evident in his concern for popular culture, is that the speech of the masses (the *allgemeinen*) also needs to evidence this same transcending movement within language – it cannot simply be reserved for the poetic and the litetrary. For Hegel, for instance, any purported purely creative act of ostension – which seems to be the intent of some Expressionists – presupposes the mediation of that act by universals (that is, by a community of consciousnesses).[34] This claim and its exploration would seem to affirm Moir's useful observation on Bloch's nascent concept of refraction, as noted above. The impression given by Moir's reading is that the 'question-like structure of the human-world relation', so key for Bloch's materialism, is only properly articulated by an *intent* of novelty in the realms of the aesthetic,[35] which need not become actualised as the concern or affair of the wider social being to which the Expressionist belongs.[36] As language is a form of collective praxis which stands at the front of the world process, one needs to see how Bloch's work

---

31   Bloch 1998, p. 501.

32   Moir 2019b, p. 321.

33   See Taylor 1990, pp. 29 and 52–7 and Lukács 1992.

34   See Forster 1998, pp. 204–5 and 207–12, which reads Hegel's 'Sense-certainty' section in the *Phenomenology of Spirit* as implying a collective backdrop for all individual speech acts: 'Hegel implies ... in a complex piece of wordplay, that any attempt to *meinen* something, that is, to *mean* it *by myself*, must fail because of the fact that "language ... is inherently *allgemein*", that is, employs *general concepts* which are *common to a whole community*'. See Hegel 1977, pp. 65–6, cf. p. 110: '"I" that is "We" and "We" that is "I"'.

35   Moir 2019b, p. 323.

36   On the importance of this point concerning novel use of language and its relationship to community in Hegel, see Forster 1998, pp. 223–5.

facilitates a view of language which sees its creativity as broader than its confinement to a *conscious, aesthetic deployment* which calls this frontal dimension of language forth in the figure of the genius. After all, as Moir notes, for
Bloch Marxist concepts had been too coldly distanced from the masses, and
thereby, in failing to reach them, they were unconvincing. The question that
goes unanswered here then is whether the creativity of language, '[l]anguage's
frontal character',[37] occupies the language of the masses, 'the speech patterns
of common people', as Bloch once wrote,[38] or whether indeed such language is
not segregated against them and left to an artistic elite, a 'literary "socialism"'.[39]
Grounds for the former trajectory become solid if one notes that Bloch was just
as much concerned with popular fiction as he was the avant-garde.[40]

Moreover, while Moir points to the left-wing tendencies of Bloch's Nietzsche-reception and to the associations Bloch draws between Nietzsche and
Marx on the score of their joint concern with transformative praxis and the
future,[41] Moir does not fully unpack how Bloch's implicit philosophy of language bears on his Marxism in any specific sense. Moir usefully highlights
that Nietzsche's prioritisation of creative subjectivity, pathos, and imagination
translate over into Bloch's attempt to draw out the 'warm stream' of Marxism,
which could help to revitalise Marxism in its task of reaching out to the masses
and bringing them to communism, yet this is not explored in depth.[42] This
insight could be pressed much further by placing Bloch's nascent philosophy of
language into dialogue with existing Marxist philosophy of language. This will
be achieved in Chapter 3, where I construct a comparative analysis of Bloch
and Voloshinov on the question of 'refraction'.

The third issue recoils back to the above point. While Moir teases out very
clearly the Nietzschean currents of Bloch's Expressionism, this is not, however,
connected back to the question of Expressionism's politics and to Bloch's fam-

---

37   Moir 2019b, p. 321.
38   Bloch 1998, p. 500.
39   Bloch 1998, p. 106.
40   See Bloch 1998, p. 109 and Freeman 2006. Despite noting their anti-authoritarianism,
      Taylor (1990, pp. 5–6) describes Expressionism and Nietzsche as 'elitist and antidemo-
      cratic'. As the well-known but otherwise dubious Russian linguist, and leading thinker of
      Marxist linguistics in Russia, Marr stated: 'All my creative linguistics ideas ... are not the
      outcome of work in the study. They were conceived and moulded in the course of my
      contacts with man and nature, in streets and market-places, in deserts and on the seas,
      in the mountains and in the steppes, by rivers and springs, on horseback and in trains –
      anywhere but in the study'. (Marr quoted in Gray 2002, p. 172).
41   See Moir 2019b, pp. 315–18. On Nietzsche's concern for the future, cf. Taylor 1990, p. 27.
42   See Moir 2019b, p. 315.

ous aesthetic dispute with Lukács. While touching on the borders of this issue, Moir's treatment does not therefore give appropriate attention to the question of fascism, nor to the connection that exists between Expressionism and the wider dispute that occupied Bloch and Lukács on utopianism.[43] Indeed, it should be recalled that as the most significant Marxist inheritor, protagonist, and defender of Expressionism, Bloch's disagreement with the 'untiring proponent'[44] of German Expressionism's fascistic essence (Lukács) is an avenue of inquiry that would significantly help to gauge the nature of Bloch's contribution to a Marxist philosophy of language. Commencing this line of inquiry will be achieved in Chapter 4.

Briefly noting one more contemporary instance that, as it were, puts Bloch to work in the context of language and materialism will be useful in order to set the record straight. In their recent analysis of how the *Logic* and the *Phenomenology of Spirit* relate as texts in Hegel's wider philosophical project, Comay and Ruda comment on the striking discrepancy between Hegel the writer and Hegel the live philosopher, between Hegel's 'legendary Swabian accent and his mesmerizingly idiosyncratic lecturing style', and Hegel as a man of the written word – that is, 'the bureaucratic style of his textbooks'.[45] On closer inspection, Hegel is said to incorporate the liveliness of speech into his texts, doing so via a punctuation mark – namely, the dash (–), placed both at the end of the *Phenomenology of Spirit* and at the beginning of the *Logic*.[46] The anacoluthon, then, is said to be the site from which Hegel's two texts meet, meeting precisely *as rupture*. And Comay and Ruda stake their reading of the Hegelian dash on 'an incompleteness and ungroundedness inherent in language ... that forces us to speak, think, and act differently';[47] an incompleteness of linguistic life that is said to be rooted in a 'notion of "material incompleteness"'[48] – indeed in an

---

43   Moir only notes that despite the evident value of Nietzsche's thought for him, particularly Nietzsche's foregrounding of creative subjectivity and dream, 'Bloch saw the metaphysics of orthogenesis that he believed underpinned Nietzsche's worldview as superficial and infused with a kind of naked heroism that was susceptible to be weaponized'. (Moir 2019b, p. 315). While revolutionary in intent, like Expressionism, utopianism was for Lukács (1971) just as subjective, idealistic, and abstract (devoid of real content). See Taylor 1990, p. 10.

44   Taylor 1990, pp. 1 and 8–10.

45   Comay and Ruda 2018, p. 128 fn. 21.

46   Comay and Ruda 2018. The figure of the anacoluthon plays an important role in the opening to Hegel's *Logic*: '*Being, pure being* – without further determination'. (Hegel 2010, p. 59). For Simoniti, Hegel's 'non-predicative anacoluthon' does not assert anything, but simply intends and means; and in that respect it – significantly – evokes a 'form of recess, leap, or even event'. (Simoniti 2015, p. 858; see Adorno 1993).

47   Comay and Ruda 2018, p. 16.

48   Comay and Ruda 2018, p. 17.

'inconsistency of materiality itself'.[49] The connection of the *Logic* with the *Phenomenology of Spirit* is thus a material connection that the dash itself performs. The dash, as I will hope to show in Chapter 2, thus becomes a written stand-in for the anacoluthon.[50] However, Comay and Ruda astonishingly pass over a fuller engagement with Bloch on this issue, justifying their doing so because Bloch himself did not comment on the dash in Hegel:

> Ernst Bloch – who astoundingly misses [the anacoluthon] in his commentary on the *Logic* – argues that the rhetorical trope is always accompanied by an 'interrupting tone of language' that brings speech into written syntax and makes them almost indistinguishable.[51]

But one need only turn to Holz (a longstanding German commentator on Bloch) to confirm that the very line of thought that Comay and Ruda stake out here was worked out early on by Bloch's utopian materialism:

> Language implicitly arises precisely from the presuppositions that are developed by the ontology of not-yet being: ... out of the presence of 'Not' in being, out of the anticipation for the future in the present.[52]

Why then the speedy criticism and the bypassing of a deeper look? Perhaps this expunction of Bloch's importance goes to the heart of what many find most distasteful and problematic with his philosophy: its assertion of the possibility of arrival. Indeed, perhaps this expunction of Bloch's importance boils down to the Lacanian slant that the dash-anacoluthon assumes as Comay and Ruda's reading progresses, and which shapes how the incompleteness of materiality is understood. Namely, the Lacanian 'tragederian subject'[53] in which this 'not' in language is built around the eternal incompleteness of nature and history. This eternality of the 'not' is expressed by the idea that perhaps '[t]here cannot be a single concept of unfinishedness ... [because] unfinishedness itself must remain unfinished', they say.[54] If 'language is *not-all* there is' because 'language itself is internally riven', then the sunderedness of language and its

---

49   Comay and Ruda 2018, p. 18.
50   The figure is itself mentioned twice. See Comay and Ruda 2018, p. 81.
51   Comay and Ruda 2018, p. 93.
52   Holz 1965, p. 117.
53   Roberts 2011, p. 133.
54   Comay and Ruda 2018, p. 36, see also p. 109.

world is insurmountable.[55] Curiously, this is a line of thought that extends back
to Voloshinov's and the Bakhtin Circle's concept of the utterance, as we will
see in a later chapter, and one that Bloch helps a Marxist philosophy of language depart from. Indeed a similar susceptibility to incompleteness marks
the fragmentary character of Adorno's paratactic method (also considered in
more detail later in the book), which exclaims a constitutive, irredeemable
disjunction. Bloch, on the other hand, holds open, I would argue, the alternative of another possibility. Contemporary radical concepts of language should
acknowledge this alternative.

At this point a brief comment on my approach to Bloch's texts should
be provided. Despite having written his *Gesamtausgabe* over the course of
decades, Bloch's corpus will be regarded here as a unitary, contemporaneous
whole. This approach of course could potentially give rise to the charge that
the treatment developed below glosses over any key shifts in Bloch's thought
that certainly, in certain instances, took place over time. The charge would be
that the treatment below is formalist, stripping the content of his work from
its precise socio-historical context. While I attempt to avoid this when possible
and necessary, my approach nevertheless contains the benefit of being able to
draw on the whole range of Bloch's conceptual resources to meet the aim of the
book, allowing me to draw out the hidden cross-connections between Bloch's
rare comments on language and his broader Marxist and materialist categories.
It is for this reason that one could call this book an applied montage: 'applied
montage', Bloch once wrote, 'shows quite rational cross-connections or analo-
giae entis'.[57] Bloch held montage in high esteem, even if, admittedly, because of

Moir's work in tracing Bloch's nascent philosophy of language back to Expressionism and Nietzsche, as well as Comay and Ruda's 'point to' and 'point
away' from Bloch are clues that there is not a ready-made, pre-existing philosophy of language in Bloch's corpus, just as there is not one in Marx's works,
but that the composition of such a philosophy can be, for good reason, sought
for within Bloch's works.[56] Since there is no fully worked out, distinct theory
of language in Bloch's writings, such therefore needs to be reconstructed from
the texts that are available to us, as well as from those rare instances in which
Bloch does concern himself with language explicitly, albeit briefly. From Bloch's
collected works (*Gesamtausgabe*) a theory of language can emerge with some
effort that acts as an alternative tendency to what is currently at hand within
Marxist concepts of language.

At this point a brief comment on my approach to Bloch's texts should
be provided. Despite having written his *Gesamtausgabe* over the course of
decades, Bloch's corpus will be regarded here as a unitary, contemporaneous
whole. This approach of course could potentially give rise to the charge that
the treatment developed below glosses over any key shifts in Bloch's thought
that certainly, in certain instances, took place over time. The charge would be
that the treatment below is formalist, stripping the content of his work from
its precise socio-historical context. While I attempt to avoid this when possible
and necessary, my approach nevertheless contains the benefit of being able to
draw on the whole range of Bloch's conceptual resources to meet the aim of the
book, allowing me to draw out the hidden cross-connections between Bloch's
rare comments on language and his broader Marxist and materialist categories.
It is for this reason that one could call this book an applied montage: 'applied
montage', Bloch once wrote, 'shows quite rational cross-connections or analo-
giae entis'.[57] Bloch held montage in high esteem, even if, admittedly, because of

55   Comay and Ruda 2018, p. 17.
56   See Alpatov 2000.
57   Bloch 1986, p. 101. See Kessler 2006.

the particular stage of capitalism that he was witnessing.[58] But for that reason montage is an immanent technique of reading when applied to Bloch's works themselves.

1   Bloch's Marxism

Briefly sketching the type of Marxist Bloch was and the sort of inheritance of Marx he developed will help to provide the reader with an initial sense of what a philosophy of language might look like when drawing on his work.[59]

Born in Ludwigshafen, Germany, in 1885, Bloch's life spanned the triumphs and tragedies of the twentieth century.[60] Cutting a marginal figure in the arc of Germany philosophy and indeed in the Marxist tradition, Bloch has been placed at times in a more anarchist current of thought – Voloshinov certainly thought that the Expressionists were anarchistic.[61] Bloch, a disruptor of orthodoxy and of theoretical dogmatism, nevertheless remained a marginal figure of the type of Western Marxism that is more associated with the better known Benjamin and Adorno, despite Bloch's obvious influence on their bodies of thought.[62] Bloch's inheritance of Marxism, entirely heterodox, nonetheless did not falter in remaining faithful to the promise of a better life that shone out of the East during the October Revolution. Not for nothing was Bloch dubbed 'the philosopher of the October Revolution'.[63] Being occupied with utopianism in all of its historical forms, Bloch has often been pejoratively portrayed as a thinker of the cook-books of tomorrow.[64] The Hungarian Marxist Béla Balázs once described Bloch as 'a Don Quixote' and not to be trusted, especially given Bloch's influence on the promising young Lukács.[65]

---

58   See Bloch 1992. Cf. Lukács 1992.
59   Detailed accounts of Bloch's Marxism can be found in Hudson 1982 and Moir 2019a. An account of Bloch's contemporary intellectual context can be found in Boldyrev 2014.
60   See Zudeick 1987.
61   See Löwy 2017, p. 19. The thesis here is that Bloch was member to 'a "metaphysical-anarchist" or revolutionary-messianic movement inspired by romanticism' (Löwy 2017, p. 40). See Bowie 2003, which fails to mention Bloch at all.
62   See Anderson 1979 and Jay 1984, pp. 174–95. Adorno and Benjamin wrote about language reasonably consistently and have been deployed for such a task by their subsequent readers. Bloch less so. See Abel 2018, Hogh 2017, Benjamin 1999a and 1999b.
63   See Negt 1975 and Jay 1984, p. 176.
64   See Jay 1984, p. 174.
65   Balázs quoted in Karárdi 2010, p. 500.

Bloch's politics were even more controversial, particularly given his support for the Moscow show trials, his 'compromise with Stalinism for a whole period'.[66] Like his intellectual companion Georg Lukács – also a 'Marxist neophyte'[67] – Bloch can, however, be credited with developing an economically non-reductionist, anti-mechanical, holistic form of Marxism, in which he developed non-economistic readings of social being, particularly of the utopian projections it produces within the superstructure, together with the causality such utopian projections can evidence.[68] Bloch is therefore said to have been an exemplar of a more *open* Marxism, displaying a remarkable familiarity with and critical absorption of diverse intellectual traditions, from Aristotelianism to German mysticism.[69] Bloch's influence on a number of theologians, such as Jürgen Moltmann and Wolfhart Pannenberg, is also notable, and made him particularly susceptible to charges of idealism.[70] And yet Habermas's notorious accusation that Bloch initiated an out of touch return to dogmatic, pre-Kantian metaphysics serves to show that Bloch can be many things to many people.[71] Indeed in his youth Bloch had held that the Kantian 'thing-in-itself' amounts to an objective fantasy (*'das Ding an sich ist die objektive Phantasie'*) – a thought Bloch would go on to unwrap and develop throughout his whole career.[72] For Bloch, the utopian desire of a better life was not, to paraphrase Cassirer, 'an illusion peculiar to representation'.[73] Rather, it abounds within objective being itself and echoes what Cassirer writes of Hermann Cohen's concept of the ethical:

> The 'actual' from experience in human history should not be made the standard of the ethically 'possible', because, on the contrary, all productivity of ethical thought consists in just that: to seek out and to establish a 'possible', which itself demands a new 'actuality' beyond anything given until now.[74]

---

66   Löwy 2017, pp. 21, 25 and 202. Cf. pp. 107–9, where Löwy discusses Walter Benjamin's support for the Soviet Union consequent to the rise of Fascism in Germany.

67   Kavoulakos 2018, p. 226.

68   Cf. Kavoulakos 2018, p. 98.

69   See Löwy 2017, p. 1. Cf. p. 22.

70   See Moltmann 1978, 2010, and Pannenberg 1968. Cf. Bloch 2009.

71   Habermas 1970. Cf. Jay 1984, p. 174 and Kolakowski 2005.

72   Bloch 1969, p. 5.

73   Cassirer 2015, p. 227.

74   Cassirer 2015, p. 228.

Bloch would write his *magnum opus* on hope as a principle. Hope was the centre around which all of Bloch's eclectic intellectual influences turned. Hope was the principle that everything returned to – hope is what drives the thing-in-itself to be other than its present actuality, it is what gives objective being its own imaginative grounding.[75] This 'new actuality' or an actuality that strives for novelty, which human history aims at, is freedom, and for Bloch it is an objective possibility of existence; thus freedom is not a first, but rather an end, cause of human action, imagination, and thought.[76] It extends into nature, too, for Bloch. This is what he terms 'the ultimate of total liberation' within and through community.[77] And, combined with nature, it has allowed Bloch to become fruitful for reconceiving the human-nature relation in light of anthropogenic climate systems breakdown.

Given Bloch's peculiar intellectual inheritances and interests, his Marxism consisted of a fragmented inheritance (*disjecta membra*) of Marx's programme. Bloch would describe his first book, *The Spirit of Utopia*, by all intents and purposes a pre-Marxist work, as 'revolutionary Romanticism'.[78] The 'young Dosto-evskian eschatologist',[79] a disruptive member of the left-wing current within the 'Heidelberg Left' around Max Weber,[80] would early on chart a similar journey to Marx as his friend Lukács would achieve, with whom Bloch would later part ways because of, among other things, Lukács's interpretation of German Expressionism.

Bloch's body of work, then, is an attempt to explore and furnish the legitimacy of the utopian postulate he took to be Marxism's real inheritance, endeavouring to take the imaginative and critical function of utopia and raise it to a new level of importance for revolutionary thought and praxis – concrete utopia. Bloch's 'remarkable renaissance of Marxist thought' coincided with and is said to have been partly inspired by a re-encounter with eschatolo-

---

75   In 1918 during his own neo-Kantian, Dostoevskian phase, the later author of *History and Class Consciousness* (1923) would speak of socialism as 'the utopian postulate of the Marxian philosophy of history: it is the *ethical objective* of a coming world order'. (Lukács 1977, pp. 419–20). For an extensive discussion of Lukács's transition to Bolshevik communism, see Löwy 1979, pp. 128–44.

76   See Cassirer 2015, p. 230.

77   Bloch 2018, p. 51.

78   Bloch 2000a, p. 279. For a very short review of Bloch's journey to Marxism, see Beck 2019, pp. 102–3.

79   Löwy 1979, p. 38.

80   Löwy 1979, p. 49, see also pp. 37–8, 43–7, 52–6. For an account of the figures around Weber's Circle, see Honigsheim 2003.

gical thought-forms in the period of Weimar Germany.[81] Some commentators therefore define Bloch's Marxism as an ethical form emerging from an internal debate within Marxism over the efficacy of neo-Kantianism.[82] In this context the old dichotomy between science and ethics, what is and what ought to be,[83] and how the new and its emergence relates to both present and possible actuality, was brought into sharp relief by Bloch's work. While at the time this rendered Bloch a figure not to be trusted, in the passing of time his contribution to Marxism has proved increasingly valuable. As Absensour has argued, the 'scientific' and 'utopian socialism' oppositional pair has become a bona fide institutionalisation of enunciations that were intended to be more theatrical than substantial, and tended to distort or mystify the otherwise demonstrable complexity of Marx's relationship to the contemporary movements of utopianism that sprung up alongside Marxism's historical emergence.[84] To reclaim utopianism for Marxism was Bloch's goal, not least in the face of the rise of fascism.

As the reader will find, reason for Bloch is not just the cold, untinctured process of critique, but also involves that dream of a better life, both its imaginations and its attempted construction. Bloch was adamant that this so-called irrational and anti-Enlightenment approach to reason need not be irrational or anti-Enlightening, not backward-looking to boot, but rather could be assessed as an expansion of reason and Enlightenment, an enlightenment of enlightenment that can contain positive political effects.[85] This 'warm stream' approach to Marxism finds its legitimacy, so Bloch thought, in Marx's famous letter to Arnold Ruge of 1843: '... the world has long dreamed of possessing something of which it has only to be conscious in order to possess it in reality'.[86] This approach was of course conditioned by the era in which Bloch found himself. One of Bloch's key interventions in the anti-fascist struggle was 'an uncompromising critique of the "socialist undernourishment of concrete phantasy"'.[87] Through the category of the 'warm stream' Bloch therefore sought to identify and harness a tendency in Marx's thought which had been subjected to what he saw as a 'one-dimensional' and 'distorted' hollowing out by 'the

---

81   Mendes-Flohr 1983, p. 633.
82   See Boldyrev 2014, pp. 4, 7 and 101, and Blackledge 2012, pp. 103, 109, 126, 132–4. See Cohen 2000. In a later chapter I interrogate Bloch's and Voloshinov's respective take-up of neo-Kantianism.
83   See Blackledge 2012, p. 16.
84   See Abensour 2016. Cf. Hudis 2012.
85   See Sayre and Löwy 1984, pp. 49–50.
86   Marx 1987b, p. 144.
87   Negt 1975, p. 11.

Marx of the apparatchiks', for whom dreams and hopes and the 'correlate of possibility' they arise from,[88] even partially and in distorted fashion, were to be discarded as unscientific detritus associated with the utopian socialists.[89] For Bloch, '[e]ssential Marxism contains in its past so much that is future still unfulfilled'.[90] Utopianism was key to this and was so particularly in the fight against fascism.

The apparent paradox of Bloch's Marxism was and remains that it sought 'the unification of reason and hope, the human and the natural, the dream and reality'.[91] Bloch supplemented the cold and hard economic analysis developed with rigour in Marx's *Capital* – a 'cool realism' as Bloch had it[92] – with Marx's 'warm stream', often neglected, but an area Bloch sought to bring to the fore. The 'warm stream' of hope, of utopian projection, in essence, the warm stream of that (human) desire to transcend what is currently given in the world in the search of a better, collective life, also had to be given its due, Bloch thought, if the proletarian revolution were to fully actualise itself. Bloch wanted to understand and unlock this desire, against fascist counter-revolution and reaction, and *for Marxism*. Indeed it was Marx who was 'in favour of the always and finally genuine idea of society'.[93]

Bloch, then – this so-called 'incurable', hopelessly utopian ideologist – stands as an increasingly germane figure for our own period.[94] Franco 'Bifo' Berardi's recent claim in *Futurability* that global society is currently witnessing the 'desertification of the future of humankind'[95] would seem to indicate that four decades after Bloch's death hope has been very much disappointed. But the consequence of this has been an upsurge in 'the felt need for utopia' – 'the possibility of some positive alternative future' grows stronger as a collective feeling.[96] For this reason the thinker of hope *par excellence*, for whom 'virtually all human beings are futuristic',[97] is needed now more than ever.[98] Bloch's

---

88   Bloch 1986, p. 206.
89   Bloch 2018, p. 159.
90   Bloch 2018, p. 168.
91   Howard 2019, p. 66.
92   Bloch 2018, p. 35.
93   Bloch 2000a, p. 243.
94   Löwy 2017, p. 2. Cf. p. 18. See Žižek 2013.
95   Berardi 2019, p. 210. On the peaks and troughs of utopianism, see Ingram 2016 and Saage 2016.
96   Ingram 2016, p. xxiii. Cf. Balibar 2016 and Fischbach 2016, especially pp. 122–3, for contemporary views on utopianism's limitations.
97   Bloch 2018, p. 31.
98   Language is not absent from Berardi's book; in the vein of Expressionism, language is said

early recognition that his utopian reading of Marx was significant[99] remains the case and is finding acceptance as a port of call in the present, with rising renewed interest in utopian and anticipation studies more broadly.[100] While for Lukács utopianism was merely the sign of an impossibility (see Chapter 4),[101] utopianism, as an expression of the wish for a better world, is something that Marxists can harness and is certainly not a layer of social being that should be left as the reserve of the far right. The manner in which this utopian desire circulates and is (linguistically) articulated should not be dismissed or left to the reactionaries. While this wider contemporary 'Blochian turn'[102] in utopian studies is sometimes viewed as far too indeterminate an approach to locate the political efficacy of utopia for the present conjuncture,[103] since Bloch's utopianism is said to constitute a 'purely theoretical' figure of the new utopian spirit[104] – 'occult' conceptual forays, as Perry Anderson has labelled Bloch's utopianism,[105] my argument below is that Bloch's categories are helpful in concretely theorising language in a Marxist framework. Connected to this is Bloch's contemporary relevance in grasping the current rise of what has been dubbed 'post-fascism'. Bloch undertook a unique analysis of classical fascism in the 1930s which centred on cultural politics. This topic is dealt with in Chapter 4.

2   Philosophy of Language as a Problem

The question of language in Marxism in not neutral of course, and something needs to be briefly said on this front. Much like Bloch's Marxism '[t]he question of Marxism and language is the site of a paradox'.[106] This is because it is still not

---

to constitute an horizon of possibility: 'We should imagine the possible political emancipation of the future essentially as an act of enunciation' (Berardi 2019, p. 196).

99   Writing to Lukács in 1955, Bloch notes that '[t]ogether we are regarded as the representatives of the intelligentsia who have made apparent in the most unmistakable way the high standards and perspectives that make up the wealth of knowledge and humanity of Marxism'. (Bloch, quoted in Karádi 2010, p. 499).

100   Poli 2006, 2009, 2010, 2011, 2017, 2019. For a Blochian critique of this tendency within contemporary anticipation studies, see Barron 2021.

101   See Lukács 1971.

102   Ingram 2016, p. xix.

103   See Ingram 2016, pp. xiii, xv and xix for a (critical) mention of Bloch; cf. p. xx, where Ingram wrongfully attributes the notion of 'educated desire' to Abensour, and not Bloch. See Saage 2016, pp. 60–1, where a similar criticism of Bloch's utopianism is made.

104   Abensour 2016, p. 43.

105   Anderson 1979, p. 66.

106   Lecercle 2008, p. 471.

entirely clear what Marx made of language in a systematic sense. As Raymond Williams indicates – himself not unaffected by utopianism,[107] comparable to other systems of thought Marxism has 'contributed very little to thinking about language itself'.[108] This is certainly a paradox if we consider that the Marxist-inspired semiotician Ferruccio Rossi-Landi insisted that '[n]o definition or characterization of man is as radical as that which places in the *definiens* his capacity to produce material (*faber*) and linguistic (*loquens*) artefacts'.[109] The Marxist tradition of thought has largely left untouched what Antonio Gramsci called *la questione della lingua* – the question of language.[110] Voloshinov's intervention was first and foremost among the rare instances which buck this trend of neglect. And while a history of Marxist encounters with the language question is yet to be written, Craig Brandist's statement concerning the Bakhtin Circle is true of much of the rare Marxist-inspired engagements with the language question: 'they are by no means pure exercises in Marxist theory'.[111]

What is more, Marxism and philosophy of language often appear as antagonistic, and for a number of reasons. Marx's already noted relatively scant treatment of language serves as one reason, as does the tendency of language theorisation to head towards idealism, contra Marx's materialism.[112] There is furthermore the common association that is made between a Marxist concern for the language question and the Stalinist and Marrist dogma emerging in Russia during the late 1920s.[113] As Lecercle writes, 'by declaring [the question] closed' Stalin's intervention on the question 'buried the issue of the relations between language and the social totality', blocking the way to investigating 'what constitutes the specificity of Marxism when it comes to thinking about language'.[114]

Thus, Lecercle's assertion that one advantage of the lack of Marxist engagement with the language question is that 'we are not labouring under the weight of a dogma'[115] does ring true if one were to note that the dogma of silence is

---

107   See Ingram 2016, p. xxvi.
108   Williams 1977, p. 21.
109   Rossi-Landi 1992, p. 193.
110   See Lecercle 2006, pp. 73–104 and Ives 2004b, p. 20.
111   Brandist 2002a, p. 87. See Tihanov 1998, p. 613 on the Circle, for which literature is the 'master refractor' of the base. Curiously, the same logic is at work in the history of utopian thought. The function of utopia predominantly belongs to literature rather than political-philosophical reflection (see Ingram 2016, p. xiv).
112   See Ives 2004b, pp. 5–6. Cf. Hartley 2016, pp. 104–5.
113   See Lecercle 2008, pp. 472–3.
114   Lecercle 2006, p. 75. See Brandist and Lähteenmäki 2010.
115   Lecercle 2006, p. 73.

present because of Stalinism. Produced in the context of socialism in one country, Stalin's *Marxism and Problems of Linguistics* (1950) – amounting to a 'fetishisation of language' in positing that language belonged to neither the base nor the superstructure, and thus not quite to social being itself[116] – is described by Lecercle as a 'spectre haunting Marxist thinking on language'.[117] This Stalinist position meant that human loquacity was seen as 'extra-revolutionary'[118] and classless, immune from revolutionary upheavals and determined only by, and subject to, a sort of technologism.[119] Bloch considered this position as truly emerging from, and residing in, 'the tradition of idealism'.[120] Naturally, the language question is drawn into wider questions of how a revolution is made, how it enunciates and articulates itself, and how the revolution is secured beyond tomorrow.

Another notable source for the paradox of Marxism's largely circumspect relation to the language question concerns the recent production of post-Marxist theorisations of language. The hangover of Stalinism on the question of language has often manifested itself in abstract assertions of the mutual exclusivity of Marxism and the significance and core substance of language: fairly or not, Pierre Bourdieu, Jürgen Habermas, Michel Foucault, and Jacques Derrida are all said to belong to the tendency which propagates a logic of separation between Marxism and language, and which went on to view language as an 'an antonym to the "matter" of materialism'.[121] To this list we might add the radical-democratic theories of Ernesto Laclau and Chantal Mouffe.[122] All in various hues these thinkers propose a kind of logology,[123] in which *everything* is language and its equivocation. 'One ... daydreams about language', writes Rossi-Landi, 'as if the rest of reality didn't exist and didn't influence it'.[124] This tend-

---

116 Lecercle 2006, p. 81.

117 Lecercle 2006, p. 74.

118 Gray 2002, p. 179.

119 See Lecercle 2006, p. 80.

120 Bloch 2018, p. 147. Stalin's intervention should alert us to the significance of the language question as a site of contestation within Marxism, a *Kampfplatz*. Prior to the First Five-Year Plan (1928), innovative theorisations on language were being developed in Russia. Voloshinov's experimentation in this field is a good example of this (see Fedorova 2010). The thorny question of Bloch's ostensible support for the wider political context of the Moscow trials and for the East German regime – even if never having become a member of the Communist Party himself – is a dimension of Bloch's life and work which Oskar Negt (1975) has sought to contextualise, but certainly not exonerate (cf. Howard 2019).

121 Ives 2004b, pp. 5–6. Cf. p. 9.

122 See Laclau and Mouffe 2001, Laclau 1990.

123 See Bosteels 2019, pp. 27–40.

124 Rossi-Landi 1992, p. 248.

ency to locate Marxism as lying at odds with the language question, arranged in a state of rivalry or opposition, seemed to develop exponentially during the course of the 1970s and 1980s.[125] The tentativeness of Marxism towards language perhaps arises, then, from the ever-present and 'obvious danger ... of making language "primary" and "original"', of seeing language as 'the founding element in humanity'.[126] The language question harbours the ever-present danger of becoming – as Johann Georg Hamann said of his own life's work, almost prophesising post-structuralism's logophilia – *a bone to gnaw on*.[127]

In *The German Ideology* Marx had already sketched out counter-positions to this trend: 'Just as philosophers have given thought an independent existence, so they were bound to make language into an independent realm'.[128] Marx subjects Max Stirner to scathing attacks on the same grounds as Voloshinov had attacked the Expressionists. Stirner's tendency to gnaw on the bone is said to be emblematic of his idealism,[129] and Proudhon, too, is castigated for traipsing down a similar *cul-de-sac*:

> In labour-commodity, which is a grim reality, [Proudhon] sees nothing but a grammatical ellipsis. ... If society wants to 'eliminate all the drawbacks' that assail it, well, let it eliminate all the ill-sounding terms, change the language; and to this end it has only to apply to the Academy for a new edition of its dictionary.[130]

In the *Eighteenth Brumaire* Marx also subjects to critique so-called revolutionaries for their use of retrograde names and phrases of the past which thereby disguises new, upcoming social conditions.[131] And yet Marx himself asserted quite famously that idealism covertly progressed the development of materialism: 'in contradistinction to materialism, the *active* side was set forth

---

125   See Lo Piparo 2010, which is emblematic of this posited separation between Marxism and language. Lo Piparo's thesis sparked a proliferation of debate (see Rosiello 2010 and Ives 2004b, pp. 16–18). Cf. Rossi-Landi 1992, Bianchi 2011, Ratajczak 2018, Virno 2004 and 2015.

126   Williams 1977, p. 29.

127   See Hamann 2007, p. xiv.

128   Marx and Engels 1976a, p. 446.

129   See Marx and Engels 1976a, pp. 231, 233, 277, 280, 299, 443, 447, and 449.

130   Marx 1976b, p. 129. Marx charges his theoretical adversaries with gnawing on the bone of language, regularly reprimanding his contemporary interlocutors for their theoretical abstractions and idealist linguistic usages which, to their detriment, bypass the benefits of *plain language* – a common stock phrase for Marx (see Marx and Engels 1976a, pp. 245 and 464; Marx 1987, p. 345).

131   See Marx 2019. Cf. Mieszkowski 2019, pp. 54–60 and 61–2.

abstractly by idealism – which, of course, does not know real, sensuous activity as such'.[132] The late Althusserian insight into the co-belonging of idealist and materialist tendencies encroaching upon each other in *one* philosophical body of work is pertinent here.[133] As Bloch wrote, because idealism 'is not yet a completely exhausted mine' it 'must be studied' and must 'be fertilized in a crypto-materialist sense'.[134] This then is another reason to study the Expressionist Bloch in pursuit of a Marxist account of language. If it is true that the subject matter of political economy is largely missing from Bloch's writings, we ought to recall what Bloch's self-stated task was: to foreground what had been largely erased from consideration within the Marxist tradition, namely the 'warm stream' of hope, precisely that *active* side of human practice which seeks to transgress given conditions via utopian projections. The idealism of utopianism contains a crypto-materialist element, and so the idealistic assertion of language's independence from its material conditions of existence contains the same.

This is something Paolo Virno's work has provided a response to. This tendency of language to give the appearance of transgressively breaking with its own social conditions of being is for Virno the very materialism of language, and is what in fact deeply ties language to modes of production and to politics. Virno contends that it is precisely the breaks of linguistic continuity, negations rooted in the *untimeliness of sense*, circulating in and constituting language, which give rise to this materiality of language:

> The untimeliness of sense involves a constant *detachment* of the speaker from the environment and the psychic drives. The voids and pauses, that is, the hesitations and postponements that punctuate the experience of the human animal, are symptoms of such a detachment. Hypothetical and counterfactual reasoning, familiarity with falsity, an imponderable intra-specific aggressiveness, the variation of techniques of production and political systems are all rooted in these voids and pauses. The detachment of statements from the environment and psychic drives is reflected within statements by the syntactic connective 'not'.[135]

As I will argue throughout this book, through Bloch's materialist categories one can contend that it is the incompletion of social existence which facilitates a

---

132   Marx 1976a, p. 3.
133   See Althusser 2006, pp. 222–5.
134   Bloch 2018, p. 133.
135   Virno 2018, p. 79.

detachment from the present, and which gives rise to the syntactic connective 'not' in language, and to other linguistic occurrences related to this, such as the anacoluthon. It is this possibility of detachment (to think and speak counter-factually, to postpone but also to hope forward) which, I will argue, is voiced in the anacoluthon of living speech. This is but one response to the question of how Bloch's 'warm stream' might inform a Marxist philosophy of language.

3   Outline of the Book

The question of how Bloch's utopian inheritance of Marx can help to reshape or reorient the rare instances of existing Marxist philosophy of language is the broad subject of this book, then. In Chapter 1, I reconstruct the key categories of Bloch's materialism to show the way in which Bloch conceives of matter as a tendency and latency-driven process, highlighting how, for Bloch, matter consists of an open process which – crucially – harbours the possibility of an emancipation from its own incompleteness, or, as I put it, the possibility of arrival.

Chapter 2 then goes on to make a linguistic incision into Bloch's materialism with a focus on the linguistic figure of the anacoluthon, which denotes a 'not-following' in the syntactical flow of speech. There I demonstrate the manner in which this figure instantiates Bloch's materialism linguistically. The general line of argument is that the very presence of a disjuncture of speech-flow in everyday social life is a particular, linguistic refraction of the tendency-latency material process. The anacoluthon is a linguistic refraction of the incomplete-ness of material existence, but equally the refraction of a tending toward latent new forms of sociality. On a methodological level, I claim that the anacoluthon constitutes a key linguistic node through which to think through Bloch's contri-bution to a Marxist philosophy of language, despite (or, as we will see, precisely because of) the figure's marginal status within Bloch's body of work. I therefore extend Moir's insights, first and foremost, by extending the material drawn on from Bloch's oeuvre.

The second part of the book (Chapters 3 and 4) locates the specificity of Bloch's contribution to a *Marxist* philosophy of language. I meet this task in two steps and with a very precise focus. Chapter 3 deals with the Marxian thrust of Bloch's contribution by placing Bloch into dialogue with the first real explicit Marxist attempt at developing a theory of language: Voloshinov and his *Marxism in the Philosophy of Language*. As a comparative chapter, I develop a discussion of the theme of relationality, which is central, I argue, to Voloshinov's philosophy of language, as well as to Bloch's. It is shown that, when read alongside Bloch's matter-categories, Voloshinov's understanding of relationality amounts to a restricted form of relationality within which the utterance is grasped. Bloch's utopian iteration of Marx contributes to a broader notion of totality than that upon and through which Voloshinov's philosophy of language rests and is developed. Equally, and in reciprocal fashion, Voloshinov's work helps to augment a more concrete version of Bloch's otherwise somewhat formalist construal of the anacoluthon. Bloch and Voloshinov's shared neo-Kantian and Freudian inheritances will play an important role in demonstrating these points of comparison. Chapter 4 seeks to edge the discussion closer to the present moment. By constructing a Blochian reading of Marx's opening passage to the *Eighteenth Brumaire of Louis Bonaparte*, which contains a neglected reference to language in a period of revolution, this chapter connects Bloch's philosophy of language as it has been developed in the prior chapters to the question of fascism. In the process, I deal with Lukács's critique of utopianism and Bloch's response to that criticism. This is particularly important for grasping language and fascism today through the lens of Bloch's utopian materialism.

CHAPTER 1

Bloch's Utopian Materialism

The distinction that Ernst Cassirer draws in *The Philosophy of Symbolic Forms* between a rational account of language, drawn out to express itself purely in a linguistic *ideal*, in contrast with empiricism's orientation to the sheer facticity and functionality of linguistic life as language presently exists – a distinction between, one might say, fact and value, a distinction so dear to the neo-Kantianism from which Cassirer derives his thought – is a distinction which Bloch's philosophy, both singularly Marxist and utopian at one and the same stroke, disputes and throws into relief. As Cassirer writes:

> Philosophical *empiricism* seems to open up a new approach to language, for, in accordance with its fundamental tendency, it strives, not to relate the fact of language to a logical ideal, but rather to understand it in its sheer facticity, in its empirical origin and purpose. Instead of losing language in a logical or metaphysical utopia, it seeks to know it solely in its psychological reality and function.[1]

A large portion of the argument of this book is that Bloch's utopian philosophy, contrary to this position of Cassirer's, allows us to grasp the present existence of language, its present facticity, its current functionality, as pointing beyond itself in the process of intimating an ideal, an 'ought' which is situated above and beyond what any mode of presence may offer up, here and now. As Virno would put it, the empiricism of language and the capacity of language to shift beyond, to transcend, its own empiricism are tightly related. For Bloch, what percolates the presence of language is that dream of a matter that Marx had intimated to Ruge.

Like Moir's account of language in Bloch's philosophy, mentioned in the Introduction, I contend that Bloch's collected writings (his *Gesamtausgabe*) possess an embryonic concept of language's materialism, one which combines the empirical and logically ideal dimensions of language (even if Bloch's logical-ideal is not of the Platonic kind that Cassirer seems to have in mind). That is, Bloch's philosophy provides a response to what Voloshinov once termed

---

1 Cassirer 1980, p. 133.

'the problem of the actual mode of being of linguistic phenomena'.[2] To tease this out requires, admittedly, a good degree of reconstructive work. I will start this work by considering Bloch's concept of matter – both the inheritances and genealogies it draws on and the innovative changes it puts to the materialist tradition. Bloch's originality in materialist thought did not mean that he began with a concept of matter *de novo*. Notwithstanding Holz's legitimate claim that it is only by way of bracketing out the presuppositions of the tradition that the proper import of Bloch's concept of matter can be ascertained,[3] it is nevertheless true that only through a knowledge of that tradition does this 'breaking free' occur. One might say that Bloch's understanding of possibility – so crucial to his concept of matter, as I will show below – is applied to his reading of the materialist tradition itself. Bloch reads traces of possibility within old concepts of matter in a quest to forge his own utopian-materialist philosophy.

Although Bloch wrote an extended book solely dedicated to the question of materialism,[4] the problem of matter spans the length of his collected works, even if his first book, *The Spirit of Utopia* (originally published in 1918, with a second edition, *der zweitern Fassung von 1923*, published in 1964) adopts a less, or at least less obvious, materialist accent.[5] Even in 1927 Bloch speaks of a '*natura nondum naturata* [nature that has not yet been brought forth]' which he will name 'the nonmateriality of a pure being-in-itself'.[6] This would align with that odd logical-ideal that I will argue Bloch conceives of within the materiality of language. But when one understands that Bloch categorises matter as possibility (see below), this is not so strange a description to make, and returns us to Comay and Ruda's claim that materiality is fundamentally characterised by an incompleteness. Matter fundamentally concerns the not-yet actualisation of possibilities. The shifts in Bloch's position in how he categorises matter is unimportant for my account of Bloch's materialism, since, as I noted in the Introduction, for better or worse here I will be treating his collected writings as a contemporaneous body of work.

The departure point of Bloch's materialism consists, I argue, in an ontologisation of a certain combination of Kant and Hegel developed in *The Spirit*

---

2   Voloshinov 1973, p. 82.
3   See Holz 1975, p. 121.
4   Bloch 1972.
5   See Münster 1987.
6   Bloch 1998, p. 409. My discussion draws on the second edition of *The Spirit of Utopia*, see Bloch 2000a.

of Utopia. To put this reading in succinct terms for now: it consists of an inscription of the question of *what* matter is into the very nature of matter itself, such that matter, for Bloch, is a searching for its own what-ness.[7] This question-answer structure of matter not only closely mirrors the incompleteness at the heart of present material actuality (a question conveys a gap in knowledge), but also begins to shed light on the centrality of language and enunciation for Bloch's materialism. To push what this means slightly further it can be said that the Hegelian moment of Bloch's reading here concerns the *possibility of arrival* that Bloch sees characterising matter's process of realising what it is. A brief inquiry into Bloch's general materialist lexicon shows that there are two substantive categories that make up this approach and which helps to further conceptualise Bloch's Kant-Hegel reading – they are tendency (*Tendenz*) and latency (*Latenz*). They are key to my reading of Bloch's philosophy of language and, as noted, they re-articulate Bloch's Kant-Hegel reception developed in *The Spirit of Utopia*. In sum, 'tendency' is a category that describes the processuality of matter's searching for its own what-ness – this is the Kantian moment of lack. On the other hand, 'latency' (the innovated Hegelian moment) deals with the nature of what-ness when essence is conceived of as 'not-yet' (*Noch Nicht*) – an important operator-term in Bloch's philosophy.

Three supplementary categories of Bloch's will also be dealt with as important off-shoots of the 'tendency' and 'latency' categories. They likely represent Bloch's true originality: the categories of 'Front', 'Novum', and 'Ultimum'.[8] Bloch describes these as the 'most un-thought through' categories in philosophy's ongoing history. While they are unique to Bloch alone, Bloch does merit Marx with having laid the groundwork for their discovery.[9]

1   Kant 'Burning' through Hegel

Bloch's Marxism acutely embodies the question of the relation of theoretical openness and orthodoxy.[10] His philosophical formation occurred in a period when questions of a 'Kantian Marxism', that is, a neo-Kantianism with socialist tendencies, was high on the agenda; it was a period in which 'a revival of

---

7   Bloch 1970a, p. 209.
8   Bloch 1986, pp. 198–205. Cf. Siebers 2012a, p. 412.
9   Bloch 1985b, p. 827.
10   See Jay 1984.

Kant after his decline' was taking place.[11] Within this context it is therefore not surprising that Bloch staged a reading in which Hegel was to be thrown back towards Kant, with Kant re-emerging through an Hegelian canvas. In Chapter 3 I will return to the topic of neo-Kantianism when I compare Bloch and Voloshinov. For now, I can unpack further the claim made above, namely that Bloch's materialism takes its starting point from a unique rehabilitation of Kant and Hegel's relation.

Whether here one can speak of a 'Kantianized Hegel' or a 'Hegelized Kant' is an open question.[12] Be that as it may, during Bloch's proto-Marxist phase,[13] the period of *The Spirit of Utopia*, this retroactive Kant-Hegel mixture is exemplified with a curious expression. In the current conjuncture philosophy must, Bloch says there, 'let Kant burn through Hegel'.[14] Staged in this imperative is Bloch's discovery of an ontology of not-yet being. I argue it captures the very essence of his materialism and thus it would be sensible to outline what precisely Bloch means by it. If after 1914 Lenin returned to Hegel and Bernstein to Kant,[15] Bloch sought a return to both.[16]

What does this imperative mean? Bloch's injunction seeks to articulate a new utopian vision through the co-ordinates of classical German philosophy.[17]

---

11   Beiser 2014, p. 17. See Kavoulakis 2018, Löwy 2017 and Moir 2019a. Ernst Cassirer, with whose remark I opened this chapter, was one such example of a generation who would stake out their thought via a mixture of Kantianism and Hegelianism (see Tihanov 2000, pp. 23–4).

12   See Beiser 2014, pp. 222 and 233.

13   See Haug 2012.

14   Bloch 2000a, p. 187.

15   See Blackledge 2012, pp. 110 and 114.

16   Habermas's (1970, p. 325) contention that Bloch 'skips' Kant is too simplistic, then. Cf. Boldyrev 2014, pp. 125–6. Kavoulakos specifies how Emil Lask's reading of Kant, for instance, was also a form of 'objectivist Copernicanism' (Kavoulakos 2018, p. 20n8). 'According to Lask's objectivist theory, the meaning of Kant's "Copernican act" was not the turn toward an epistemological elaboration of the synthetic acts of an ideal judging subject, but the revelation of the principle of the so-called *logos-immanence of the object*'. (Kavoulakos 2018, p. 20). The repercussion of this was that 'Lask is obliged to drastically downplay the constitutive role of the subject' in forming the object; as such the subject is reduced to a contemplative, not spontaneous stance, which passively correlates itself with 'objective meaning'. (Kavoulakos 2018, p. 23; cf. pp. 26–9). Lask was influential for Bloch and is mentioned in Bloch's important review, discussed in Chapter 4, of Lukács's *History and Class Consciousness* (1923). For a critique of Habermas's own post-metaphysical position and the Kant-Hegel reading that it relies on in developing a discourse ethics, see Hammer 2007.

17   Despite Bloch's curious expression apparently announcing a 'return to Kant' that echoes Eduard Bernstein's revisionism (see Willey 1978, p. 175), Bloch never did subscribe to reformist Marxism.

Margaret Susman anticipated this when describing Bloch's thought as prefiguring a new German metaphysics.[18] This new metaphysics was a metaphysics of the new and it led to a new vision of matter. It is useful to note first off that Bloch's imperative stages a tension of opposition which he perceives takes place between Kant and Hegel. Like a number of neo-Kantians who dominated German philosophy during the period prior to Bloch's first book, such as Emil Lask, and like Georg Lukács's neo-Kantian period, Bloch develops a Kant-Hegel reading that presents the two thinkers as representatives of 'two great opposing poles of classical Germany philosophy'; as Kavoulakos puts the matter in Lukács's case – like Lukács, Bloch attempted to chart 'a *middle theoretical perspective* that would lie between them'.[19] As I will show, this 'middle' condition is one of a threshold between incompletion and possible arrival. It is very much what defines matter in Bloch's eyes.[20]

This middle, threshold condition aligns with the reference to 'burning' mentioned in Bloch's Kant-Hegel imperative. It is a burning opposition which turns on the *Sein und Sollen* problematic – what is and what ought to be, the very essence of utopia and utopian projection. It is a tension over which, as Bloch says, two philosophical schools 'conflict' but 'between which one may not simply choose'.[21] Bloch therefore asks for the power of 'both' – Kant must burn through Hegel. And it is through this 'burning' – *durchbrennt* – that the excess power of a 'both, and ...' is produced.[22] It is a 'both, and ...' which is 'neither strictly Hegelian nor recognisably Kantian', as Blechman has argued in a slightly different context.[23] I argue that this is the fundamental, principled departure point of Bloch's utopian materialism. As such it is therefore key for developing a Blochian philosophy of language.

A further grasp of precisely what, for Bloch, Kant and Hegel each stand for in this injunction is required. A sense of this can be gleaned by working backwards to the sections that precede the injunction within *The Spirit of Utopia*. In

---

18   See Susman 1992.

19   Kavoulakos 2018, p. 42, see also p. 58.

20   The *Materialismusstreit* of 1854 was indeed a 'spur to the early neo-Kantian movement'. In his own manner Bloch followed the mantra of that time, namely, '[t]o understand Kant is to go beyond him' (Willey 1978, p. 36). Bloch arguably developed the 'dark spaces in Kant', as the Marburg neo-Kantian founding editor of the *Kant-Studien* described neo-Kantianism's aim in 1897 (Vaihinger quoted in Willey 1978, p. 155).

21   Bloch 2000a, p. 185.

22   As Heinrich Rickert (2015, p. 385), on whom Bloch wrote his dissertation, stated on the question of antecedent between ontology and epistemology: 'Realistically, there is no *either-or* but rather a *both-and*'.

23   Blechman 2008, p. 182.

the relevant exposition Bloch begins with Kant, who, chronologically preceding Hegel's philosophy of course, is nevertheless meant to re-assert his philosophy *after* Hegel. Kant is meant to burn through the Hegelian edifice. What then is Kant's burning standing for, according to Bloch?

Kant's role in Bloch's imperative can be summed up in two steps. The first concerns Bloch's rejection of the *regulative* approximation to the fullness of being that defines Kant's philosophy as a principle. As Pierre Kerszberg, re-counting Heidegger's ontological reading of Kant, put it, Kant's 'critical philosophy wants simultaneously to reach the absolute and to get by without *the* Absolute'.[24] Arguably Bloch was not content with Kant's 'transcendental principle of waiting – the postponement of reason's fulfillment in being – or a displacement of this fulfillment'.[25] It is because of the dynamic regulativeness that is generated from the Kantian undecidedness of fulfilment that Hegel was required to step in and serve up something besides disappointment and abandonment, resulting from this Kantian heterogeneity of *Sein und Sollen*. Secondly, despite the drawback of Kant laying in his requiring the services of Hegel, Bloch's imperative signals a discernible merit of Kant's transcendental ego, which, as Bloch argues, possesses a powerful surplus in knowing 'how to postulate morally beyond a bad existent'.[26] In other words, however detrimental the infinite approximation to a fullness of being is in Kantianism, there still is registered in this endless movement an acknowledgement of a gap and a hope for a future in which the gap is reconciled. This hope represents an outright rejection of what presently is given (even if in the long run Kant eternalises this inadequate present) and carries in itself that critique of appearance when appearance is considered in its non-relation to totality. To frame things along the lines of language here, it can be said: *the empiricism of language does not subsume the possibility of what can linguistically be otherwise.*

While, then, Kant eternalises the fissure between what is and what ought to be, in which a conclusive goal is only approximated asymptotically, Kant's philosophical integrity and revolutionary flavour is to be located in his bringing to the fore the very implacability of a gap in the present, and thereby his philosophy intimates a potential surplus in that interstice of being, a *potential point of opening* within the real existence of the human being and its world. However, Kant thereby is caught between, on the one hand, an acceptance of the present

---

24   Kerszberg 2000, p. 35.
25   Kerszberg 2000a, p. 42.
26   Bloch 2000a, p. 147.

as unfulfilled, and, on the other, an equally intense and jarring acknowledgement that this same present is – *precisely unfulfilled*, it requires something more that is currently missing. For Bloch, it is this sense that 'something's missing' which needs to burn through the coordinates of the present: 'The Not is lack of Something and also escape from this lack; thus it is a driving towards what is missing'.[27]

Such incompletion and hope give rise to process, even if Kant shuts the motivation of this radical process down by rendering an arrival at what is aimed-for, in this life at least, impossible for reason. Kant disenfranchises the gap's potency, one might say. An ultimate arrival, an identity, is persistently and forever receding into the horizon of being in the Kantian frame of things. The Kantian striving is one that 'only always approximates the infinitely remote goal', as Bloch says –[28] the striving never seizes the thing. Kant's virtue – his recognition of the gap between fact and value – turns into his weakness. Kant therefore practises 'the art of talking about what we have not yet experienced', but only so to *end* all talk of it.[29]

Contrary to Kant, Bloch holds onto the possibility of the gap's overcoming, an overcoming that was rendered poignantly available in its absence in Kant's thought. Hegel is thus required to bring it to a type of half-ripeness. Indeed at first blush more accord seems to obtain between Bloch and Hegel, for Hegel is also averse to the goal's 'remotion',[30] to 'the fiction of a completion', a completion not 'actually attained or ever attainable'.[31] Hegel too struggles against the Kantian theorisation of an irreparable dualism between the 'ought' and the 'is', Hegel 'discards any mere ought-to-be' and indeed 'scoffs at Kant's infinite approximation'.[32] To Hegel's mind, Bloch says, the Kantian subject is left 'starving [*Hungerleiderei*]' for what would be its 'good and proper meal [*einer tüchtigen Mahlzeit*]' – an 'ought' for which it craves – that 'actualization of the new'[33] which, situated in the unreachable domain of the 'eternally non-present' in Kantianism, is far from nourishing for the mind and the body.[34] This bad infinite, a strictly Protestant form of desire Bloch stresses ('the bad

---

27   Bloch 1986, p. 306. Bloch was fond of deploying this famous line from Brecht's lyrics in the *Mahagonny* (1927). 'Something's missing' (*etwas fehlt*).

28   Bloch 1969, p. 375.

29   Bloch 1986, p. 24.

30   Bloch 1962, p. 446.

31   Natorp 2015, p. 192.

32   Natorp 2015, p. 190.

33   Boldyrev 2014, p. 126.

34   Bloch 1962, pp. 446–7.

infinite of Protestantism'),[35] 'eliminates the surplus' as an utterly unattainable beyond, and, as has been noted, does so in the very act of recognising it.[36]

If Kant's striving in the present is merely 'the ideological reflex of the early capitalist economy',[37] simply a Protestant 'distrust of human striving and an aversion to the end, to the arrival of striving',[38] then it would seem that, if the choice is between Kant and Hegel, it is Hegel who turns out to be the better of the two options. After all, Hegel is prepared to entertain the notion of arrival. And yet, while Kant eliminates the surplus of what has not yet come to be by casting its attainability aside as a strict impossibility, as irrevocable and as separate from and without immanence in being,[39] Hegel, Bloch argues, liquidates the power of the 'ought' in another equally, perhaps even more perilously unacceptable manner.[40] Despite Hegel's antipathy towards a 'melancholic' Kantianism that honours its own incapacity to attain the ultimate 'What' of its desire ('a desire to believe but an inability to'),[41] Hegel's proposed alternative is just as suspect in Bloch's eyes, for it leads to a certain quietism,[42] best embodied by Hegel's *Philosophy of Law*: 'To comprehend *what is* is the task of philosophy, for *what is* is reason'.[43] The remotion from what ought to be, rendered *a priori* and thereby fixed in Kant, in Hegel no longer takes on the colouration of pure absence, but pure presence. The gap is levelled to 'the perfect Now'.[44] This is because 'Hegel', writes Bloch, 'with great correctness, goes against the perennial Ought, but with the effect that there is generally no more un-realised [*Unverwirklichtes*] remaining, and so no future'.[45] Hegel discards the bad infinite of Kantian striving and in doing so discards the impossibility of a real future arrival. But Hegel pushes too far, is too impatient. No need or demand

---

35   Bloch 1962, p. 448.

36   Bloch 1962, p. 447. For a more subtle discussion of the 'confessional-political background' to Kant's philosophy, see Hildebrandt (2007, pp. 477–8): 'The description of Kant as the philosopher of Protestantism has a long tradition'. See also Adorno (2001, pp. 71–3), who makes a similar argument concerning the tight relation between Protestant theology and infinite striving as a type of anti-utopian tendency of thought; there is a danger that the not-yet of the reality of reason is suspended into an infinite task, Adorno suggests.

37   Bloch 1969, p. 370.

38   Bloch 1969, p. 28.

39   See Boldyrev 2014, p. 128.

40   Bloch 1969, p. 28.

41   Bloch 2000a, p. 173.

42   Bloch 1962, p. 446. Cf. Rose 2009, pp. 84–97.

43   Hegel 1991, pp. 21–2.

44   Bloch 2000a, p. 179.

45   Bloch 1962, p. 446.

for striving occurs here, for no incompletion remains whatsoever.[46] The good and proper meal has been cooked up, is served, and simply awaits its recognition:

> Hegel's theory that everything rational is already real concludes a premature and total truce with the world, but Kant's only approximative infinity of reason, practical reason in particular, makes of the world an ocean without a shore.[47]

This 'shore' is the utopian hoped-for arrival. Here *in nuce* lies Bloch's suggestion that, while Hegel forgot the future (Hegel closed down the possibility that the very notion of the future was necessary), the future will not forget Hegel. The future of Hegel's reception will not forgo Hegel's admission of the possibility of arrival.[48] In sum, then, while Kant recognises the gap and yet posits its overcoming as an impossibility – such that here there is *too much* beyond,[49] on the other hand, Hegel recognises the possibility of overcoming the gap (this is why the future will not forget Hegel), but Hegel does so only insofar as the gap has already been overcome – such that here there is *too little* (in fact, no) beyond. On the one side, there is a language that is ultimately cut adrift from any logical-ideal (Kant), while on the other stands a language of a logical-ideal that totally subsumes the incompleteness of empiricism (Hegel). Bloch's imperative to let Kant burn through Hegel rejects both of these outcomes, and posits both in their very combination.[50] Bloch's imperative demands a recognition of the gap while holding open the possibility of its overcoming. 'So it seems necessary at

---

46   Bloch 1962, p. 448.
47   Bloch 2000a, p. 178. Following a common neo-Kantian train of thought against Hegelianism in force in the late nineteenth century, Bloch rejected a 'Hegelian *Versöhnung* with reality' (Löwy 1979, p. 92). In the case of the early Lukács, this tendency to veto against an appeasement with present reality would translate itself into a proclivity for a mystically oriented 'sharp rejection of the world' (Lukács quoted in Löwy 1979, p. 94n12. Cf. p. 210).
48   See Bloch 1962, p. 12: 'Hegel leugnete die Zukunft, keine Zukunft wird Hegel verleugnen'.
49   '... the shoreless ocean of infinite tasks that we have dared to embrace. For we do not wish to be saved: *navigare necesse est!*' (Natorp 2015, p. 193). As Chapter 3 shows, this Kantian formulation reverberates in Voloshinov.
50   Bloch may well recapitulate what Roberts (2011, p. 86) terms 'the Hegel of bourgeois caricature'. Roberts will argue that Hegel's focus on actuality's realisation in the present is materialist insofar as it expresses the notion of an 'active mode of the actual' (Roberts 2011, p. 90) in which actuality is emergent from the appearances of the present as emancipatory tendencies, as negation; hence Hegel being 'a formidable critic of unrealizable ideals' (Roberts 2011, p. 91).

this point to let Kant' – the yearning will of a striving amidst the not-yet – 'burn through Hegel'[51] – the objective possibility/power of arrival. Such is the spirit of utopia, the starting point, and such is just what matter is for Bloch.

The incomprehensibility of the Kantian thing as it is in itself (the gap)[52] is now inscribed into matter's objective constitution, and the question of what matter is turns over into a question that matter fundamentally poses of itself. And an arrival at an answer to this *objectively real* question remains entirely possible. A materialist philosophy of language that is constructed in the framework of Bloch's thought would have to, I argue, contend with this Kant-Hegel reading. As Bloch writes:

> What is matter? This question is ... the own most question of *all matter itself*, its resolution-experiment in progress. It is the What-problem of human contents together with not only our sustaining but cosmically enormous, encompassing nature.[53]

The surplus of the real unknowability that structures Kant's philosophy is not an epistemologically outstanding element of the real that is unknowable for the human mind. Rather, this surplus is a *really extraterritorial* state of matter's existence – a residue or ontological surplus, an indeterminacy in the being of matter in which human beings find themselves. In fact, as Ivan Boldyrev notes, it is Kantian ethics and not Kantian epistemology which is 'truly significant for utopian philosophy' and which is that dark space in Kant which, in Bloch's philosophy, and 'along neo-Kantian lines',[54] merges the phenomenal and the noumenal realms that were left fractured in Kant. Bloch, then, displaces Kant's metaphysics of knowledge into the light of a new metaphysics of being, indeed a *materialist metaphysics of the new*, and does so with the help of Hegel, or better, with a Hegel burned by Kant. As Hegel writes: 'In a living relation, insofar as it is free, the indeterminate is nothing but the *possible*'.[55] For Bloch, then,

> ... the substance of the world, the matter of the world, is itself not yet concluded, but is located in a utopian-open, that is, on a not yet self-identical, manifested footing.[56]

---

51   Bloch 2000a, p. 187.
52   See Kant 2003.
53   Bloch 1970a, p. 209.
54   Boldyrev 2014, p. 125. Cf. Levinas 2000.
55   Hegel 1977a, p. 146.
56   Bloch 1970a, p. 102.

Matter's what-problem, the 'kernel of the world',[57] is not yet resolved. It is located within its own objective blind spot. This indeterminacy in the substance of the world, which humans themselves live out and live through, aligns with Bloch's category of the 'darkness of the just lived moment',[58] a category that expresses a recognition of the incompleteness of material being in the immediacy of its being experienced. Within empirical immediacy lies an incomplete logical-ideal. Following Friedrich Engels, Bloch holds that a fundamental facet of materialism consists in an immanence of philosophical explanation, i.e. materialism explains the world from out of the world; it avoids at all costs the postulation of a transcendental beyond that is bereft of matter and yet is utilised as the principle by which to explain matter's very existence.[59] Matter must be explained from itself. Writing to Theodor Adorno in 1935, Bloch puts a seal on his guiding philosophical insights: 'the darkness of the just lived moment, the form of the inconstructable question, not-yet-conscious knowledge, and a new utopian substance'.[60] It is the first insight – the darkness of the just lived moment – that articulates Bloch's Kant-Hegel reading in another form and which captures this materialist principle of explaining the world from out of itself. Indeed Bloch employs an ocular analogy to clarify this root idea:

> What is very near, what immediately rises up before my eyes, I cannot see. It must give a distance there. Then it can first be objective. Otherwise it is not yet shaped at all, and much less representational. In proverbs it is simply felt: what he weaves, no weaver knows – at the foot of the lighthouse there is no light – the prophet is never honoured in his own land ...[61]

Significant for my discussion of exotopy in the Bakhtin Circle in Chapter 3, what makes one's visual field possible is not *in* one's visual field, but extraterritorial to it. Bloch sometimes enlists the verb *'ausstehen'* to make this point, literally meaning 'out-standing', both in the sense of 'standing outside of' and 'yet to be given', 'yet to be determined'. Matter itself, for Bloch, is an attempt to step beyond this immediacy of itself and arrive at an uncontrived encounter with itself, overcoming this blind spot in the darkness of the just lived moment.[62]

57   Bloch 1969, p. 146.
58   Bloch 1969, p. 149.
59   Bloch 1972, p. 169. See Vilmar 1965.
60   See Bloch 1985a, p. 435.
61   Bloch 1978, p. 340. Cf. Zimmermann 2001, p. 17.
62   See Moltmann 1978, p. 73 and Barron 2021.

Indeed, insofar as the possibility of arrival mediates this blind spot, contrary to a Wittgensteinian silence, matter becomes creative, enunciating new forms. Thus Bloch understands matter as 'a fruitful world-womb experimenting with forms, figures, [and] shapes of existence'.[63]

2 Tendency

This *process* of material creativity is matter's determination as 'tendency'. The 'disparity of the substance with itself',[64] to paraphrase Hegel, does not entail a silent condition or stasis, but a productive process that for Bloch is inherent to matter: 'it is possible to define "Tendency" according to a fundamental thesis of Marx, as the "dream of the actual"'.[65] Mediating the material process, then, is both the current lack of, and the possibility of, arrival.

'Tendency' describes a chiasmus of process and matter: 'there is no process without matter', Bloch says, 'no matter without process'.[66] This inseparability is established by Bloch with the term 'process-matter [*Prozeßmaterie*]'.[67] Fundamentally, then, matter is not the a-historical *Klotzmaterie*. It is not an 'it', not the mechanistic clump whose movement is only externally communicated to it, as is the case in Kant's Newtonian doctrine of motion, which, as a consequence is forced to hypothesise a transcendent origination of material movement,[68] and which therefore contravenes the materialist principle that the world must be explained from out of the world.[69] For Bloch, the origination and the continuing production of material process must instead be grasped immanently. As Hegel wrote, 'free matter moves spontaneously',[70] such as Marx perceived in Epicurus's swerving atoms, the *clinamen*:[71]

---

63   Bloch 1972, p. 17.
64   Hegel 1977b, p. 21.
65   Bloch 1998, p. 108.
66   Bloch 2000a, p. 122.
67   Bloch 1972, p. 121.
68   See Kant 2004, pp. 15 and 25, Guyer 2005, p. 84, Hegel 2012, p. 258, Bloch 1978, pp. 250–60, Bloch 1972, pp. 17 and 246, Bloch 1970a, pp. 230 and 234, Bloch 2000a, p. 185 and Bloch 1986, p. 237. Mechanical materialism refers to the mathematically oriented materialisms of the early modern period. Galileo Galilei (1564–1642), Thomas Hobbes (1588–1679), René Descartes (1596–1650), and Isaac Newton (1642–1726/27) are the most prominent figures of this scientistic materialism in relevant compendia (see Wallace 1977, pp. 300–1).
69   See Bloch 1972.
70   Hegel 1970, p. 49.
71   See Bloch 2018, pp. 153–8.

> Among the qualities inherent in *matter*, *motion* is the first and foremost, not only in the form of *mechanical* and *mathematical* motion, but chiefly in the form of an *impulse*, a *vital spirit*, a *tension* – a *'Qual'*, to use a term of Jakob Böhme's – of matter.[72]

Bloch's concept of matter is in some sense an opus of confrontation with mechanical materialism, the latter of which has, for Bloch, certain repercussions for aesthetic linguistic production: 'The substance that finally can be adequate to poetry is not merely mechanical, space filling matter, but that which blossoms forth historically, as a realisation of the possible'.[73] Here one has a more fundamental, temporal mode of materiality. Incidentally, the exteriority to language that is often attributed to the figure of the anacoluthon mirrors this mechanical notion of matter on the score of process – the anacoluthon's disruption of syntax, as I will show, is said to derive from a place external to the proper functioning of language (see Chapter 2).

The category 'tendency', then, accords with Bloch's intention to re-think process as an 'existential mode of matter',[74] and in doing so Bloch to a large extent is guided by Heraclitus' famous dictum that 'everything flows' or 'everything is in a state of flux' (*panta rhei*). Akin to Hegel's notion that one must think substance as subject, Bloch says one must think 'substance as process',[75] thereby emphatically breaking with metaphysical substance doctrines. Process, for Bloch, is anterior to being, just as the burning will for fulfilment precedes what fulfilment can be.[76]

Since matter is not thrown into process by a cause external to it, so then its 'tendency' names matter's self-causative, autopoetic process. 'Tendency' therefore points to an incomplete, self-causative materiality. This moves us towards further determinations of Bloch's materialism, 'contradiction' and 'anticipation'.[77] These further Blochain determinations of matter indicate that process-matter is at one and the same time a discontinuous process (it is contradictory), and a future-directed process (it is anticipatory). These determinations are borne out by the genealogical heritage of the 'tendency' category as it was first worked-out in Leibniz's monadic metaphysics, in which the most ele-

---

72   Marx and Engels 1975c, p. 128.

73   Bloch 1998, p. 113.

74   Bloch 2000a, p. 176.

75   Bloch 2000a, p. 160.

76   See Zimmermann 2014, p. 66, Geoghegan 1996, p. 28 and Hudson 1982, p. 69. See Bloch 1986, pp. 201–2 for a sense of Bloch's critical stance towards Bergsonianiam.

77   Bloch 1986, p. 336.

mentary constituents of reality – 'monads' – are said to pass from confused to clear representations of themselves.[78] Since these basic constituents of reality undergo a passage from confusedness to clarity, they, according to Leibniz, actively appetite for, intend, and anticipate a certain self-clarity. As Zeilinger writes:

> The root of the concept *tendency* [...] lies in the old-Greek verb *teinein*, with the central meaning of 'to stretch', 'to tension', 'to expand or extend itself', 'to tend toward something'. This meaning survives in the Latin *tendere*. *Tendere* [...] means 'inclination', 'striving', 'direction', 'aim or purpose', 'intention', and is akin to *appetitus, conatus*, and *inclinatio*.[79]

'Tension' derives from matter's contradiction, namely, it is objectively blind to itself as what it is but wants to have that what-ness; and in this wanting it creatively and actively anticipates its what-ness, or essence. As Leibniz wrote: 'one can say that in the soul, as indeed everywhere, *the present is great with the future*'.[80] Bloch's inheritance of this Leibnizian idea of an ontological confusedness that tends towards a future clarification of itself – 'an understanding of the future', therefore, 'as the greater dimension of the present'[81] – places its own unique stamp on the idea, refunctioning it to Bloch's own purposes. Here, matter's 'passage of clarification' is defined by contradiction and discontinuity, and of a process of self-clarification the content and form of which does not precede the searching for it.[82] Indeed, Leibniz's understanding of nature was premised on a pre-established harmony – *lex continui natura non facit saltus*.[83] According to Bloch, on the other hand, the very existence of the human being demonstrates that nature certainly does make leaps and is constituted by ruptures:[84] '[t]his inceptive Not and what it searches for grows exacting in us humans, like nowhere else. We are transcending ourselves but so too is everything in our compass'.[85]

---

78   Bloch 1972, p. 55.

79   Zeilinger 2012, p. 555, my translation.

80   Leibniz 1970, p. 580.

81   Bloch 2018, p. 32.

82   Bloch 1972, p. 54.

83   See Schneider 2006.

84   Leibniz's (1998, p. 268) claim that monads 'have no windows, through which anything could come in or go out', for instance, is altered by Bloch into the following: 'form [*Gestalt*] is significant only when it has a window that heads towards the path of morning'. (Bloch 2000a, p. 315).

85   Bloch 1975, p. 172.

3   Possibility

It is difficult to see where the relationship of materialism to utopia can be found: 'At first glance such a connection appears foreclosed'.[86] Not least because of the critical eye Marx and Engels cast over the idea of a utopian tendency of thought, one that Lukács continued in his own manner (see Chapter 4). But the connection between matter and utopia lies in possibility, for possibility names the relationship of incompletion to actuality. The history of the world teaches us quite clearly that not every relation of possibility to actuality is realised, or that not all possibilities are possible at once. But *that* there is a relation of possibility to actuality – this points to the ontological incompleteness that still defines material existence.

'Possibility' is a category which provides a connective in Bloch's materialism between 'tendency' and 'latency', the latter grasped as a goal of process which is 'not-yet' (a utopian actuality – 'no-place'). That is to say, if 'tendency' names an interruptive and anticipative process it is also a process of realisation from possibility to actuality. The anticipatory and discontinuous process which moves to what is not yet, and which Bloch calls matter, is born of possibility; matter's process of self-clarification is merely another name for Bloch's re-formulation of Aristotle's classical determination of matter as tied to the movement of possibility to actuality.[87] While 'Aristotelian possibility' ultimately never realises itself in a novelty of actuality, nevertheless 'Aristotle was the first to recognise possibility in real terms, in the world-stock itself'.[88]

Possibility is therefore matter's principal modality for Bloch and materialism is indeed a philosophy of radical possibility. The emergence of novelty in the material process is premised on this priority of possibility. Compared to

---

86   Bloch 1978, p. 265.
87   As Brentano (1975, p. 27) states, for Aristotle, potential being and matter are 'coextensive'. Bloch (1962, p. 113) considers Aristotle a 'process thinker' (Bloch 1962, p. 113) and Adorno (2000, p. 56) asserts that, relative to Plato, Aristotle renders ontological speculation 'incomparably more dynamic'.
88   Bloch 1986, p. 235. See Bloch 1986, pp. 207–8 and Bloch 1972, p. 235. As Bloch notes, this precedence plays itself out in the matter-form couplet. If it was the virtue of Aristotle's anti-Platonism to have re-immersed forms in the things as the form-matter composite (see Ricoeur 2013, p. 223), then Aristotle remains beholden to the Platonic form as pre-existing matter. Aristotelian form is thus un-engendered: 'certainly ... an immanent quiddity', but 'for all that they are no less entities removed from time', 'no less immutable than the Platonic real', as Ricoeur (2013, pp. 226–7) puts it. Aristotle's desire to avoid a Platonic dualism fails to hit its target, then, insofar as form is 'dualistically separated from matter' (Bloch 1986, p. 235).

actuality, Bloch declares, 'the ocean of possibility is much greater'.[89] Of course, often things are presented in reverse order, particularly by those who benefit most from present actuality. Bloch's refunction of the Aristotelian concept of entelechy demonstrates the precedence of possibility well. Entelechy denotes 'having a goal in itself' and, as Bloch writes, entelechy names 'the idea [the end] endeavouring to shape itself in matter', 'the active principle of realisation' that is 'contained ... in the appearance'.[90] In this regard Bloch speaks of the 'utopian' notion of 'incomplete entelechy'[91] which emphasises the incomplete locus of the natural generative process, the not-yet decided principle of realisation which realises itself through history. Here, then, one has 'a latent goal working from a latent idea of shape'.[92] Here again then is that not-yet logical-ideal embedded within the empiricism of language. Thus matter itself is conceived of as a process of self-formation, an idea that is important for my reading of the anacoluthon in Chapter 2.

Forms *emerge* from or are *given birth to out* of matter's radical possibility, insofar as the locus of its process itself is still undergoing realisation.[93] Matter is now also implicitly taken to constitute a *forward* forming developmental process, one in which possibility is set-free from its initial subordination to an external, already constituted form. Matter's process of realisation now truly becomes an *open material process of real realisation*. These shifts in the Aristotelian problematic, first given to Bloch by Arabic heretic readers of Aristotle, constitute the beginnings of what Bloch will call 'a futural materialism', or what I shall call a utopian materialism.[94] Bloch's admiration for the etymology of 'matter', a word derived from *mater*, meaning 'mother', exemplifies this idea of matter as a womb of possibility.[95] An emphatic, objective sense of self-causation, self-creation, and self-clarification take centre-stage in Bloch's categorisation of matter here. Matter is 'the fermenting womb of a substance which so to speak first gives birth to itself, i.e. develops, clarifies and

---

89   Bloch 1978, p. 356. Bloch formulates this priority of possibility in a propositional form: 'P is assigned to S in the mode of Can-be'. (Bloch 1986, p. 226). As Hogh (2017, p. 3) notes, the dichotomy of matter and form arises in early analytic approaches to language which, on the whole, 'determine language as an autonomous form' separate from non-linguistic reality, i.e. nature/matter.

90   Bloch 1978, p. 409.

91   Bloch 1983, p. 304 and Bloch 1986, p. 223.

92   Bloch 1986, p. 984.

93   See Bloch 1970a, p. 234 and Bloch 2000a, p. 173.

94   Bloch 1970a, p. 233.

95   Bloch 1972, p. 17 and Bloch 1970a, p. 231.

qualifies itself'.[96] Matter is for Bloch, as Siebers writes, 'the world-womb, the birthplace of possibility'.[97]

However, Bloch's 'Moduslehre'[98] develops a twofold modal definition of possibility which will be important for my comparative discussion of Voloshinov and Bloch in Chapter 3. Bloch distinguishes between matter 'according to possibility', which relates to 'the respectively conditioning element according to the given measure of the Possible', and 'What-Is-in-possibility' as the 'womb of fertility from which all world-forms inexhaustibly emerge'.[99] In other words, according to Bloch, 'matter' as possibility is at one and the same time 'what can appear in respectively determined historical-materialist conditions',[100] namely, a new emergence which is in accordance with prevailing possibilities tied to the here and now, which would include a 'critical *consideration of the attainable*',[101] *and* 'the correlate of objective-real-possibility, or pure beingness',[102] namely, the interwoven possibility of arrival, '*the founded expectation of attainability itself*'.[103] This twofold definition of possibility maps neatly onto Bloch's notion of 'cold' and 'warm streams' of Marxist critique, its 'two ways of being red', a notion which avoids positivist economism just as much as it tempers utopian opportunism.[104] Indeed the 'real possible', as Bloch writes,

> ... has two sides, a reverse side as it were, on which the measures of the *respectively* Possible are written, and a front side on which the Totum of the *finally* Possible indicates that it is still open.[105]

The '[f]orward materialism' as the 'warmth-doctrine of Marxism' thus entails a goal-openness to it, not only in the sense that the goal is open in its content, but also in the sense that the goal's achievement is entirely possible.[106] True to its nature as possibility, Bloch divides this ultimate possibility along the lines of two potential outcomes: the possibility of the 'All', that is, of pure being-ness, and the possibility of 'Nothingness':

---

96   Bloch 2000b, p. 173.
97   Siebers 2014, p. 3.
98   Schmidt 1978a, p. 66.
99   Bloch 1986, p. 207, emphasis removed.
100   Bloch 1970a, p. 233.
101   Bloch 1986, p. 207.
102   Bloch 1970a, p. 233.
103   Bloch 1986, p. 207.
104   See Bloch 1986, pp. 208–9.
105   Bloch 1986, p. 206.
106   Bloch 1986, p. 210.

> The *Not-Yet* characterizes the *tendency* in material process, of the origin which is processing itself out, tending towards the manifestation of its content. The *Nothing* or conversely the *All* characterizes the *latency* in this tendency, negative or positive towards us, chiefly on the foremost Front-field of material process.[107]

The possibility of Nothingness does not deny the possibility of arrival but indicates the contingency of process-matter's ultimate realisation. It signals the extent to which a consummation of the ultimate possibility is held open: an ontological equivalent of Rosa Luxemburg's 'Socialism or barbarism!'[108] This as of yet undecided and ultimate possibility, balanced on the scale of history's vicissitudes and struggles, points to 'the unresolved utopian tension constantly undermining everything shaped'.[109] What undermines the already-become shaped-ness of matter is that which allows matter to open out towards a newness of itself. As Bloch writes, the 'tendency' to interruption of 'exodus forms'[110] within the material process is born of inadequacy[111] and signals that matter has not yet exhausted what it can become:

> The womb of matter is not yet exhausted with hitherto becomeness; the most important forms of existence of its history and of its nature still stand in the latency of real possibility.[112]

Bloch's notion of 'Front' crystallises this conception of matter as a process towards what is not yet, both as the possibility of the Nothing and the All. The 'Front' concerns that state or moment *between* the two modes of possibility dealt with above. To 'cling to a world without Front'[113] is, for Bloch, not only to cling to a world without that undecided ultimate possibility which tensions already-become material shapedness. The Front is, as Schmidt writes, the *'threshold-condition* of conditionedness' as such, the borderline of material shapedness.[114] To stand within this threshold-condition is, for Bloch, to stand

---

107 Bloch 1986, p. 306. Cf. Berardi 2019, pp. 9 and 103.
108 Luxemburg 2004, p. 350. See Münster 1986.
109 Bloch 2000a, p. 228.
110 Bloch quoted in Moir 2013, p. 134.
111 Bloch 1962, p. 138.
112 Bloch 1972, p. 524.
113 Bloch 1986, p. 5.
114 Schmidt 1978b, p. 305.

on the Front of the world process. It implies a *threshold-condition of realisation within matter itself*.[115] As Bloch writes of this:

> The being that conditions consciousness, and the consciousness that pro-
> cesses being, is understood ultimately only out of that and in that from
> which and towards which it tends. Essential being is not Been-ness; on the
> contrary: the essential being of the world lies itself on the Front.[116]

4   Latency

Sometimes Bloch employs another term for 'tendency', the 'That [*Daß*]'.[117]
'That-ness' (*Daßheit*), 'the state or condition of being there', stands as a cat-
egorial determination of what is a pre-categorial state of being.[118] Existence as
simply being there (recall Bloch's departure point in immanence) is poverty
and hollowness of being. That-ness is the in-determination of what-ness, of
essence, and is a condition which seeks that determination in process. Bloch
therefore speaks of the 'completely empty *Daß*'.[119] But the poverty of the not-
having instils dynamism into matter, as we have already seen:

> ... the That is intending, tensioning, driving, addiction; gives itself as
> intensive, namely as drive, hunger, need, longing, but also as a question
> which not only intends what it asks for, but also in the end *intends itself*.[120]

For Bloch, what is ultimately intended by matter as 'tendency' (as 'That-ness') is
that which is new, a *Novum*: 'the What itself – in the still pending expression of
its contents – is ultimately the Novum'.[121] Indeed, 'the essence of the world lies
on the Front'.[122] Were That-ness eventually to have itself as it truly intends, this
would amount to having a novelty of itself, for it would be something that has
not yet arisen in the history of material becoming. Chepurin usefully describes
a similar thought with reference to 'the revolutionary production of newness

---

115   See Siebers 2012b, p. 163.
116   Bloch 1986, p. 18.
117   Bloch 200b, p. 255.
118   Bloch 2000b, p. 256.
119   Bloch 2000b, p. 255.
120   Bloch 2000b, p. 256.
121   Ibid.
122   Bloch 1970a, p. 275, emphasis removed.

from the in-itself'.[123] This idea is the other, equally important determination of matter in Bloch's utopian materialism, and it concerns the category 'latency'.

The very existence of a relation between 'That-ness' and 'What-ness', that is, between 'tendency' (the Kantian acknowledgement of a gap and a hope to close it), on the one hand, and 'latency' (the Hegelian possibility of arrival), on the other, is fundamental. As Bloch writes:

> But *that* between That and What there can obtain a relation at all: this relation itself is the most fundamental category and all other categories merely perform it, all others are only the continued opening out of the That emanating Something-multiplicity through a road network.[124]

Language as such too must thereby perform this relation. Through the category of 'tendency' ('That-ness') Bloch had invited a consideration of matter as a process with 'Front' – matter as the open horizon of the real. But Bloch goes a step further: a realism that does not *realise* anything – one of pure openness – will only fail to grasp the 'realisms of possibility'.[125] For Bloch, realism cannot simply amount to 'a description of reality', but rather it must additionally contain 'an attainment of the real as significant and essential'.[126] Thus realism involves something more occurring than the real as it is now presents itself as being – for Bloch, the real of material existence involves those two ultimate possibilities which were touched on earlier. The 'All' and 'Nothing'.

The difficult issue of purposiveness or teleology in Bloch's philosophy arises here and can be dealt with briefly. Bloch's categorisation sees matter as an open process but it is, paradoxically, a *directed* openness, that is, it is said to contain an invariant of direction, a 'utopian invariant'.[127] Bloch therefore does not conceive of material process only as Heraclitean becoming. Rather, as Gross observes, for Bloch matter is a 'process of *becoming itself*, of achieving its own structure and proper form'.[128] 'The genuine utopian will is definitely not endless striving', as Bloch writes.[129] In seeking what-ness, matter seeks a kind of completion or fulfilment of itself. It is this dimension of matter as a directedness

---

123   Chepurin 2015, p. 339.
124   Bloch 1975, p. 71, my emphasis.
125   Bloch 1986, p. 15.
126   Tihanov 2000, p. 28.
127   Bloch 2000b, p. 365.
128   Gross 1972, p. 122, my emphasis.
129   Bloch 1986, p. 16.

towards a proper form of itself that indicates a *teleological moment* in Bloch's materialism. The question of whether this approach to goal is not a delayed Hegelian reconciliation with reality is an open one. What it does speak to is the importance, for Bloch, of forms of fulfilment, or projections of forms of fulfilment, which circulate material existence, and which Bloch centres in his analysis of classical fascism (see Chapter 4). A materialist philosophy of language that is derived from Bloch's materialism must tarry with the nature of this non-fated goal-bearing quality of process-matter. Insofar as Bloch's is a materialism of possibility, so then the question of actuality, in its ultimate iteration, is necessarily encountered within it.[130]

The nub of *Kant's* account of teleology holds that purposiveness is simply what the human mind presumes to be working in nature as a whole, but that, given this mind's limited architectonic, the assumption lacks convincing theoretical proof; however, purpose in nature should not be considered totally irrelevant.[131] For Kant, natural purposiveness cannot be posited 'in the object' but rather must be viewed as 'strictly in the subject', namely as merely a representation of nature; purpose is thus not as 'a property of the object outside me, but merely a kind of representation in me'.[132] Now, for Kant, one can *assume* that nature harbours an end towards which it '*specifies itself*' in accordance with a certain principle (or idea of system)'.[133] We can assume that this natural specification-towards-an-end leads to the human being as the ultimate form of *free* life as such – 'that nature must be conceived of as an arena for the realisation of our moral ends'.[134] Such an end, however, insofar as its confirmation remains out of the reach of theoretical reason, is no more than an anthropocentric, practically useful projection onto an unknowable nature in itself.[135] It is a 'methodological fiction' – a 'teleonomy'.[136]

---

130   See Feser 2014, p. 160. There can be no question that purposiveness characterises Bloch's materialism. Münster speaks of a 'goal quality' inscribed in matter's 'tendency' (Münster 1982, p. 18). And Bloch casts matter as impetus (*Anstoß*), drive (*Trieb*), hunger, need (*Bedürfnis*) and longing (*Sehnsucht*), all of which suggest something sought for (*Nicht-Habens*) (see Bloch 1975, p. 73). Elsewhere, Bloch asserts that 'things have been thought as process and so precisely as purposive'; '[i]n each process is direction' (Bloch 2000b, p. 366). And he extends this to the broadest of philosophical terms: '[T]he *world* is full of propensity towards something, tendency towards something, latency of something, and this something means fulfilment of the intending'. (Bloch 1986, p. 18).

131   Kant 2000.

132   Kant, 2000, 20:216, and 5:365.

133   Kant 2000, 20:215.

134   Guyer 2005, p. 353, see also p. 171.

135   Guyer 2005, p. 281.

136   Varela and Weber 2002, p. 98.

The directedness of material process in the compass of Bloch's materialism deals with the issue of teleology in the following way, and mirrors Bloch's Kant-Hegel reception that was dealt with earlier on. Firstly, Bloch retains a dimension of the in-determination that we see in Kant's suggestion that teleology is merely *regulative* – for Kant, merely a representation of the subject – but then Bloch inscribes this back into the object, re-positing goal-directedness as an objectively real feature of process-matter – a 'real mode of being'.[137] In sum, Bloch retains in-determination of sorts because we currently cannot know what the common purpose is that binds us to nature (the possibility of the non-realisation of this purpose also steps in here), since the forward specification of materiality contains no pre-conceived idea of system, and indeed no guarantee of its achievement. But then neither is this question of purpose simply reduced – as it is in Kant – to a helpful fiction of our own making. *It is rather a real question of material existence itself*, matter's 'most important truth'.[138] Here, once again, Bloch's notion of matter as an 'intention-for-meaning' or 'intention-for-realisation'[139] does not so much 'skip' Kant as fundamentally re-work the routes that Kant's philosophy made possible to pass down.[140] In sum, purpose is in the object, but it is not pre-conceived purpose. It is open purpose, demanding creativity.

Bloch will at times speak of this in-determinate outfall of the material intending as 'home [*Heimat*]', but also more familiar philosophically as essence ('What-ness', or *quidditas*), or the highest good as 'the non-existing all ... that holds ... together' the openness of the material process.[141] As Bloch writes, 'matter does not have its *Totum* in the horizon of the past' but in 'the future'.[142] What holds the material process together in its openness is that 'dream of a matter' which Marx calls up in his letter to Ruge. Here one can speak of an 'immanent teleology' of sorts.[143]

The nub of the issue lies in whether direction to process can be preserved in a process which is radically open in this way. Bloch wants to avoid a closed-ness of the goal, rejecting pre-determination, yet simultaneously he wants to maintain a notion of directionality, a determination of destination. But process for

---

137   Weber and Varela 2002, p. 111.

138   Bloch 1986, p. 1374.

139   Bloch 1986, p. 121.

140   Cf. Mendes-Flohr 1983, pp. 644–5, who incorrectly reads Bloch in a regulative vein, as does Norris 1989. Cf. Bloch 1975, p. 152.

141   Bloch 1983, p. 303.

142   Bloch 1962, p. 410. See Bloch 1986, pp. 306–13.

143   Bloch 1972, p. 447.

Bloch is precisely *directed to the new*, to novelty. Direction and openness are not incompatible, then. What makes the process directional is therefore also what makes the process open, for process is directed to the really new, which is its goal. As Bloch writes,

> ... it is not something like nonsense or absolute fancy; rather it is something not *yet* in the sense of a possibility; *that* it could be there if only we could do something for it. Not only if we travel there, but *in that* we travel there does the island of utopia arise out of the sea of the possible – utopia, but with new contents.[144]

For Bloch, this purpose of material process arrives only off the back of experimental probing, through accidental turnings, and thus it arrives only through its openness to being imprinted by those accidents. Here again arises the basic premise of Bloch's Kant-Hegel reading: namely, to have a possibility of arrival (contra Kant) without necessitating the type of closure which traditional teleology imposes on the notion of purpose (contra Hegel). Insofar as teleology in Bloch's concept of matter is tied into a Novum that can only reside on the Front of material becoming, so then there is a *real* 'future character' to teleology in Bloch's materialism – for the goal of process is u-topic – a utopian teleology.[145] From an indeterminacy of a final cause's contents to, nevertheless, an invariant of direction to a final cause, leads Bloch to speak of the goal of material process as 'an objectively-real *real problem*'.[146] In other words, it is an *objective* problem – unlike Kant's position, it does not merely name a representation within us, being merely 'an artifact of our own judgment'[147] – but it is also a *real* problem of the object itself, since the contents of purpose within the object are not pre-laid out before the process towards it – or not, as the case may be. As Bloch writes:

> [T]hat which is meant by the highest good, formerly called God, then the kingdom of God, and which is finally the realm of freedom, constitutes not only the purpose-ideal of human history but also the metaphysical latency problem of nature.[148]

---

144   Bloch 1988, p. 3.
145   Bloch 1972, p. 254.
146   Bloch 1986, p. 1324.
147   Guyer 2005, p. 300.
148   Bloch 1986, p. 1324.

Bloch's 'latency' categorises this peculiar teleological moment of matter. 'Latency' 'comes from *latere*', meaning '"being hidden [*versteckt sein*]", "being concealed [*verborgen sein*]", "having not yet emerged [*noch nicht herausgetreten sein*]"', and for Bloch names 'the existence of the not-yet goal-contents in tendency'.[149] This 'latent' goal of material process possesses a 'frontier characteristic'[150] and thus could just as well be 'the All' as 'the Nothing'. 'Latency', then, names that final cause of the material process which has, as it were, fallen 'out of changelessness into movement', 'out of the sphere of identity' and 'into the river of the world fire'.[151] Bloch's proclivity to 'drive the totalizing impulse in Marxism to ... imprudent extremes',[152] as Martin Jay puts it, may be a correct assessment in light of this form of teleological thinking. And yet Bloch's understanding of goal was just as privy to the disasters of previous history, and how these must shape our thinking of historical goal, as it was just as determined to refuse to relinquish the notion of the goal all the same.

---

149 Bloch 2000b, p. 352.
150 Bloch 1998, p. 131.
151 Bloch 1983, p. 300. Cf. Siebers 2012c, pp. 583–84, where the Ultimum of material process is described as standing as a productive limit whose function is to act 'as a (negative) measure for the critique of existence'.
152 Jay 1984, p. 174.

CHAPTER 2

Bloch's Anacoluthon

The task now is to open up the question of language to the 'blossoming field of questions' that Bloch's utopian materialism gives rise to.[1] After all, if, according to Bloch, a utopian logic imbues both being ('not-yet being') and, as I will show in Chapter 3, thought too (the 'not-yet conscious'), so then it would seem appropriate that language be defined by the same prospective logic.[2] The 'mode of being of language' – the expression is Voloshinov's[3] – must undergo a similar re-conception as do being and thought under Bloch's pen. But just as Bloch's body of work carries no explicit, self-standing aesthetic theory, despite Bloch having a lot to say about aesthetics,[4] neither does his work provide an explicitly self-standing approach to language. But as with the topic of aesthetics, there are instances in Bloch's work which point to a more systematic grasp of the language question. The syntactical figure of the anacoluthon, as I will show below, supplies us with one site within language that not only speaks to the basic structure of Bloch's utopian materialism, but is an instance of language which Bloch himself treated, though cursorily only in a single essay.[5]

Moving, then, in the same direction as Cat Moir's fruitful contribution to this topic, I nevertheless chart a slightly different path. As I discussed in the Introduction, Moir focuses on the entangled Nietzschean and Expressionist derivations that make-up Bloch's implicit philosophy of language, singling out Bloch's first and last works.[6] Construction of the Blochian philosophy of language that I develop below has its starting point not in the influences which can be said to have made it up, but in what I call its 'immanent starting point' – the anacoluthon. My approach follows the materialist principle that one must explain the world from out of the world, applying that principle to Bloch's texts themselves, and this entails an exploratory speculation on language in and through Bloch's material. Like the principle of montage – which Bloch made use of during his analyses of fascism – Bloch's corpus can become 'a kind of laboratory, an open experimental space' for the materialist philosopher of

---

1   Bloch 1986, p. 6.
2   See Cunico in Bloch 2000b, p. 451.
3   Voloshinov 1973, p. 67.
4   See Jung 2012, p. 670.
5   Bloch 1998.
6   See Moir 2019b.

language; the texts can become a 'Front', as it were, a 'middle space' of con-ditionedness.[7] The texts themselves tense with latency, but one must begin in them, in their immediacy, to crack the latency open.

Resorting to the basic categories of Bloch's materialism can nevertheless furnish a sort of guide to this exploration: 'tendency' and 'latency', but also the 'Front', the 'Novum', and the 'Ultimum'. Reading these categories alongside the anacoluthon figure – this central and yet unassuming and rarely treated instance of thought on language in Bloch's work – allows me to make a lin-guistic incision into Bloch's materialism. An inquiry into the anacoluthon can help to show that 'the capacities and mechanisms [sic] of language can capture its realist ontological dimension'.[8] As I will show in Chapter 3, despite the mer-its of Voloshinov's Marxist attempt to theorise language, this attempt tends to remain – to paraphrase Bloch here – somewhat 'deficient in utopian thought and lacking an adequately *prospective* view'.[9] With the help of Bloch's philo-sophy it is possible to begin to address this deficiency in Voloshinov's work, and wider Marxist philosophy of language. Developing a Blochian-materialist read-ing of the figure of the anacoluthon begins to highlight this and move things forward.

If the anacoluthon marks a *concrete* beginning here then the question to pose in this chapter is how this linguistic figure embodies the material process which for Bloch is an open process of searching for its own essence, one that entails possible exodus forms. In what manner does matter's 'tendency' and 'latency' mark the anacoluthon? How can the underlying notion that 'the hori-zon of the future ... gives reality its real dimension' be brought to bear on the anacoluthon as a node through which Bloch's Marxist philosophy of language can begin to be built?[10] Where can 'a day break, a movement forwards'[11] be dis-cerned in the anacoluthon, and so on?

Insofar as the anacoluthon is a figure of syntax, I have therefore chosen to explore the materialism of language in Bloch's work neither in the sign nor in the propositional form. It is of course plausible that Bloch's concept of mat-ter could produce a broad semiotics of sorts, a utopian-semiotics that avoids the type of 'archaising recourse' to retrospection[12] of, say, Peirce's semiotics, in which the sign's basic function is seen as one of re-presenting an absent object –

---

7   Bloch 1991, p. 226.
8   Avanessian 2016, p. 200.
9   Bloch 1998, p. 55, my emphasis.
10   Bloch 1986, p. 285, emphasis removed.
11   Bloch 1980, p. 48, emphasis removed.
12   Bloch 1975, p. 158.

an object or a part of an object that already was but is no longer or is no longer here in this present moment.[13] The sign's referent in a Blochian semiotics would no longer be a 'not-any-more' but a 'not-yet' in the process of its becoming.[14] The sign's temporal direction (*Zeitrichtung*) would be a process forwards, the rudiments of a semiosis of anticipation or an anticipatory semiosis, as opposed to one of re-collection (the very thing, it seems, that Marx called for in the *Eighteenth Brumaire*, which I discuss in Chapter 4).[15]

Although there are other legitimate possibilities for inquiry in this context, I will explore the materiality of language for Bloch's philosophy via syntax; or better, via a rupture of syntactical normality; 'where', as Bloch will say, 'meaning's former context is split open'.[16] One could legitimise this path of inquiry by recalling the general tendency of thought set-out by Humboldt, for whom, as Cassirer writes, 'the true vehicle of linguistic meaning is never to be sought in the particular word, but only in the sentence; for the sentence reveals the original force of *synthesis* upon which all speech and all understanding are essentially based'.[17] The question of synthesis relates to the question of totality. The Marxist semiotician Ferruccio Rossi-Landi once suggested that the syntactic dimension of language, that is, the manner in which signs relate to other signs, is never free of the sign's semantic dimension, which concerns the relationship between a sign and its *significata* and possible *denotata*; nor is it free of the pragmatic dimension of the sign (which concerns the relationship between a sign and its interpreters and interpretants). No sign, then, simply belongs to just one dimension of language alone, whether the semantic, pragmatic or syntactic,[18] instead one always has 'the *simultaneous presence* of the three'.[19] In this light, in concerning the totality of a sentence the anacoluthon concerns totality, but is it not a figure with merely an internal concern to language, but also with

---

13   See Peirce 1998.

14   Cf. Kübler 1975, p. 273.

15   It is equally plausible to explore the implications of Bloch's materialism for re-configuring logical-grammatical and/or subject-predicate constructions. It has been argued that the conventional subject-predicate construction remains coextensive with the elemental teachings of substance metaphysics (see White 2014), precisely that metaphysical tongue that Bloch and Marx and Engels assail. Siebers has treated of this potential in Bloch for language speculation, placing particular emphasis on the role of the Novum category (see Siebers 2013a, p. 66; see Bloch 1975, pp. 39 and 41).

16   Bloch 1998, p. 100.

17   Cassirer 1980, p. 160.

18   See Rossi-Landi 1992, p. 40.

19   Rossi-Landi 1992, p. 40. Cf. Davidson: 'Questions of reference do not arise in syntax, much less get settled'. (Davidson 2001, p. 223).

its world and with the people who speak it. In this way Voloshinov provides
further good reason for moving in the direction of syntax. As he writes,

> ... problems of syntax have immense importance for the proper under-
> standing of language and its generative process. In point of fact, of all
> the forms of language, *the syntactic forms are the ones closest to the con-
> crete forms of utterance*, to forms of concrete speech performances. All
> syntactic analyses of speech entail analysing the living body of an utter-
> ance and, therefore, powerfully resist relegation to the abstract system
> of language. Syntactic forms are more concrete than morphological or
> phonetic forms and are more closely associated with the real conditions
> of discourse.[20]

So syntax leads close to the real conditions of discourse. If it is true that Wittgenstein once said that at times a whole treatise of philosophy is or can be
condensed into a drop of grammar,[21] then the (a-)syntactical figure of the
anacoluthon, I argue, condenses within itself Bloch's utopian materialism. But
just why begin with, and just what is, the anacoluthon? Probing these questions will establish, first, the nature of the figure, and second, the manner in
which the anacoluthon's status as a *trace* in Bloch's philosophy leads to its significance as a node through which to develop a Marxist philosophy of language
from Bloch's corpus.

1   The Anacoluthon

One can begin with Sanders's commentary on the anacoluthon, which provides
an initial response to the question of what, in the old world of rhetoric, the figure stands for:

> The anacoluthon qualifies as a grammatical-rhetorical technical term
> for a linguistic 'derailment in construction [*Konstruktionsentgleisung*]'
> or, if one wants to avoid a negative valuation, an 'inconsistent syntax
> [*Satzbau*]'.[22]

---

20   Voloshinov 1973, p. 110.
21   See Virno 2018, p. 2.
22   Sanders 2014, p. 485. Incidentally, the editor of the book in which Sanders's singular com-
      mentary appears, is a one-time student of Bloch's, Gert Ueding, a prominent figure behind
      the revival of rhetoric in the German academy.

The anacoluthon represents, then, an 'inconsistent mode of expression [*nicht folgerichtige Ausdrucksweise*]'.[23] It is this sense of not following that essentially corresponds

> ... to the etymological derivation of the notion from the Greek ἀ(ν)- 'not' and the adjective ακόλουθον (*akólouthos*), 'accompanying [*begleitend*]', 'corresponding [*entsprechend*]', 'following [*folgend*]'.[24]

The anacoluthon's 'chief form [*Hauptform*]' is therefore a 'not-accompanying', a 'non-corresponding', or more simply a 'shift in construction [*Konstruktion-swechsel*]' in the flow of a sentence.[25] All of this is captured in the original German term '*ein Satzbruch*', originally coined by Eduard Engel, denoting the same sense of the anacoluthon albeit with more intensity. '*Ein Bruch*': 'a violation', 'a breach', 'an infringement', 'a flaw', 'a failure', 'a rupture', 'a fracture', 'a breakage, break, breaking(-off)', 'a disruption', 'a crack', 'a discontinuity', 'a parting'. As Most has more recently written:

> Ancient grammarians and rhetoricians observed such irregularities in the texts that they dealt with, and ... they applied to them such terms as ... (anakolouthia), 'lack of succession', and ... (anakolouthos), 'lacking succession', in order to describe them. These words derive from the negation (ἀν-) of the verb ... (akoloutheô), which means 'I follow or accompany': the basic idea is that the elements of a discourse must not only follow one another in the sense of mere temporal succession but must accompany one another, 'follow' them in the richer sense of 'obey' or 'comply with' them. Mere temporal sequence is only a necessary condition for a well-formed text but not a sufficient one: the text's components must additionally be linked with one another by established grammatical relations of consistency and compatibility if it is to form a satisfactorily unified whole. Grammar, we might say, lends significance to the brute temporality of a linguistic utterance and thereby redeems it, demonstrating that it is not simply arbitrary but is instead meaningful; anacoluthon puts into question this local redemption, and, by implication, other, even larger ones.[26]

---

23   Sanders 2014, p. 485.
24   Ibid.
25   Sanders 2014, p. 487.
26   Most 2019, p. 242.

Not only then is there a temporal break within the anacoluthon's appearance in the flow of speech, but so too is there a break in the sense of disobedience, an infraction of a rule, an intractable speech. These senses of the anacoluthon are corroborated by other definitions given in the literature. Newmark defines the anacoluthon as an occurrence of speech in which 'one syntactical pattern, one grammatical construction' is discontinued 'by another before the first [pattern] is allowed to complete itself'.[27] The anacoluthon therefore touches on incompleteness (that erasure of a local redemption just mentioned above), and it could be described as a question that is posed or posited within the speech act, seeking after what completeness *is*; it is that which interrupts the 'normal' circulation of spoken language, disrupts the normal totality to which language is meant to obey. As if language were out of step with itself, the figure stands for 'a deviation, a rupture or a break within an overall movement that could otherwise be integrated into one system of meaning'.[28] The speech movement is disallowed from running its usual course.

Richter similarly defines the anacoluthon as that which 'has no logical following in the syntax of a sentence'; it is a disjunction in 'the scheme of sequential speech or writing to mark a point where the linearity of a discourse and its logic breaks down'.[29] The becoming of the word, that is, its place within the sentence's temporality and wider developing sense, becomes unstuck and is thus disrupted. What is crucial here in this definition is that the anacoluthon is considered not as objectively augmentative of a new beginning – which is where I think Bloch places his emphasis, as I will show – but as an objective breakdown – which is where Adorno places the emphasis in his treatment of parataxis.[30] Indeed, Sanders stresses that the *Satzbruch* should not be understood

---

27   Newmark 2012, p. 93.

28   Ibid.

29   Richter 2000, p. 110.

30   See Adorno 1992, pp. 109–52. Adorno's (1992, p. 138) analysis of the 'paratactic method' in Hölderlin's hymnic poetry touches on the anacoluthon as a figure antithetic to synthesis. Adorno (1992, pp. 142–4) associates the paratactic with rupture, through which identity, i.e. synthesis of subject-object, the very 'watchword of Idealism', is cast aside. In the German original of the essay on Hölderlin, Adorno (1974, p. 480) claims that the 'fragmentary [*fragmentarischen*] character' of Hölderlin's paratactic hymns perhaps marks a 'constitutive inability to be complete [*konstitutiv unvollendbar*]'. However, Bloch's reading of a similar figure of rupture associates the anacoluthon with the possibility of a genuinely real arrival. Bloch's position is subtly, but fundamentally, different to Adorno's, something Bloch is well aware of. As Bloch wrote to Adorno: 'It is true that the utopian conscience [...] has remained alive, quite explicitly, in your rich and successful writings. But the snag [is] the abandonment of the great line, the *unum necessarium*' (quoted in Claussen 2008, p. 272).

as a 'termination [*Satzabbruch*]' but more as an 'interruption [*Satzunterbruch*]' of speech.[31] That is, not a termination but rather a *turning point* of speech, a disruption of syntactical order which potentially strikes upon novelty.[32]

The anacoluthon's presence in language also points to an immanent sign of the utterance to which, as I will show in Chapter 3, Voloshinov refers to: interlocution between at least two speaking subjects. This is because, of the three forms of anacolutha reviewed by Sanders it is prolepsis (Latin: *anticipatio*) that is just as significant as is the more literal *Satzbruch* (the final form being the particle).[33] In its most essential character, prolepsis is 'anticipation [*Vorwegnahme*]' in debate – indicating the conflictual aspect of the figure in the life of language, the anacoluthon is often a strategy deployed to pre-empt or forestall any potential objections on the side of one's interlocutor.[34] The anacoluthon therefore touches on a prefiguration of the future, a prefiguration of what is not-yet placed squarely in the context of potential struggle (see Chapter 3).

It has already been noted that Voloshinov foregrounded the importance of syntax for understanding the real conditions of discourse. Voloshinov will elaborate on this idea with a discussion of paragraphs, which are essentially 'a vitiated dialogue worked into the body of a monologic utterance',[35] and as such paragraphs constitute 'a type of partitioning that takes the addressee and his active understanding into decisive account'.[36] In other words, although here the point is made by way of Voloshinov's well-known extension of dialogue into the literary word, syntax and its rupture points to an 'anticipation of possible objections'[37] within the utterance, that is, it leads us to a 'fundamental' aspect of dialogue, to 'the real unit of language that is implemented in speech

---

31   Sanders 2014, p. 487.
32   The anacoluthon need not be merely a syntactical figure. One might also speak of 'semantic irregularities' in which the norms of syntax are respected but 'the meaning of at least one of the terms stands in more or less violent contradiction to that of one or more of the others' (Most 2019, p. 244). One can also, within the visual arts, speak of 'a visual anacoluthon' (Most 2019, p. 246). Examples: 'Horace's anacoluthic painter' in the opening of the *Ars Poetica*, as well as in works of Cubism and Surrealism which have 'generalized visual anacoluthon into a fundamental compositional principle ... consisting of multiply perspectival, jaggedly fragmented, arbitrarily created meanings' (Most 2019, p. 246). Bloch's connection to German Expressionism and indeed to Surrealism's artistic exploration of the Freudian unconscious belong here (see Bloch 1998, pp. 97–113).
33   Sanders 2014, p. 486.
34   Ibid.
35   Voloshinov 1973, p. 111.
36   Voloshinov 1973, p. 111n3.
37   Voloshinov 1973, p. 111.

(*Sprache als Rede*)', namely 'the *active reception of other speakers' speech*'.[38] To a word there is always a 'reply (*Gegenrede*)',[39] not merely, we could say, in the sense that there would be no word without its reply, without an addressee, without an 'other' to which one word is directed, but also in the sense that one word implies a counter-word, a conflicting word, discontinuity. Indeed, to imagine a speech without an addressee, a speech 'that absolutely ignored the addressee', would be to imagine language 'with organic partition reduced to the minimum'.[40] The anacoluthon could therefore be described as the organic partition of speech within speech for which class bears the responsibility as an expression of the inadequate and incomplete condition of material existence.

In light of these different aspects of the anacoluthon, it becomes clear that this syntactical figure significantly resonates with – echoes, even – the fundamental tenets of Bloch's materialism. Not only is the presence of an incompleteness (a not-having) expressed through the figure, but the figure is also stamped by conflict and anticipation, alongside an openness to novelty. It bears upon the idea that the not-yetness of matter renders speech not so much silent as creative, searching for and productive of the new. The anacoluthon equally provokes questions concerning the existence of a proleptic cadence in language, of anticipatoriness *in* language, or better of language *as* anticipation. And its curious position of being a syntactical figure that paradoxically marks an upheaval of syntactical normalcy demands further reflection. The Greek derivation of syn-tax, as σύν- 'together' and ταξις 'an ordering', highlights that the anacoluthon is not necessarily *anti*-syntactic, but nor, in its discontinuity, is the figure strictly speaking purely syntactic either. This point leads to further consideration of the anacoluthon as a border figure, that is, as a figure on the Front of linguistic movement – a 'frontal figure'[41] which, as such, bears witness to a linguistic 'refraction' of the disjunction of being, and an anticipation for something new. As Miguel Abensour says, 'utopia has always been the search for an insular utopia, for a parenthetical place, tentatively cut off from the rest of the world'.[42] The question of utopianism's 'positive intentionality'[43] – the question of where the desultory heads towards and how it gets there, the question of rupture as discovery – and its link to the figure of the anacoluthon will

---

38 Voloshinov 1973, p. 117.
39 Voloshinov 1973, p. 118.
40 Voloshinov 1973, p. 111.
41 Cf. Moir 2019b.
42 Abensour 2016, p. 23.
43 Abensour 2016, p. 24.

be dealt with in more detail soon. The anacoluthon, 'not only a flagrant error, but ... a more or less latent tension suggesting multiple and indeed conflicting interpretative possibilities'.[44]

The anacoluthon, then, is a point (perhaps a starting point), it lacks any clear logic (it is an evident illogicality, a *non sequitur* – the German '*Satz*' means 'sentence', 'proposition', but also 'leap', thus the anacoluthon is an 'interrupting leap'), it is a deviation, a rupture, a break; it marks an incompletion (but what is it to be complete?), it is unsystematic (what is a system?), it is non-linear, irregular, heteroclite, and it seemingly spurns the almost naturally integrative movement of a sentence (but what is a sentence?).[45] The anacoluthon will turn out to be many things – but certainly not nothing!

2   The Anacoluthon as Trace

Besides the young Bloch penning his dissertation on Rickert's epistemological method in historical science (*die Geschictswissenschaft*), for which, like much neo-Kantianism, the singular, non-repeatable event constituted the proper concern of historical studies,[46] there are two reasons, internal to Bloch-scholarship, for taking-up the anacoluthon as a starting point for constructing a philosophy of language from his utopian materialism.

Firstly, the anacoluthon suffers from a lack of reception in extant Bloch-scholarship despite it constituting a clear, though rare, instance in which Bloch explicitly deals with the question of language (another instance is dealt with in the last chapter concerning fascism). This is the 'minor' trace. It is notable that those who have treated of the anacoluthon stand as unworked-out intimations and therefore more or less follow George Steiner's lead, who also had the merit of touching on the truth of the matter but ultimately failed to systematically unfold the line of thought at stake. There are three instances of this 'minor trace': Richter's,[47] Witschel's,[48] and Landmann's.[49] Richter suggests

---

44   Most 2019, p. 246.

45   As Mieszkowski (2019) shows, what a sentence is, is commonly presupposed, but unearthing the question throws up all kinds of philosophical (metaphysical), psychological, rhetorical and political questions. Of course, Hegel's (1977b, p. 38) delineation of 'the speculative proposition' is a prime attempt to un-fix the rigid subject-predicate construal of the sentence, and he does so for definite philosophical purposes.

46   See Bloch 1978, pp. 55–107.

47   Richter 2000.

48   Witschel 1978.

49   Landmann 1965. See the English version, Landmann 1975.

that the anacoluthon may relate to 'Bloch's understanding of non-self-identity, both in the aesthetic and the materialist utopian sense'.[50] However, he fails to systematically explain why or indeed in what way the anacoluthon relates to this incognito as a starting point, nor how it relates to matter as pre-categorial 'That-ness' ('tendency'). Equally Witschel asserts a confluence of utopian matter and the anacoluthon, suggesting that the anacoluthon 'reflects'[51] the reality of which it speaks. However, the connection is stated only in the manner of a passing comment and merely repeats what Bloch himself says of the figure (Bloch's essay on the anacoluthon nowhere directly mentions matter or materialism either, though). This issue of the anacoluthon reflecting material being, however, needs to be overcome, for it does not properly capture the nature of speculation for Bloch. For Bloch, speculative materialism is not one that reflects material being, but one that sees in that same being incompleteness, openness, and novelty. I meet this task below by showing that the anacoluthon does not merely linguistically reflect but, using Voloshinov's work in Chapter 3, *refracts* the structure of what Bloch takes matter to be.

Finally, there is the interesting case of Landmann, whose remarks are drawn from his recollections of a lecture which Bloch is said to have given on the anacoluthon in Berlin in 1964. In Landmann's account of that lecture the anacoluthon is said to have been associated with 'spontaneous language' and the 'liveliness of speech', and the anacoluthon is said to be a linguistic testimony to the fact that 'reality always breaks through our logically smooth image of it'.[52] But Landmann takes up the same general position as Richter and Witschel, failing to move beyond a simple positing of the inextricable relation between the anacoluthon and Bloch's materialist categories. On all counts, a systematic exposition is missed.

This 'minor trace' also moves in the opposite direction in Bloch-scholarship, too. While some commentators have insightfully treated of language in Bloch's philosophy, there persists a near-universal omission to mention or invest in the anacoluthon any degree of significance. Steiner is a representative of this omission, as too is Holz, an otherwise keen commentator on Bloch's writings.[53] Another is Siebers's analysis of Bloch's *Traces*, which Siebers reads alongside Johann-Peter Hebel's *The Treasure Chest* (1811);[54] curiously, Hebel is counted as that writer who best preserves the *viva vox* within the written word for Bloch

50   Richter 2000, p. 110.
51   Witschel 1978, p. 103.
52   Landmann 1965, p. 354.
53   Holz 1965.
54   Siebers 2013. Also see Siebers 2011.

in his anacoluthon essay.[55] Siebers not only intimates the utopian directedness of language in speaking of the 'utopian core' and 'horizon' 'necessary to human communication',[56] but Siebers also recognises this anticipatory horizon of language as emerging from – and being only comprehensible within – the structure of Bloch's materialism.[57] Siebers does not, however, incorporate the figure into his discussion. And finally, Moir's treatment of the place of Expressionism in Bloch's concept of language also omits the anacoluthon from mention.[58]

The anacoluthon becomes a trace for a much more immanent reason, however, beyond simply lacking the appropriate attention from numerous commentators on Bloch's work. This is because there is a 'major' trace which defines the anacoluthon in Bloch's corpus – namely, that the anacoluthon is a trace *in Bloch's corpus itself*. Alongside Landmann's recollections of the already mentioned Bloch-lecture in 1964 – which incidentally is itself a trace, for, to my knowledge, no text of the actual lecture exists – the only other explicit appearance of the figure in Bloch's oeuvre can be found in the *Literary Essays*. Beyond this and the abovementioned lecture, no explicit mention of the anacoluthon surfaces in the collected works, perhaps serving to explain why the figure has been given scant treatment in Bloch-scholarship up to now. It seems Bloch himself gave it little scrutiny.

And yet the anacoluthon is not only inconspicuous in Bloch's corpus, nor just in commentary on Bloch; it is in fact near-universally neglected in the field of rhetoric to which it traditionally belongs. If one were to cast an eye, for example, to Vickers's otherwise comprehensive index of rhetorical terms, it will be found that the anacoluthon is absent there.[59] Sanders's exception to this rule of abandonment helps to explain it. The anacoluthon's continuous negligible status presumably lies in the fact that neither Donatus nor Priscian nor Quintilian treated of it. Naturally those rhetoricians who followed the masters did not think to either.[60] It is a custom that stretches back a long way, then, to ignore the anacoluthon.[61] There is thus something vaguely consequential when in the opening to *The Principle of Hope* Bloch states that '[i]n his first attempt at a Latin grammar, M. Terentius Varro is said to have forgotten the future tense;

---

55   Bloch 1998, pp. 499–500.
56   Siebers 2013, pp. 190–91.
57   Siebers 2013, p. 204.
58   See Moir 2019b.
59   Vickers 2002.
60   Sanders 2014, p. 490.
61   Cf. Smith 2012, p. 16 on the lack of scrutiny given to the intentional device of interruption in Ancient texts on rhetoric.

philosophically, it has still not been adequately considered to this day'.[62] Perhaps fondness for the strictures of grammar and for the steady flow of speech have often precipitated against an appreciation of the future tense – that is, against a higher estimation of the anacoluthon?

But as important as all this may well be, it does not help to explain why the unassuming anacoluthon warrants attention in this context, and why it might constitute a starting point to the task at hand. This changes when we acknowledge the significance of that which is marginal and inconspicuous for Bloch's philosophy itself. This is clear if we turn to a composition of *Traces* (*Spuren*), a parabolic text which, as Boella notes,[63] Bloch chose, far from fortuitously, to open his collected works with. Bloch thereby once again inverts Adorno's approach, who *closes* his corpus aphoristically with a turn toward the micro of life, the 'hidden recesses' of life, in *Minima Moralia*.[64]

In *Traces* Bloch gives a piece of important advice: 'One should observe precisely the little things, go after them. What is slight and odd often leads the furthest'.[65] Here one might recall Voloshinov's stance with regards to syntax – it is precisely because of syntax being on the peripheries of speech that it leads to concrete totality. At stake in this rather innocuous statement of Bloch's, then, is not a realism of 'reproductive naturalism', of mere mirroring, but a realism of concentration that leads to a vision of the cracks and openings of material existence.[66] Bloch invites his readers to practice a *Spurenlesen* – a reading of traces. And it is through concentration on the ostensibly incidental things where hope indeed begins to blossom:[67]

> What was that? Something moved! And it moved in its own way. An impression that will not let us come to rest over what we heard. An impression on the surface of life, so that it *tears*, perhaps.[68]

---

62   Bloch 1986, p. 6.

63   Boella 2012, p. 510.

64   Adorno 2005, p. 15. Adorno's final aphorism in *Minima Moralia*, 'Finale', famously opens by drawing a connection between the small recesses of life and redemption (see Adorno 2005, p. 247). Interestingly, Adorno charges Bloch with monism – despite Bloch asserting that 'being is no universal gravy' (Bloch 1970, p. 285). Just as everything is for the psychoanalyst a road to a sexual interpretation, 'so too there is nothing which cannot be regarded as a Blochian trace, and this indiscriminate use of everything comes close to meaning nothing'. (Adorno 1992, p. 210). Adorno, however, will deny the possibility of the power to arrive: 'it is', he writes, 'the utterly impossible thing'. (Adorno 2005, p. 247).

65   Bloch 2006, p. 5.

66   Bloch 1986, p. 216.

67   See Bloch 1986, p. 302.

68   Bloch 2006, p. 6, my emphasis.

It is precisely its inconspicuousness in Bloch's work, in commentary on Bloch, and indeed in the discipline of rhetoric itself to which it traditionally belongs, that permits one to treat of the anacoluthon with a serious concentration when the task is to develop a materialist philosophy of language from Bloch's works. Although it seemingly occupies a marginal place in Bloch's corpus, the anacoluthon thus carries its weight in gold, *precisely because of its marginality*. In sum, Bloch's imperative to turn and pay attention to the inconspicuous can be practiced on Bloch's corpus itself, being immanently applied to the texts in question. By observing and going after what is slight and odd – a micrology of sorts, something Bloch prized in Benjamin – one can go the furthest in speculating on a Blochian-materialist philosophy of language. 'Attentiveness', as Bloch quotes Malebranche, 'is the natural prayer of the soul'.[69]

One more point on this theme of 'following the small' can be made with regards to linguistics itself. Indeed one cannot deny the importance of the anacoluthon's marginality in relation to such a significant thinker of language as Saussure. Saussure famously undertakes the project of separating 'language from speaking', from *parole*, 'the embryo of speech', that is, the 'execution' of language as a system; in this separation, Saussure will relegate *parole* to the insubstantial life of language, to 'the heterogeneous mass of speech facts'; indeed he will assert that the particular usage of language in a given socio-historical moment of becoming, the singular linguistic event, is the less 'true', unscientific side of language, it is 'accessory and more or less accidental' to language as a homogenous system.[70] Saussure would have one photograph a language – translate it 'into a fixed visual image' – rather than observe language in the movement of its historical flux, in the crevices of its becoming.[71] Perhaps the anacoluthon, then, as a small site of speech production, captures the essence of *parole* very well. It is not for nothing that, turning to Lukács's and

---

69   Malebranche quoted in Bloch 1992, p. 41, emphasis removed. Cf. Comay and Ruda 2018, pp. 1–8, who enact a similar operation of 'indiscriminate attentiveness' to the seemingly trivial on Hegel's texts – and do so precisely on the figure of the dash. Beck (2019, pp. 105–6) states that Bloch's concern with the everyday ciphers of the utopian is a modern rendition of old Jewish messianic thought-forms; while Bennett (2003, p. 50) gives a clue concerning perhaps the Tolstoy-provenance of this approach to the small: 'Tolstoy's narrative style' is one of 'close attention to detailed, almost naturalist description of minutiae', the latter of which is said to serve as a 'device of "bestrangement"' in relation to processes of assimilation to the (literary) given. More broadly, Roberts gives a wider idea of what is behind this practice of following the small: 'for both psychoanalysis and modern art, no thing, no matter how insignificant or marginal, fragmented or mistaken, is without signification or effect' (Roberts 2011, p. 233).
70   Saussure 2011, pp. 13–15.
71   Saussure 2011, p. 15.

Bloch's respective readings of Hegel (readings which are not without their echo in the *Expressionismusdebatte*), Dick Howard has noted that in Bloch the connection between a concern for the marginal and a concern for the discontinuous go hand-in-hand, and in fact, both touch on the tendency and latency of the 'not-yet'.[72] Unlike Saussure, it is the case that, for Bloch, if the anacoluthon were the smallest embryo of *parole* it would possess the power to modify what structural linguistics took as un-modifiable – the system of language itself.[73] The discontinuous implies history, contradiction, and Saussure sought to omit, to bracket out from a theory of language the vibrational effects of discontinuity – the anacoluthon. The boundaries of language, for Saussure, were located at the limits of the historical. To borrow a distinction Hegel brings to bear in the *Philosophy of Nature*, we can stress that while Saussure treats language as a 'materialized *space*', Bloch would like to see language treated as 'materialized *time*'.[74]

To see how the anacoluthon can be conceptualised as materialised time one can turn to a number of assumptions that Bloch makes in the one explicit discussion of the anacoluthon within his corpus. In 'Spoken and Written Syntax: Anacoluthon',[75] Bloch conveys the anacoluthon as a figure of speech that linguistically depicts or re-presents the objective world.[76] Bloch's reasoning for this is that what the anacoluthon depicts, and thus what language 'confronts', is a 'world that is less closed than ever'.[77] As Bloch writes:

> Ultimately, in order to narrate by means of rupture, something else is needed that was missing also in the preliterary period. When the old-time storyteller commenced his tale, using the *viva vox* to weave new

---

72   'Where Lukács' analysis [of Hegel] is continuous, systematic, and well-rounded, Bloch's disconcerts, leaps, doubles back on itself only to stride forward toward that Now, the spheric totality opening onto a we-subject. Lukács' analysis is useful to the reader wanting to know why Hegel could have been so important to Marx; Bloch's intention is to situate Hegel in the world .... He specifies ... the need for "attention to instances in the sense that no detail is a priori designated as inessential is unavoidable for concrete philosophizing". ... The contrast with Lukács appears again in a short essay in which Bloch stresses Walter Benjamin's "sense for the incidental" as "that which so unbelievably lacked [*sic*] in Lukács"' (Howard 2019, p. 55, cf. p. 60).

73   'Language as a well-defined object ... is the social side of speech, outside the individual who can never create nor modify it by himself' (Saussure 2011, p. 14).

74   Hegel 1970, p. 137.

75   Bloch 1998, pp. 497–504. 'Gesprochene und geschriebene Syntax; das Anakoluth' (Bloch 1965).

76   Bloch 1998, p. 503.

77   Bloch 1998, p. 504.

patterns from the well-worn material that was most familiar to himself and his listeners, the surrounding environment of spinning rooms and marketplaces showed hardly any trace of rupture; the social hierarchy was fixed and apparently stable. Today, however, the still-existent unity of the epoch – if not the even deeper dialectical identity of opposites – no longer emits the false luster of an *ordo sempiternus rerum* [eternal order of things]. In accordance with this objective situation, the newborn élan of the old-time storyteller, like the spirit of freely creative speech itself, is at last returning home. Hence the particular timeliness of the appropriate anacoluthon, of the most fluidly mobile discourse, in the face of a nonclassical world ...[78]

At the same time, Bloch seems to base his whole discussion on the anteriority of the spoken word: 'The fact is, oral and written modalities have existed for different lengths of time. Speaking, storytelling, even singing appeared much earlier than writing'.[79] '[W]riting is a late development'.[80] While Bloch's prospective and anticipative form of speculation opposes at a fundamental level any explanatory arguments that are drawn from a logic of retrogression, here Bloch lends precedence to spoken over written language on account of the former's supposed temporal precedence. The fissure that disjoins the spoken word from the word that is 'mediated by written signs' is said to lie in the obvious temporal anteriority of oral-acoustic culture.[81] Writing is thus seen by Bloch as merely derivative of sounded speech, of verbal interaction, for the anacoluthon 'best captures the difference between spoken and written syntax. For living speech always begins anew and breaks up along the way'.[82] This certainly recalls the phonocentrism that Derrida rallied against, signalling a potential return to a Socratic-Platonic prioritisation of the spoken word, the *phoné*, 'the pre-eminence of voice', as Alain Badiou puts it.[83] Voloshinov would agree with the broad direction here, however, since 'verbal interaction is the

---

78   Ibid.

79   Bloch 1998, p. 497.

80   Bloch 1998, p. 498.

81   Ibid.

82   Bloch 1998, p. 502.

83   Badiou 2019, p. 163. 'It is indisputable that the philosophical strategy, as a strategy of mastery, has always privileged the oral face-to-face confrontation with those that it calls upon to become disciples (which means: to become, within thought, *disciplined*)'. (Badiou 2019, p. 163). 'Let's say that philosophy's mother tongue is the lesson, or even the exercise, at best the manual (which is to the taste of Descartes). The book, in the sense of the oeuvre, always comes second'. (Badiou 2019, p. 164). 'The consequences of this secondariness of

basic reality of language'[84] (rather than being an earlier stage of language that has fallen away and should be returned to), and thus Marxism 'should and must stand squarely on the utterance as the real phenomenon of language-speech'.[85] As Bloch suggested in the earlier quotation, the objective conditions of the utterance are key, but it is on that score that Bloch and Voloshinov part ways, as I will show in a later chapter. The point for now is that spoken language is more dialectical than written, for the 'the corporeality of speech displays totality resumed into individuality', as Hegel writes.[86] And as Bloch says, the language of the *viva vox* is 'created and received differently' to the written word, emphasising the interactive nature of the spoken word as opposed to 'the silent, lonely labor of forming letters with meticulous care at a writing desk'.[87] Fissure characterises the utterance immanently, and fissures in writing are merely '*acte accessoire*' of the spoken kind, a type of 'Mecator projection' of the spoken word into a 'nonacoustic' artificial form (exceptions exists of course, such as Luther's Bible, which, according to Bloch, narrows the gap between spoken and written words expertly).[88]

Besides assertions that the anacoluthon depicts an objective world in rupture and is tied more closely to the spoken word, Bloch also makes a point concerning the figure's relation to rationality, tempering any easy conflation of the anacoluthon (associated for him, as mentioned, primarily with speech) with a pejorative sense of the irrational. As Bloch writes:

> The pattern of living speech that flows and flourishes as such, and that still sounds within lettered speech, is not inimical to reason; rather, it constitutes its own – or even more, the actual – *music* of reason.[89]

Here Bloch is not advocating for the idea of a 'natural voice', comparable to a child's speech 'that issues forth irrationally or spontaneously' and which bears close connection to 'that false immediacy' of the archaic Heideggerianism of

---

the book concern above all the syntax. The philosophical discourse ... is assembled with an eye on obtaining assent, which must be extorted even by anticipating, as much as possible, the eventual objections'. (ibid). The figure of the anacoluthon is also defined by an anticipation in speech, however.

84   Voloshinov 1973, p. 94.
85   Voloshinov 1973, p. 97.
86   Hegel 1979, p. 116.
87   Bloch 1998, pp. 497 and 498.
88   See Bloch 1998, pp. 498–500.
89   Bloch 1998, p. 501.

'blood and soil'.[90] In a left-wing Nietzschean register (indeed Bloch mentions Expressionism's 'authentic immediacy' here),[91] irrationality is not viewed as hostile to reason but as proximate to its 'warm stream' – the anacoluthon is the music of language in this sense. Here un-grammatical speech, or more broadly speech that is erroneous by exiting normative standards, is not seen as adverse to a clarity of expression but as proximate to what is new and needs articulation. John Roberts might term this extended rationality of the anacoluthon its *'conjectural reason'*;[92] as he writes, shunning this expansive notion of reason leads to 'the fear of error [which] produces forms of rationalization that may produce detrimental or irrational effects'.[93] A Marxist philosophy of language, then, would need to locate and harness this music of language. Bloch seems to be suggesting that the anacoluthon reveals another side of rationality or indeed that the supposed error of the anacoluthon can be seen as 'prepar[ing] or enact[ing] the death of an ungiving and unworkable rationality, and the birth of a new rationality'.[94] The musicality Bloch attributes to the anacoluthon indicates the anacoluthon as an expression of the utopian art form *par excellence* for Bloch, and points further towards Bloch's association of the anacoluthon with the anticipatory dimension of time and with the temporality of the future more generally.[95] The significance of the anacoluthon is held up quite explicitly with Bloch's reference to music here.

This musical dimension of the anacoluthon can be pressed further by tying Bloch's comment of it here with the Marxist inflection that Bloch lends to the warm stream of reason elsewhere in his work. Countering suggestions that Marx's thought ought to be discarded on the basis that it fancifully sought to peer too far ahead of the present moment and thus cannot but be unrealistic (this charge is premised on positivist dreamlessness that 'one cannot see around the corner'[96]), Bloch responds with the simple statement: but 'reason has an acoustic sense of significance' since 'it is entirely possible to hear around a corner'.[97] If we follow Gillian Rose in noting that Walter Benjamin's 'emphasis on the visual is itself derived by Benjamin from the nature of modern life – the decline of listening',[98] then to hear around the corner is to sense that bet-

---

90   Bloch 1998, p. 500.
91   Bloch 1998, p. 501. See Taylor 1990, pp. 1–7.
92   Roberts 2011, p. 111.
93   Roberts 2011, p. 143.
94   Roberts 2011, p. 146.
95   See Korstvedt 2010.
96   Bloch 2018, p. 32.
97   Bloch 2018, p. 32.
98   Rose 2017, pp. 202–3.

ter otherness which modernity harbours within itself and is to place a futural accent on the Herderian prioritisation of the spoken (hearing) over the written word (vision).[99] And indeed, to Bloch's mind, one of Marx's lessons in the *Theses on Feuerbach* is that Feuerbach's 'epistemological inactivity',[100] along with other previous contemplative and inert materialisms, remains trapped in ancient ideas of knowledge 'as mere reception, as sight, *visio*, or passive reflection as retained in the concept of *"theoria"*, ...: *vision*'.[101] That there is such a thing as an 'around the corner' to be heard in the objective world signals that that world is ripe for making, that the world is not just something to be passively received, that it remains incomplete and open to the new. It could therefore be suggested that the figure of the anacoluthon embodies an active, linguistic sensuousness – contrary to an exaggerated '"non-active" perception'[102] which becomes pure unto itself: 'Being, which determines everything, has men, who are themselves active, within it'.[103] 'The truly total explanation of the world in terms of itself ... also presupposes the transformation of the world from itself', as Bloch also says.[104] This fact linguistically expresses itself within the anacoluthon. Hence, the anacoluthon does not just simply re-present objective reality, but rather, as this active linguistic sensing of that reality, it has the potential to help change it. The main issue with this idea, which stems from the Expressionists, is the tendency it contains towards the *meinen* of the individual, rather than the *allgemein* of the community.

The figure of the anacoluthon, connected in Bloch's mind to the music of reason, namely to the future of reason, can also be connected to the temporal concept of the instant (*Augenblick*, literally meaning, 'in the blink of an eye') as it features in Bloch's work. There is a close association between the anacoluthon and Bloch's concept of the darkness of the just lived moment. As Humberto Beck's study into rupture and fragmentation as the proper regime of historical consciousness in Germany during 1914–40 reveals, sudden and abrupt discontinuity became the overarching historical and perceptual aura of that period.[105] The 'instant' becomes a key concept for figures such as Bloch and Benjamin who 'resort to the language of instantaneity'[106] in order to explore

---

99   See Forster 2011, p. 147. Cf. this notion at work in Hegel (Forster 2011, pp. 154–5 and 166).
100 Bloch 2018, p. 66.
101 Ibid.
102 Bloch 2018, p. 69.
103 Ibid.
104 Bloch 2018, p. 80.
105 See Beck 2019.
106 Beck 2019, p. 4.

disoriented consciousness and 'the exceptional and unexpected'.[107] As Beck notes, however, the 'instant' as a new concept for the German expression of a discontinuous mode of temporality was first articulated by Plato, for whom the instantaneous moment is 'an *atopos* – a *non*-place but also a non-*time*',[108] and which relates the anacoluthon to the 'contradictory components' of the figure of the instant, which give it its hue of sudden discontinuity; namely, the encounter of those juxtaposed (like a montage) 'ideas of time and eternity'.[109]

The instant is also said to express an experience and consciousness of time that is singular and, in Bloch's work, radically antihistoricist and non-linear:[110] neither an historicist concept of time in which there is a progressive and transitory movement into an open future, nor a contemporary presentist notion of time in which no anticipation exists because the present is considered perfectly fulfilled, and so entirely immobile.[111] In this light the anacoluthon comes to touch on Bloch's admonition that Kant should burn through Hegel (see Chapter 1). The 'time of instantaneism'[112] – and so this time linguistically enacted via the figure of the anacoluthon – therefore touches on Bloch's concept of the Novum: completion by interruption. Curiously, too, Beck speaks both of 'the language of instantaneity'[113] and the rhetoric of instantaneity,[114] but not the *instantaneity of rhetoric* or the *instantaneity of language*. The figure of the anacoluthon opens the door to both, and I would suggest that Bloch's anacoluthon essay is a key text in the language of instantaneity which Beck stakes out in Bloch, precisely as the *instantaneity of language*. The anacoluthon, it could be argued, stands as the moment of the linguistic materialisation of consciousness, which stutters in expressing itself because it comes very near to itself: it is the material 'now' of language. This instantaneity of language aligns with Bloch's category of the darkness of the just lived moment. And, to prefigure Chapter 3's comparative discussion of Bloch and Voloshinov, it is important to note that this notion of instantaneity in Bloch's philosophy is said to be grounded on an analogy 'between the experiences of subjective tem-

---

107   Beck 2019, p. 3.
108   Beck 2019, p. 7.
109   Beck 2019, p. 10.
110   See Beck 2019, pp. 97–8.
111   See Beck 2019, pp. 13–14.
112   Beck 2019, p. 14.
113   Beck 2019, p. 4. This language of instantaneity is described as 'new language' (Beck 2019, p. 12). Cf. Moir 2019b for a discussion of this new language as intimately connected to the rise of Expressionism.
114   See Beck 2019, p. 9.

porality and collective historical time'.[115] This is also Bloch's path away from the charge of individualism that has often been levelled at the Expressionists.

3   The Anacoluthon as Linguistic Tendency

As was outlined in the previous chapter, 'tendency' in Bloch's philosophy names an incomplete, self-causative, self-clarifying materiality that is future-directed insofar as it possesses the potency of producing novelty. Two thinkers, in varying degrees, disclose the 'tendency' dimensions of the anacoluthon. Indeed Steiner and Mieszkowski[116] clarify the way in which the anacoluthon expresses the incompleteness of material existence and an intending towards its own consummation. Steiner is assigned to my discussion of the 'latency' category later on. Unlike Steiner's contribution here, Mieszkowski's insights neither mention Bloch nor explicitly draw into their discussion the issue of materialism. Mieszkowski does, however, inadvertently illuminate the figure as expressing linguistic 'tendency', in Bloch's sense of 'tendency'. His work helps to elaborate on Bloch's ideas further.

Mieszkowski's first observation is that the very existence of the anacoluthon in the life of language reveals something essential about that linguistic life. Instead of being an appendage to language the anacoluthon is seen as 'a window onto an essential feature of signification'.[117] The first crucial claim of Mieszkowski's is therefore that the anacoluthon should be viewed as *intrinsic* or immanent to language, and Mieszkowski shows how this perspective on the figure has been commonly denied. The mandate for the figure's exclusion from importance is it being shunned as mere linguistic detritus. As Mieszkowski argues, unless the figure is compositionally or rhetorically utilised by a Shakespeare or a Cicero or a Luke (as in the Acts of the Apostles) as an epideictic effect *a consilio* – intentionally as an artistic device (*Kunstmittel*) – and not *a casu* – accidentally, so then the anacoluthon is commonly ignored as unimportant and inessential to the true realities of linguistic life.[118] The anacoluthon

---

115   Beck 2019, p. 98.
116   Steiner 1965 and Mieszkowski 2009.
117   Mieszkowski 2009, p. 649.
118   See Smith 2012, pp. 1–2 and 10–11, which does not mention the anacoluthon by name but does outline how Luke's employment of interrupted speeches – *Redeunterbrechungen* or *Nichtausredenlassen* – are said to index the experiences of early Christian missionaries. Most, who tends to praise the figure in his reading of the anacoluthon in Kafka's writings,

comes from the outside of language, and corrupts it. Some commentators have picked up on the class character of the anacoluthon in an aesthetic context, a point which Bloch fails to tie into his anacoluthon essay in any clear manner:

> A special form of naïve anacoluthon is the literary representation of the quoted speech of uneducated characters, for example in modern American fiction. Already in Aeschylus, the speeches assigned to such lower-class characters as the messenger in *Agamemnon* or the nurse in *The Libation Bearers* contain such patent violations of grammatical norms that scholars have sometimes been misled into trying to emend them, against the manuscripts, into syntactic regularity. In literary representations of this sort, anacoluthon is concentrated into a restricted quoted passage while, like a cordon sanitaire, the surrounding discourse remains quite unexceptionable, and the local irregularity serves to characterize these speakers, in contrast with others or with the narrator, and to create an emotional link of some kind between them and the recipient.[119]

Most's reference to the depiction of the lower classes of Greece via the anacoluthon has undertones of Hegel's lord-bondsman dialectic in the *Phenomenology of Spirit*, in which the slave only recognises the master and is herself not recognised.[120] The division in the text discussed by Most expresses well the division between the lord, 'the consciousness that exists *for itself*', and the bondsman, 'a consciousness whose nature it is to be bound up with an existence that is independent, or thinghood in general'.[121] It is the recognition of non-recognition, 'a recognition that is one-sided and unequal'.[122] In commonly being deemed to be an imperfection of speech, then, the anacoluthon is seen as something (*etwas*) which intrudes upon speech exogenously (the rising crisis of class?) – even if the purpose of its intrusion seems to have been the intent of someone like Aeschylus (after all, posterity had tried to *correct* his 'mistakes'). Or at least, the anacoluthon is pejoratively considered as an unwelcome attribute of linguistic life that remains downplayed as insubstantial or indeed parasitic to the core of that life (a kind of linguistic reformism). But if anacoluthic speech

---

still discerns, in an elitist vein of thought (Most 2019, p. 249), an axis within the figure along the lines of a 'naïve anacoluthon and refined anacoluthon' (Most 2019, p. 246), one which essentially mirrors the *a consilio* and *a casu* distinction.

119   Most 2019, p. 247.
120   See Hegel 1977b, pp. 113–15.
121   Hegel 1977b, p. 115.
122   Hegel 1977b, p. 116.

bears a similar logic of being held in subjection insofar as the anacoluthic speech of a lower class distinction is materially 'marked off' in a text as a barrier (a *cordon sanitaire*), then she who truly works on the thing, which the lord merely enjoys, is the worker of language.[123] Hence the anacoluthon must be expunged or silenced, not allowed to speak, gagged, detained, and marked-off to stop a crisis of infection,[124] opposing to it a conception of language which conceives of it as an orderly flow, corresponding to – perhaps the idea is implicit here, but no less axiomatic – an orderly, structurally totalised world, classical.[125]

This levelling down of the anacoluthon's waywardness to a pathological error which intrudes into language from its outside could be connected up with a theory of error itself. John Roberts has developed just that, which he calls 'a materialist and historical account of the error'.[126] Bloch thus would give to Marxist thought the idea of the importance of error for a Marxist philosophy of language,[127] one in which 'the ... ontological implications of error'[128] are brought to the fore in language. As Roberts helpfully notes, the 'error elimination' behind Karl Popper's philosophy of science and of scientific discovery more generally – Popper's theory of the scientific subject in particular – is of an objectivist provenance insofar as it seeks 'the radical and continuous expunging of error'[129] to obtain progress in objective knowledge. Of course, the main critique of abstract objectivism in linguistics, given by Voloshinov (see Chapter 3), shows how abstract objectivism neglects *parole* and, not coin-

---

123   See Hegel 1977b, p. 116. 'Desire has reserved to itself the pure negating of the object and thereby is unalloyed feeling of self. But that is the reason why this satisfaction is itself only a fleeting one, for it lacks the side of objectivity and permanence. Work, on the other hand, is desire held in check, fleetingness staved off; in other words, work forms and shapes the thing'. (Hegel 1977b, p. 118). Anacoluthic language could then be an independence of the working speaker from the present normality of language: here language shows resistance to what needs to be expressed. On the other hand, the language of the master is *dependent language*: the master moves freely in it without resistance, enjoys it, the master sees language as its own. '... the lord, who has interposed the bondsman between it [the thing] and himself, takes to himself only the dependent aspect of the thing and has the pure enjoyment of it. The aspect of its independence he leaves to the bondsman, who works on it'. (Hegel 1977b, p. 116). Cf. Roberts' critique of Kant for not having rationality appear in 'lower forms of culture' (Roberts 2011, p. 41).

124   Cf. Roberts 2011, p. 69.

125   Mieszkowski 2009, p. 649.

126   Roberts 2011, p. 19.

127   See Roberts 2011, p. 12.

128   Roberts 2011, p. 78.

129   Roberts 2011, p. 65.

cidentally, the diachronic.[130] Sanders has also pointed to this time-honoured negative valuation of the anacoluthon as merely error. The figure's 'disruption [*Störung*] of syntactical texture', its 'improper transformation of sentence construction', its 'transgression [*Verstoß*] of the written norm' are conventionally held to be conditioned by a 'sloppy way of speaking', by 'excitation', by 'forgetfulness' and/or 'disjointed thought', by a 'spontaneous speech that is reducible to intellectual deficiencies' or simply to one's 'losing the thread of a complex sentence-construction [*Satzbildung*]'.[131] This judgement lays claim to the anacoluthon belonging to the mere vagaries of an individual psyche, which, to paraphrase Voloshinov's critique of 'individualistic subjectivism',[132] becomes, above and beyond the social conditions of its being, the 'source of language'.[133] The social purport of the anacoluthon is lost, just as, in mechanical materialism, motion is externally communicated to the real life of matter.

In sum, the anacoluthon as linguistic disruption is seen as strictly the purview of the *parole* of those in good possession of the literary language, tying *that* use of it to art and aesthetic creation, exemplified by Vossler, as well as Croce's view of language.[134] When attributing anacoluthic utterances either to erroneous individual linguistic usage or to a distanced, artful linguistic deployment, the possibility that such 'errors' point to the social nature of language, to the socially determined nature of language's existence, is closed down. Contrary to this, if the anacoluthon is an inherent feature of language by dint of language always being of a community, it is because both its emergence and direction of travel always involves, as Voloshinov might say, 'a *social situation*', a concrete mode of social existence.[135] If 'the sign and its social situation are inextricably fused together', then the interstices of the sign, the syntax and its

---

130   See Voloshinov 1973, pp. 57–63.
131   Sanders 2014, p. 487.
132   See Voloshinov 1973, pp. 48–57.
133   Voloshinov 1973, p. 48.
134   See Voloshinov 1973, pp. 48 and 50–2.
135   Voloshinov 1973, p. 37. Cf. Hartley 2016, p. 97. Franco Berardi (2019, p. 11) will say that the origin of power is 'the insertion of automated selections into the social vibration' – that is, we might say, grammatical insertions into the selection of present possibilities. Grammar is automation, 'engendered determinism' (Berardi 2019, p. 12). Grammar as such, as a 'determinist strategy', 'aims', we could say, 'to subjugate the future, to constrain tendency into a prescribed pre-emptive model, and automate future behaviour'. (Berardi 2019, p. 12). Grammar attempts to subjugate the 'incomputable', that is, 'the vibrational, indeterminable quantum leaps that are inscribed in ... linguistic excess'. (Berardi 2019, p. 88). This linguistic excess Berardi grounds in humanism: 'humanist freedom is consciousness, imagination, linguistic construction in the absence of ontological foundations'. (Berardi 2019, p. 89).

breakdown, express a social situation, too.[136] Thus the anacoluthon's presence in language, far from being an error intruding from the outside, signals rather that 'the *alternating lines of a dialogue*' are taking place here in this moment, and that language concerns us here and now.[137] What is in play with it is 'the living interaction of social forces'.[138] To paraphrase Voloshinov, the anacoluthon involves 'alternating lines of dialogue, not grammatical connections but connections of a different kind', namely *'total impressions of utterances*' which 'are joined with one another and alternate with one another not according to the laws of grammar or logic but according to the laws of *evaluative* (emotive) *correspondence, dialogical deployment*' and 'in close dependence on the historical conditions of the social situation and the whole pragmatic run of life'.[139] The anacoluthon, then, while being that supposed detritus of *parole*, concerns a totality above and beyond the merely lawfulness of a language. Indeed, by 'total impressions' Voloshinov means

> ... the still undifferentiated impression of the totality of an object – the aroma of its totality, as it were, which precedes and underlies knowing the object distinctly. So, for example, we sometimes cannot remember a name or a word, though 'it is on the tip of our tongue', i.e., we already have a total impression of the name or word but the impression cannot develop into its concrete differentiated image. According to Gompertz, total impressions have great epistemological significance. They are psychic equivalents of the forms of the whole and endow the whole with its unity.[140]

---

136   Voloshinov 1973, pp. 37 and 111, emphasis removed. As Voloshinov elaborates: 'Each word, as we know, is a little arena for the clash and criss-crossing of differently oriented social accents. A word in the mouth of a particular individual person is a product of the living interaction of social forces'. (Voloshinov 1973, p. 41). And further: 'If, instead of the physiological act of implementing sound, we take the implementation of word as sign, then the question of proprietorship becomes extremely complicated. Aside from the fact that word as sign is borrowing on the speaker's part from the social stock of available signs, the very individual manipulation of this social sign in a concrete utterance is wholly determined by social relations. The stylistic individualization of an utterance that the Vosslerites speak about represents a reflection of social interrelationships that constitute the atmosphere in which an utterance is formed. *The immediate social situation and the broader social milieu wholly determine – and determine from within, so to speak – the structure of an utterance*'. (Voloshinov 1973, p. 86).

137   Voloshinov 1973, p. 38.
138   Voloshinov 1973, p. 41.
139   Voloshinov 1973, p. 38.
140   Voloshinov 1973, p. 38n15.

While an uncompromising grammar teacher may, then, decry this enthusiasm and disjointedness, this forgetfulness, this linguistic zig-zagging and out and out rule-breaking as personal linguistic deficiencies, and thus allot it to a corruption that exists outside the otherwise proper operations of language, the merit of Mieszkowski's first insight is to give us to think that this dis-order(ing) *of* language points to something *in* language, endogenous to language insofar as language is endogenous to our world and our communication of that world.[141] To take a key position of Gramsci's thoughts on language, in being endogenous to the core life of language I am not saying that language can be explained purely linguistically (with recourse to parthenogenesis),[142] since 'outside' of language stands the historical and political developments which language continues to be determined by and open to. Rather, the anacoluthon could be said to linguistically capture a total impression of a totality not-yet there, but sought for. It is clear from the *Literary Essays* that Bloch does not view the anacoluthon as exogenous to language – it is the music of reason, *logos* – and that the figure's interruption of normal linguistic flow derives from objective conditions in which language participates – it depicts an un-classical world. Echoing the Renaissance's prioritisation and deep appreciation of stylistics over Scholastic grammar,[143] Bloch will write that the 'world was not built by schoolteachers, neither its poetry nor its forming-transforming forces that provide the basis for a poetry of universal style'.[144] Against the regulation and governance of grammaticalness, Bloch indeed argues elsewhere that:

> There is good German that is thorough if it expresses what it has to say. Naturally there can be grammatical transgressions. Yet the German language can be good and great insofar as grammatical errors are also necessary, since language has been ruptured until fit and pliant enough to express what in common grammar, which is good for undialectical objects, is incommunicable.[145]

---

141   Cf. Comay and Ruda 2018, p. 15.

142   See Ives 2004b, p. 45.

143   See Cassirer 1980, p. 127.

144   Bloch 1998, p. 116.

145   Bloch 1985c, p. 14. 'Heraclitus situates the particular object in the constant stream of becoming, in which it is both preserved and destroyed; and for him the particular word is related to "speech" as a whole in the same way. Consequently, even the ambiguity inherent in the word is not a mere deficiency of language, but is an essential and positive factor in its power of expression. For in this ambiguity it is manifested that the limits of language, as of reality, are not rigid but fluid. Only in the mobile and multiform word, which seems to be constantly bursting its own limits, does the fullness of the world-forming logos find

Here Bloch is not endorsing any old error for any old sake, but an error in speech that makes possible the emergence of something new, of something that could not be expressed in the current present state of language, an expression close to the 'tendency' of material process ('That-ness' as imprecise). As Roberts notes, not all errors are productive 'in all circumstances', and so one cannot speak of 'the virtuous "error" in the abstract'.[146] And yet one can speak of 'the purposefulness of the error', which Roberts says 'derives from the desire *for* truth'.[147] With Gaston Bachelard one can speak of '*objective* errors!'[148] An 'objective error' is a 'not-following' in the fibre of present being. 'Errors', Roberts writes, are 'the daily of language of that which doesn't arrive',[149] and one can hope to find such errors in language itself, precisely as expressions of such a non-arrival, an arrival that has not yet occurred (*etwas fehlt*) in 'all the routine failures that make up everyday activity'.[150] As Bloch writes with reference to Soviet Russia: 'a path which has never been travelled before can only be skipped or jumped over with some failures'.[151] But for Roberts, while errors 'are identifiable with the missteps, omissions, oversights and mistakes involved in the execution of a particular activity, or pursuit of a set of ideals or programme', a failure points towards 'the dissolution, collapse, breakdown of a given programme, project or systematic endeavour'.[152] The anacoluthon is potentially both error and failure, and potentially leads to what Bloch calls 'the All' or 'the Nothing'.[153]

What is incommunicable for Bloch is the 'Novum' as that which ultimately has not yet arrived – the 'dream of a matter' which Marx spoke of in his letter

---

its counterpart. Language itself must recognize all the distinctions which it necessarily effects as provisional and relative distinctions which it will withdraw when it considers the object in a new perspective'. (Cassirer 1980, pp. 120–1).

146 Roberts 2011, p. 16.
147 Roberts 2011, p. 25.
148 Bachelard 1964, p. 100.
149 Roberts 2011, p. 136, emphasis removed.
150 Roberts 2011, p. 191. For an account of Marxism, the revolutionary, and the 'everyday', see Roberts 2006: 'the critique of the everyday is ... a utopian and historically discontinuous space through which struggles over the cultural form of art, technology, technique and aesthetic experience and *Bildung* are fought out'. (Roberts 2006, p. 123).
151 Bloch 1986, p. 205.
152 Roberts 2011, p. 190.
153 'The execution and recognition of "errors" implies correction and continuity, failure implies cessation, and perhaps, at a later point, the basis for new beginnings. "Errors", of course, can lead to the 'failure' and cessation of a particular project or systematic endeavour, indeed errors consistently produce failures, but errors in themselves are not specifically identifiable with the collapse of a given project or endeavour overall'. (Roberts 2011, p. 190).

to Ruge. And since what is truly new has not-yet been experienced, articulating it with clarity turns paradoxically into a 'precise vagueness'. Indeed matter's incompleteness and its 'tendency' forwards does not entail the most austere (*Entsagung*) language imaginable, nor for that matter does it entail (*pace* Wittgenstein) a reversion to silence:

> Vagueness can be identical with expression of the highest precision; because materiality, that in itself is not yet determined, likewise cannot be expressed in the usual sense of preciseness, otherwise one falsifies it.[154]

The otherwise erroneous anacoluthon is, then, that potential point of language becoming otherwise than itself, moving beyond its given linguistic forms – what Voloshinov might have termed the 'regular linguistic formations in syntactic patterns'[155] – which otherwise hamper the articulation of what is emerging as something new.[156] The anacoluthon is, as Bloch says, 'a space of suspension, of probing, of deliberation'.[157]

While commonly treated of as an impropriety infiltrating speech from its outside, and thereby customarily considered as reducible to peculiarly psychological or emotional interferences in the otherwise smooth flow of linguistic life, much like Saussure's dismissal of 'history as an irrational force distorting the logical purity of the language system',[158] Bloch claims that the spurning of grammatical correctness or conformism – as seen with the anacoluthon – strikes at an essential and *necessary* feature of language production; that is, when that language is seen as occupying an unfinished world, limited by a contrived (and class imposed) sense of already achieved Hegelian arrival.[159]

---

154   Bloch 1978, p. 293.
155   Voloshinov 1973, p. 125.
156   As the American linguist Edward Sapir noted, '[w]ere a language ever completely "grammatical", it would be a perfect engine of conceptual expression. Unfortunately, or luckily, no language is tyrannically consistent. All grammars leak' (Sapir 2014, p. 38).
157   Bloch 1998, p. 504.
158   Voloshinov 1973, p. 61. Consider: 'With respect to living language, systematic, grammatical thought must inevitably adopt a conservative position, i.e., it must interpret living language as if it were already perfected and ready-made and thus must look upon any sort of innovation in language with hostility. Formal, systematic thought about language is incompatible with living, historical understanding of language. From the system's point of view, history always seems merely a series of accidental transgressions'. (Voloshinov 1973, p. 78).
159   Cf. Voloshinov: 'Only in abnormal and special cases do we apply the criterion of correctness to an utterance (for instance, in language instruction). Normally, the criterion of lin-

If language occupies an incomplete and unfulfilled world, as Bloch's mater-ialism lays-out, then that which is to be communicated requires a novelty of expression. As Roberts has written: 'in an open world inconsistency, incom-pleteness and errors are ineliminable'.[160] But the anacoluthon does not express the Vosslerite notion[161] that the root of all linguistic phenomena is the vicis-situdes of psychologism or a subjective transgression gone too far in the form of a stylistics: 'Language breaks down, but the fault is said to lie with the speaker rather than with language itself'.[162] Rather, its deviation or *swerve* away from normative grammaticalness, from 'the plane of the repeatability of lan-guage',[163] indicates the proximity of the anacoluthon to the incompleteness of material existence; a materiality that, as Bloch claims, is a constant tension-ing of already achieved become-ness (repeatability). Bloch's anacoluthon essay, however, fails to tie the figure directly to class, or at least only discusses the anacoluthon's closeness to 'That-ness' with reference to the misuses and abuses of it in the petite bourgeoisie, susceptible as they were to fascistic moorings (see Chapter 4).[164]

The second and final merit of Mieszkowski's is to heighten this sense that the anacoluthon inextricably belongs to language. He does this by suggest-ing that the figure does not merely count as one essential feature of language among other essential features, but that it instead constitutes *the very site of linguistic generativity as such*. Read alongside Bloch, the suggestion here would

---

guistic correctness is submerged by a purely ideological criterion: an utterance's correct-ness is eclipsed by its truthfulness or falsity, its poeticalness or banality, etc'. (Voloshinov 1973, p. 70). Cf. Ives's detailed discussion of Gramsci's dialectical distinction between an immanent spontaneous grammar, and a normative grammar – a dispute with Benedetto Croce located at the culmination of the *Prison Notebooks* (Ives 2004, pp. 40–4). For Gram-sci, immanent spontaneous grammar is not abstractly opposed to normative grammar, but precisely arises through such normativity (read power and law): 'Gramsci is ... not positing some sort of original spontaneity, or some immanent grammar that is devel-opmentally separate from all normative grammars'. (Ives 2004, p. 42). Here we have the relation of Bloch's twofold definition of 'possibility'.

160 Roberts 2011, p. 101. Roberts will, however, emphasise the importance of the 'need for a critique of open-endedness in the spirit of the second negation and the Absolute'. (Roberts 2011, p. 101). This second moment of open-endedness speaks to Bloch's category of latency.

161 See Voloshinov 1973, p. 26n1.

162 Mieszkowski 2009, p. 649.

163 Ponzio 1993, p. 139. Cf. p. 147: 'Enclosed within ... the constriction of speech according to laws, conventions and habits, the signs loses its character as a challenge, as a provocation with respect to identity and the closed totality'.

164 See Bloch 1998, p. 500.

be that the anacoluthon is the linguistic manifestation *par excellence* of the driving 'That-ness' of matter ('tendency') insofar as it is seen as the site of the productivity of linguistic phenomenality or figuration as such. It is the fundamental site where wider material being and linguistic materiality coincide. The idiosyncrasy of the anacoluthon is that it is a linguistic phenomenon that is located '[a]t the border of figuration and disfiguration'.[165] The anacoluthon is

> ... both super-figural – the extension of creativity in language use to transformations in the rules of syntax and grammar themselves – and sub-figural, almost too deviant to register as a coherent representational gesture. As a figure for the difference between a departure from literal language and a mistake, anacoluthon is at once *the figure of figures and a figure for the dissolution of figure*, the collapse of sustained comparisons between figurative and literal instances of language that allows for figuration to emerge in the first place.[166]

The anacoluthon could therefore amount to a clear – exemplary, even – instance of what Voloshinov called a 'borderline form'. As he writes:

> ... the demarcation of a strict borderline between grammar and style, between a grammatical pattern and its stylistic modification, is methodologically unproductive and in fact impossible. This borderline is fluid because of the very mode of existence of language, in which, simultaneously, some forms are undergoing grammaticization while others are undergoing degrammaticization. It is precisely these ambiguous, borderline forms that are of the greatest interest to the linguist: this is precisely where the developmental tendencies of a language may be discerned.[167]

The anacoluthon constitutes not merely, then, a material figure of linguistic generativity, but rather the site of material linguistic generativity as such, the

---

165   Mieszkowski 2009, p. 653. Jacques Derrida (2002, p. 167) has also touched on the anacoluthon's speculativeness in this regard: 'Doubtless more than a figure of rhetoric, despite appearances, it signals in any case toward the *beyond* of rhetoric *within* rhetoric. Beyond grammar *within* grammar'.

166   Mieszkowski 2009, p. 652, my emphasis. Cf. Comay and Ruda 2018, p. 16.

167   Voloshinov 1973, p. 126. See Chapter 3 for a clearer comparison between Bloch and Voloshinov.

tendential flow of linguistic life. The unassuming anacoluthon really does take us far! As the site of figuration and disfiguration it is that place of tensioning that undermines everything already linguistically shaped. It embodies the open 'That-ness' of material existence which marks the ontological incognito, the real incompletion of matter, within language. As Bloch writes:

> ... it is at all times the immediate that beneath everything is the throbbing Am of the That, that expresses itself in these utterances, unfolding itself in these expressions. Only because this ground is not yet certain, remains speechless, does it come to voice, does it attempt to say and clarify itself.[168]

The anacoluthon would thus constitute the productiveness of language, or what Hillis Miller terms 'the nonsignifying and *nonphenomenal* syntactic aspects of language'.[169] Mieszkowski explicitly touches on this reading through his reappraisal of Kant's concept of 'self-affection'. Read as language's 'self-affection', the anacoluthon stands as 'the dynamic in virtue of which language becomes what it is by relating to itself as something that it has not yet become'.[170] As the site of the figuration and disfiguration of linguistic being, the anacoluthon expresses an immanent self-relation of language to itself as an incompleteness; an incompleteness which, I would add, only derives from an incomplete materiality. As Bloch writes, this is because 'reality itself is undergoing upheaval and breaking apart'.[171] The anacoluthon in language is language's sharpened percipience of the incomplete actuality from which it speaks, a refraction of it, to use Voloshinov's concept.

But the anacoluthon is therefore not a passive reflection of the *referent* since the referent is not itself settled but rather requires work's intermission. Any linguistic productivity stamped by the material process as Bloch conceives it would thus be neither a perfected speech that exists prior to the saying of it – is not pre-constituted or pre-fabricated – 'a code which has been fixed and definitively established prior to communication', as Ponzio would put it,[172] nor would it be a saying that refers to or expresses a completed world: otherwise the speaker would be 'a spokesman of a totalization of reality' – again, as Ponzio

---

168   Bloch 2000a, p. 208.
169   Hillis Miller 1990, p. 110, my emphasis.
170   Mieszkowski 2009, p. 654.
171   Bloch 1998, p. 503, emphasis removed.
172   Ponzio 1993, p. 12. Cf. p. 14.

puts it.[173] To think the anacoluthon as expressive of 'That-ness' ('tendency') would be to think it as expressive of an ontological incompletion enjoying process forwards into the 'dark open'.[174] The anacoluthon is a threshold condition of speech which arguably is a speech which

> ... does not know the Intended-for [*Gemeinte*] positively as what it is, but negatively as what it is not. In such a way that it can be said after all, with things and solutions supplied: 'that was not meant'.[175]

This brings the discussion to Bloch's concept of narration – an underlying theme of Bloch's anacoluthon essay. For Bloch, a narrative style of language attuned to the incomplete reality from which it speaks must be free of an 'incestualised continuity', enjoying an anacoluthic leap at its heart.[176] A narrative form of continuity exudes falseness. Indeed, in *The Spirit of Utopia*, leading up to Bloch's imperative that Kant must burn through Hegel, Bloch criticises Hegel's penchant for systematising and his 'flawlessly communicated [*sprunglos vermittelten*]'[177] form of philosophising, summarising it with the following image:

> It is easy to discern ... whether a man tested by life is speaking, or a Münchhausen. Who only tells a story – say, 'We left Peking and got to Canton; on the fourteenth we were in Canton' – is simply changing locations, not himself, and so the continuous form of narrative is in order [*der verändert nur den Ort, nicht sich selbst und daher ist die unveränderte Form des Erzählens in Ordnung*].[178]

Thus Bloch repeats on the plane of narrative his disputation with mechanical materialism, for which motion is deemed an *external* attribute of extended matter. Bloch's opposition to this arid form of materialism has a bearing on a general mode of expression, as Landmann says:

> The logical mastering style [of these sciences] corresponds to the faith in a perfect, complete and harmonious world. Its perfection reflects itself

---

173   Ponzio 1993, p. 55.
174   Bloch 1969, p. 72. See Holz 1975, pp. 44–5.
175   Bloch 1969, p. 75.
176   Bloch 1969, p. 491.
177   Bloch 1971a, p. 281.
178   Bloch 2000a, p. 180; Bloch 1971a, p. 277.

in the closedness, in the unbroken beginning, in the smoothness of its expression. But for Ernst Bloch ... there is still work and ferment in all things, which are undetermined, un-concluded potentiality.[179]

Kant will also speak of the straightness of mathematical reason in comparison to the 'incomplete', 'approximative' and thus 'defective definitions' of philosophy: 'In mathematics, definition belongs *ad esse* [to the being], in philosophy *ad melius esse* [to the improvement of being]'.[180] 'To the improvement of being', the *music of reason*, one might say. For Kant, this 'music' would relate to 'those highest ends that most closely concern humanity', for which 'mathematics can yield no satisfaction'.[181] As Bloch describes the process of materialist definition, it can 'include determination from something and determination to something'; while 'determination from something (*definitio*) ... is only formal and not yet material', '[d]etermination to something (*destinatio*) moves with the passage of the matter, conforming to its objective directedness [*Gerictetsein*]'. Hence Bloch will call a proper materialist definition, one which accords 'with material directedness', a 'destinatory [*destinatorisch*]' definition.[182] The continuous, well-rounded form of narrative is a ruse – a *Münchhausen* – insofar as it observes and communicates the ups and downs of the world process – indeed if it communicates them at all – from a detached, un-dialectical position. And so the journey from Peking to Canton is without events, advents, transformations, detours, errors, failures, regrets, hopes, new perspectives and unanticipated awakenings. Rather, the discontinuity of the journey that Bloch deems to better capture material existence springs forth from the vicissitudes of history in which the narrator herself, and her work, are transformed by such tests and trials.[183] In a discontinuous narrative form one changes with the world which is also changing. As Bloch writes, 'the passage of matter is not only a depict-

---

179 Landmann 1965, p. 345. This mechanical materialist-inspired narrative accords with what the anticipation studies scholar Roberto Poli argues is a dominant physical science framework for understanding temporality, which he calls a 'commutative' mathematical framework, for which 'the only relevant information ... is provided by the starting and ending points'; 'the details of the specific routes', Poli says, 'are irrelevant'. (Poli 2009, p. 20).

180 Kant 2007, p. 588. See Roberts 2011, p. 53.

181 Kant 2007, p. 423.

182 Bloch 2000b, pp. 361–2.

183 One need only think of the breaks and the new beginnings that constituted Marx's writing of *Capital*: 'The long pause between the first part and the continuation is due to an illness of many years' duration, which interrupted my work again and again'. (Marx 1990, p. 89; see Heinrich 2016).

ing [*abbildendes*], but a shaping-forth [*Fortbildendes*]'.[184] Truthful speech thus 'runs ahead of itself, retreats, shifts the emphasis, reemphasises, and otherwise *communicates by means of discontinuity*'.[185]

4   The Anacoluthon as Linguistic Latency

How then can the anacoluthon also embody the matter-category of 'latency'? Bloch's strong emphasis on the openness of the material process at the same time always cautiously reminds us that this openness is not an end in itself – Bloch does not propagate an openness for the sake of openness. I have already argued in Chapter 1 that this purposive feature of Bloch's materialism would need to be contended with in any philosophy of language that is stamped with his name. The question of purpose in linguistic 'tendency' is briefly touched on in Bloch's anacoluthon essay. The context of the passage below is one in which Bloch is in dispute with Lukács's more formalist approach to narration.[186] Bloch holds that narration, understood as 'a literary form for representing linear succession' is not apt to capture 'the *viva vox*, which has its own form and its own style of preliterary narration'.[187] But as Bloch goes on:

> We should reiterate that this conclusion in no way affirms a merely affected or even made-to-order immediacy, nor does it seek the supposed resurrection of spontaneity marked by irrationalism. The authentic mode of narration intended here cannot be objectified in itself, nor can it stand forth as a purely autonomous form, capable of serving as a *counterforce* against rational poetics (however much it has always burst through the limits of that poetics, whenever the latter has devolved to artificiality à la Gottsched). But otherwise, the well-conserved *viva vox* is the *conditio*

---

184   Bloch 1975, p. 55.

185   Bloch 1998, p. 503. What is identical between language and matter is their shaping forth, and thus their identity is found in non-identity: there would be no need for shaping-forth if matter or being were already complete. Depiction as *fortbilden*, Bloch says, is 'the simplest form of the bridge between Percipere and Esse' (Bloch 1975, p. 55). In the anacoluthon essay, Bloch (1998, p. 504) states that 'the point of discourse is not to rhapsodize but to perceive – without maintaining discursive pretensions to a purely idealistic and rhetorical totalization of the world'. Cf. Hotho quoted in Adorno 1993, p. 120 and Roberts 2011, p. 41.

186   See Bloch 1998, pp. 501–2.

187   Bloch 1998, p. 502.

sine qua non of every poetry that has not become an end in itself, and resounds throughout the art – not least as an *anacoluthon* within an ever so magisterially closed system.[188]

I would argue that here the anacoluthon's two moments as 'tendency' and 'latency' are present but not clearly articulated. That for Bloch the 'authentic immediacy' of the *viva vox* – which the anacoluthon embodies – cannot be objectified, acting not as separate form but as a counter-force to rational poetics, speaks, firstly, to what I have suggested above concerning the anacoluthon's sub-figural status, its non-phenomenality. Like material productivity itself the anacoluthon cannot be objectified nor be made into a purely autonomous form, an end for itself, for the figure constitutes the site of the productivity of expressive form as such ('That-ness'). Bloch's passage also speaks to the anacoluthon's super-figural status, that is, its condition as one of tending beyond what is given through a generation of novelty in speech. Devoid of an anacoluthic rupture all poetics is said to reduce to an end that simply closes in on itself: such poetics, which the anacoluthon would remedy, possesses no openness of a goal. Contrary, then, to what the passage might at first suggest, the anacoluthon is, for Bloch, not a feature of linguistic life that is adversarial to all endings. Locating the passage within the context of Bloch's materialism, as laid-out in the Chapter 1, it can be argued that this thwarting of a poetics of closure frustrates a propensity in language to close itself off from the objective correlate that it expresses: the relation between incompletion and possible realisation. The anacoluthon, then, is not thwarting a linguistic 'tendency' to an end goal, but rather is curbing – indeed countering – a linguistic 'tendency' to otherwise gloss over this goal-direction, precisely a direction towards a goal that is not only 'not-yet' arrived at but 'not-yet' fully determined in and of itself. Bloch's point here, I would suggest, is that the anacoluthon closes off an all-too premature, supposed-Hegelian truce with existence.

Anacoluthic language is never an end in itself but always a means to an end. This was where I found the drawback in Comay and Ruda's reading of the dash in Hegel (see the Introduction). If the anacoluthon points to a mode of 'open expression'[189] that finds its correlate in a material ontology of not-yet being, then in the context of Blochian materialism the anacoluthon must constitute the threshold of linguistic conditionedness as such. The anacoluthon therefore lies at 'the threshold of expression [*der Schwelle der Äußerung*]', on the

---

188   Bloch 1998, p. 502.
189   Bloch, 1978, p. 122.

linguistic 'Front' of the becoming of material incompleteness in its linguistic iteration.[190] Bloch's point seems to be that the anacoluthon marks a borderline in language between what has and what has not yet become linguistically. The figure therefore touches on 'What-ness', since for Bloch 'ultimately the What itself is ... the Novum'.[191]

As Chapter 1 showed, Bloch's 'latency' category concerns this orientation to a still unsettled goal of the world process, which can be applied to language in the case of the anacoluthon. As Bloch himself puts it, 'the river is strongly oriented to the still outstanding outfall [*Mündung*]'.[192] The anacoluthon arguably can be said to possess a double register. As the previous section argued, the figure marks the incompleteness of material existence, that is, *the counter-force of incompletion* ('That-ness'), but within this also a purposive movement of that incompletion towards an outfall is present – an *unum necessarium* of the process, *a counter-force*, at one with the previous, *of an invariant of direction*. And it is precisely this invariance of direction that is the harbinger of the leaps and breaks that are found within linguistic life. For when it is considered that what this process aims towards is a goal that is 'not-yet' in existence and 'not-yet' determined in its substantive contents, so then only daybreaks of historical novelties can mark its course. As Bloch writes:

> There exists exactly in the interruptions, concrete montages, appropriately utopian indeterminacies of open-systematic thought always an *Invariant of direction*, straight through all cross-connections and in particular all through the Open itself.[193]

The linguistic openness of the anacoluthon is not an end in itself. While anacoluthic events in the life of language express their ontological correlate as an incompleteness of material 'That-ness' – the very starting point of Bloch's philosophy – they simultaneously border on the 'nameless *a priori*' that is their very provenance. From within and yet against 'the darkness of the incompleteness of material existence' the anacoluthic leap presents attempted determinations of a better life which is suitable for the liberation of mankind. All this takes place in the closeness of language to itself, in those small moments of interruption in the actual life of language, between interlocutors. So the

---

190   Bloch 2000a, p. 256.
191   Bloch 2000a, p. 256. 'A sentence has wishes as an event', as Gertrude Stein (1973, p. 18) once put it.
192   Bloch 1978, p. 30.
193   Bloch 1978, p. 30.

anacoluthon does not signal interruption for interruption's sake, a constant transgression for the sake of transgression, but rather points beyond itself to something new, the Novum, which for Bloch constitutes the 'not-yet' extant totality which is always intended.

The anacoluthon thereby creates a linguistic opening for a linguistic experimentation of 'What-ness'; the figure is 'a space of suspension, of probing, of deliberation, according to a different state of mobility than that of the all too settled condition that subsists behind the past perfect of eternal letters'.[194] Rupture necessarily creates space for a new turning in the constitution of 'not-yet' totality, bearing in mind, once more, that syntax concerns the totality of signs in their relation to one another. Following the recent work of Franco Berardi in *Futurability*, one could therefore argue that the anacoluthon is the 'vibration of the linguistic being'. As Berardi writes: 'When facing an alternative between different possibilities, the organism enters into a vibration, then proceeds making a choice that corresponds to its potency'.[195] Rupture and totality do not constitute mutually exclusive alternatives but rather rupture is the proper manner of the becoming of totality when totality is 'not-yet'. As Bloch writes: 'the non-existing all, not the existing whole, is the goal of the dialectical movement that *holds it together*, exactly as need is its impulse and motor'.[196] It is the 'non-existing all' that holds together the syntactical movement; it is the inkling that 'something's missing' that forms, re-forms, and perhaps trans-forms linguistic life, and then attempts to give that life its proper outline. The anacoluthon's disruption of an otherwise orderly syntactical flow not only, therefore, linguistically expresses the non-existence of totality – it equally and in the same moment expresses a real and open intending towards such a non-extant totality.

As I mentioned earlier in this chapter, George Steiner was a rare commentator to have identified the hidden potential in Bloch's philosophy for speculating anew on the core nature of language. While Steiner does not refer to the anacoluthon by name but to what he calls the 'Pythagorean genre',[197] the anacoluthon clearly demonstrates this genre's logic, as Steiner conceives it, and which, as I will show, is clearly in agreement with the general thrust of the 'latency' category. The Pythagorean genre principally concerns novelty of expression and in Steiner's estimation Bloch was, during his own time, the 'foremost living writer' of the Pythagorean genre; Bloch is said to have 'broken the generically ponderous, clotted norms of German syntax', giving 'unique

---

194   Bloch 1998, p. 504.
195   Berardi 2019, p. 1.
196   Bloch 1983, p. 303.
197   Steiner 1965, p. 341.

voice' to an 'an unprecedented need'.[198] This of course should recall Bloch's own admission that 'erroneous' language is sometimes apposite for calling forth the new which cannot presently be articulated in the limits of given language. The disruption of a syntactical norm is therefore evidently at the centre of Steiner's understanding of the Pythagorean genre. This genre's breaking free of syntactical uniformity is said to emerge from an urgency to give voice to the new, the unprecedented, the unheard-of, what is on the horizon. The prevailing view among Bloch's intellectual circle was indeed that philosophy had to succumb to a new mandate so that it may renew its vision and articulation of reality.[199] Bloch saw this renewal in the avant-garde of the Expressionists, in its recognition of the human incognito and a simultaneous directedness towards a search for outfall.[200] And insofar as Bloch believed that his philosophy had broken with longstanding conceptions of being, so then he considered it as anacoluthic with regards to the history of philosophy.[201] As Holz says, the novel movements of material becoming 'requires [philosophy's] own linguistic reproduction'.[202] Adorno equally considers that the return of philosophy to its speculative mandate renews (philosophical) expression.[203] But like the Expressionists before him, Steiner only grasps this novelty in linguistic production by way of a focus on artistic expression, and not the mundane expression of the workers.

The 'Novum' – and thus the 'latency' category – enters Steiner's considerations in his suggestion that Bloch's stylistics represent a kind of *aubade*-prose (*Tagelied*). This is an intriguing assertion which, given the history of this prose which I briefly touch on below, indicates that Bloch's own style of expression exemplifies the possibility that material process could both lead to 'the All' or 'the Nothing'. The point that Steiner's account misses is indeed the idea, so key to Bloch's materialism, that the need that gives birth to syntactical breaks is the need for a 'not-yet' existing nor determined totality. The claim that Bloch's philosophy constitutes a sort of dawn song, then, is not too far off the mark. Bloch was frequently moved to express the drive to utopia with the Latin phrase *ex oriente lux* ('light from the East'). Bloch also quotes Hebel to the same effect: 'The Orient, where our faith, our fruit tree, and our blood reside'.[204] But Steiner's

198   Steiner 1965, p. 342.
199   See Gluck 1985, pp. 143–73.
200   See Bloch 1971b, p. 160.
201   See Bloch 1986, p. 6. Cf. Holz 1975, p. 38.
202   Holz 1975, p. 43.
203   See Adorno 2008, pp. 107–8. On the question of Bloch's writing style, cf. Bense 1978, Richter 2000, p. 107, and Geoghegen 1996, p. 30.
204   Bloch 1998, p. 154.

claim needs to be read back into the categories of Bloch's materialism. The Latin *albus*, 'aubade' denotes the overwhelming whiteness or clarity of dawn and is rooted in the old Occitan form of the *alba*: 'Traditionally *aubade* is a joyful poem that celebrates the coming of morning':[205]

> The category of the dawn song or poem is vast: they are found in almost all cultures and have been composed since the earliest times. Perhaps originally religious, dawn poems are also associated in most of these cultures with secular eroticism.[206]

But the aubade moment equivocates in its meaning between, one might say, looking in one's own direction, on the one hand, and disappointment, on the other. As Rowe notes, the aubade does not simply convey the positivity of a 'joyful dawn song' in the troubadour tradition; in fact, in much of the poetic tradition the emergence of a new day announces the need for lovers to part – the aubade can thus also be understood as a cursing of the dawn.[207] This is taken further with Philip Larkin's poem 'Aubade' (published in 1977), which itself is a reflection on death and on entropy – no dawn shall dawn again.[208] Indeed the aubade in this sense captures the heart of utopia itself, the failure and the optimism tied up in utopia's history. Against the co-ordinates of Bloch's materialism this equivocity of the dawn song merely highlights the undecidedness of the goal of the world process – not only in content, but in victory. There is an indication here that 'the All' or 'the Nothing' circulates the possibility of arrival. Of course, this reading is abstract and continues the very path I suggested in the Introduction was contrary to a real Marxist inheritance of Bloch's nascent philosophy of language. It remains within the confines of an aesthetic reading of Bloch on the figure of the anacoluthon. Chapter 3 will seek to remedy this.

This aesthetic and formalist problem is in fact located in Steiner's discussion of the Pythagorean genre, published in 1965, which is prefigured with a claim that there was a sense that a growing inadequacy of expressive form was developing but that new expressive forms, 'other possibilities of form', tentative but real, were being constructed.[209] Steiner's account of why these changes take place within expressive form is formalist because its treatment implies that aes-

---

205   Anon 2013, p. 1.

206   Fryatt 2012, p. 200.

207   Rowe 2011, p. 171.

208   The different interpretations of the anacoluthon provided by Bloch and Adorno are, I would suggest, therefore woven into the very history of the *alba* form.

209   Steiner 1965, p. 336.

thetic expression exists in its own enclave away from the social materiality that is its condition of being. Because Steiner misses the importance of these conditions the Pythagorean genre is painted in quite abstract terms which tend to lead to Wittgensteinian statements and admissions:

> Wherever it reaches out toward the limits of expressive form, literature comes to the shore of *silence*. There is nothing mystical in this. Only the realisation that the poet and philosopher, by investing language with the utmost precision and illumination, are made aware, and make the reader aware, of other dimensions which cannot be circumscribed in words.[210]

Steiner holds the likes of Kierkegaard and Nietzsche, Karl Kraus and Walter Benjamin as figures who belong to these tentative explorations in expressiveness, through whom old, congealed expressive forms shine in the light of their own inadequacy. Steiner here formulates the idea of 'latency' in worn-out notions of genius, in the type of 'individualistic subjectivism' which Voloshinov rallied against (see Chapter 3). Bloch himself is privy to this new tendency in literary and philosophical expression which Steiner holds dear: the 'great cultural works ... expose "meaning" to its own utopian content', a process in which meaning's former context is 'split open'.[211] In so doing Bloch tends towards a more Frankfurt School obsession with high art's emancipatory potential, even if Bloch is otherwise set apart from that propensity through his lifting up popular culture to a serious treatment of how it enables the Novum to be glimpsed.[212] Steiner certainly intimates a more objective grasp of this genre when he suggests that the 'common factor in these works' is

> ... the reaching out of language toward new relations (what we call logic), and in a wider sense toward a new syntax by which to tempt reality into the momentary but living order of words.[213]

And in their striving 'toward new potentialities'[214] these nascent forms of expression are said to 'modify, by the very fact of their existence, our sense of

---

210   Steiner 1965, p. 341.
211   Bloch 1998, pp. 110 and 100.
212   See Bloch 1986.
213   Steiner 1965, p. 336.
214   Steiner 1965, p. 338.

how meaning may be communicated'.[215] But as Ferruccio Rossi-Landi notes, the 'latency' and emergence of new linguistic form must be solidly rooted in a non-formalist manner, precisely in its social conditions:

> Within revolutionary movements throughout the world the new desire can be traced to give back meaning to words and to set up new constructive mediations between the linguistics and the nonlinguistic or to find again mediations that have been lost. This amounts not only to an initial recognition, intuitive but collective, of linguistic exploitation and alienation; it amounts also to the forming of a conflictuality directed against exploitation of codes by ruling classes and nations and the alienation of language and communication. Linguistic disalienation, in fact, belongs to the future; it necessarily requires revolutionary praxis. No real operation on language can be only linguistic. To operate on language, one has to operate on society. Here as everywhere else, politics comes first.[216]

Thus, when one sets Steiner's Pythagorean genre in its social conditionedness, which would entail situating Bloch and the anacoluthon in the same context, what is disclosed is that the anacoluthic interruption which arguably stands 'at the front of immediacy [*an der Unmittelbarkeits-front*]'[217] is a linguistic 'experience of Front [*Fronterlebnis*]'.[218] And so, contrary to Steiner, the genre's exploration of new linguistic form does not lead to confirming Wittgenstein's assertion that '[t]he limits of my language mean the limits of my world'.[219] Instead, as Berardi writes, 'if language is a limit, this implies also that there are more possibilities beyond that limit'; there is thus an 'excess' or a surplus to this 'linguistic creation' that is not reduced to silence.[220] Even if Berardi once more follows the Vosslerite tendency of asserting that it is poetry that constitutes 'the linguistic activity that exceeds the limits of our language',[221] as is the case for Alain Badiou, for whom poetry should not be reduced to a 'verbal instance of silence',[222] one nevertheless can say that the anacoluthon possesses the pos-

---

215   Steiner 1965, p. 336.
216   Rossi-Landi 1992, p. 265.
217   Bloch 1969, p. 147.
218   Bloch 1969, p. 147.
219   Wittgenstein 1974, p. 68, emphasis removed.
220   Berardi 2019, p. 195.
221   Ibid.
222   Badiou 2019, p. 109.

sibility of a *common* disentanglement among people in their everyday limits and not poets in their masterpieces.[223] Berardi himself taps into this broader capacity of language on this score:

> Language enabled the emergence of society, the differentiation of human beings from their environment, and enabled the jump beyond their existing reality that, according to Paolo Virno, was made possible through the faculty of negation. In the space of language, the double process of negation and imagination became possible.[224]

If anacoluthic language is expressive of the darkness of the 'That' of material existence, then the 'advancing intention [*das fortschreitende Meinen*]'[225] of linguistic production expresses the desire for the 'Ultimum' – 'a *Lösewort*',[226] the, after all, 'fundamental concept [*Grundbegriff*] of utopian philosophy'.[227] Via the figure of the anacoluthon, this would have to be located in the linguistic intercourse of the workers.

For Stalin, the question of the multiplicity of human languages was always contoured by a vision of historical unification. Smith speaks of Stalin's 'Marxian "eschatology" of language development', which, following Nikolai Bukharin, was premised on 'the ever developing and perfecting forms of human life', including language, which was ultimately dependent on the economic base, moving from the many to the one.[228] This supposed movement towards world-linguistic uniformity was also, of course, shaped by Marr's understanding of language development.[229] Marr himself advocated in 1930 'the need for com-

---

223 Badiou will write that '[t]he poetic act is neither descriptive (even if it practices description) nor "monstrative" in the sense of the mystical element (even if it practices suggestion). It aims rather to organize a verbal totality (a poem by itself composes *a* proposition) in such a way that a presence-of-being be named by this totality, whereas nothing in ordinary language named this. Poetry is the creation of a name-of-being that was previously unknown. The sole axiom of poetry is: "Everything that participates in being, whether simple or infinitely multiple, has a name. The difficulty lies in inventing it". It is not for nothing that poetry, for this unhead-of invention, uses the maximal resources of *difference*, including sonorous, between the names from inherited language'. (Badiou 2019, pp. 108–9).
224 Berardi 2019, p. 107.
225 Bloch 1978, p. 75.
226 Bloch 1969, p. 214.
227 Ibid.
228 Smith 2010, p. 113.
229 Ibid.

plete "speech revolution" using "new language material".[230] This possible link with some of the worst (scientific) excesses of Soviet Russia serves to raise the ever-present spectre of Bloch's complicity with the Stalinist authorities, especially during the period of the show trials – certainly not Bloch's finest hour. Whether Bloch theoretically 'colluded' on the question of language with this application of 'latency' to the question of language remains to be determined and cannot be automatically assumed. In the context of the question of Marxism in linguistics, Vladimir M. Alpatov has argued that one ought not to confuse a person's political positions and activism with their stance on linguistics and theories of language.[231] The question of Marxism and language, and Bloch's place within it given my reading of the anacoluthon, is the topic of the next chapter.

---

230   Marr quoted in Gorham 2010, pp. 139–40. Cf. p. 146, where Marr himself is said to have advised grammar be exiled from Soviet classrooms. Cf. Gramsci's opposition to the Fascist educational reforms of Giovanni Gentile, on the basis that 'normative grammar', insofar as it is the unifying force of this normativity, empowers a higher level of expressiveness for the masses – a precondition for withering away parochialism and of developing a new hegemonic power bloc (see Ives 2004, pp. 43–7).

231   Alpatov 2000, p. 173.

Bloch and Marxist Philosohpy of Language

In proposing that the anacoluthon can act as a starting point with which to construct a Blochian philosophy of language, the theme of relationality has arisen, a relationality that is premised on the incompleteness of (human) material being, and a tendency to a possible arrival of what is missing. This processual relationality is precisely what Bloch names 'matter'. The reading of the anacoluthon outlined in the previous chapter can now pave the way for this processual relationality to act as a site of comparison – a *tertium comparationis*. Indeed, a parallel reading will help to elucidate some philosophical-linguistic commonality *and* divergence between Bloch (1885–1977) and Voloshinov (1895–1936). In doing so, the proper stakes of Bloch's contribution for Marxist philosophy of language can be better gauged.

Bloch's categories have helped to delimit language in a certain way, within the purview of a tendency-latency dialectic, and the anacoluthon has been that node through which this dialectic has been shown to play itself out linguistically. By placing Bloch into dialogue with Voloshinov's self-described Marxist philosophy of language, however, this Blochian delimitation can be pushed further by specifying how the material tendency and latency of *not-yet being* can contribute to the philosophy of language within the purview of a properly Marxist thematic.[1] If, as I argue, the figure of the anacoluthon acts as a node through which Bloch's nascent philosophy of language can emerge and be read, then the parallel reading of this with Voloshinov's work supplements Bloch's contribution with the important concept of *dialogue*. Equally, Bloch's contribution supplements Voloshinov with a broader notion of the *being or objective conditionedness* which the word exists within and refracts.

Voloshinov's name is well-known. The much vaunted question of authorship vis-à-vis Voloshinov and the legacy of the Bakhtin Circle does not have a real bearing on the argument below. For the sake of brevity I will simply employ the name of Voloshinov.[2] Voloshinov is significant because he first produced an

---

1 Not all Marxist contributions to the philosophy of language can be taken up for consideration. For more recent work, for instance, on Gramsci, see Carlucci 2013, Ives 2004a and 2004b.

2 Like Vladimir M. Alpatov (2000, p. 181), here *Marxism and the Philosophy of Language* will be

explicit Marxian account of language. *Marxism and the Philosophy of Language* (1929) has been central to the further development in this otherwise marginal area of Marxist studies. Indeed the work has been a clear port of call for the type of comparative task that will be my method of approach in this chapter.[3]

Previous comparative work of this type is not, however, the only reason which grants a comparison between Bloch and Voloshinov legitimacy. As far as the record goes, Bloch and Voloshinov did not know of, nor comment on, the other's work. Initially only flimsy points of contact appear between Bloch and Voloshinov. But once the surface of the matter is scratched, 'immanent' reasons for such a comparison emerge. Just below the surface there are remote connections. Both thinkers could be, and have been, defined as post-Marxist.[4] The post-Marxist tenor of Bloch and Voloshinov's respective bodies of work unite them only very loosely, of course. Another faint connection here belongs to Bloch's relationship to Russia. Bloch, taken as the philosopher of the October Revolution, heralded the Revolution as that *orient lux* which could redeem humanity of the vicissitudes of capitalist civilisation.[5] Voloshinov himself was a key figure in the great burst of creative thought and culture that emerged from that period. Moreover, Bloch, alongside his great intellectual companion Lukács, held Russian literature aloft as an expression of utopianism, particularly the work of Dostoevsky and Tolstoy, literary figures who held particular gravity for the Bakhtin Circle, too.[6] Finally, somewhat analogous to Bloch's own neophyte journey to Marx, Voloshinov had briefly undergone a 'dalliance with mysticism'[7] and had shared with Bloch a

---

considered as a collaboration of both the authors in question. Much of the work developed during the 1920s within the Bakhtin Circle was fittingly the product of collaboration. While the identity of the man behind *Marxism and the Philosophy of Language* is disputed – two Russian editions were printed in Leningrad, 1929 and 1930 – I will focus on the substantive issues the work deals with (see Tihanov 2000, p. 8; Brandist 2002a, pp. 4 and 9; Holquist 1990, pp. xxxii–xxxiii; and Lecercle 2006, p. 106).

3   Sućeska (2018) has compared Voloshinov's approach with Gramsci's work on language, while Abel (2018) compares Adorno with Voloshinov's philosophy of language in relation to music. Beasley-Murray (2007) compares Bakhtin and Voloshinov with Walter Benjamin's account of language.

4   See Lecercle 2006, p. 105. Cf. p. 124, where post-Marxism is contrasted with 'para-Marxism', defined by 'displacement by translation' rather than 'succession and supersession'.

5   See Negt 1975.

6   See Löwy 1979, p. 113n80. For a sense of Dostoevsky and Tolstoy's importance for the Circle respectively, see Bakhtin 1994 and Medvedev 2004.

7   Alpatov 2000, p. 181.

strong aversion to mechanical materialism.[8] Both thinkers also held an equivalent interest in the philosophy of music.[9]

More substantial points of contact obtain between the two thinkers, however. These concern Bloch and Voloshinov's receptions of two commanding intellectual traditions during the late nineteenth and early twentieth century: neo-Kantianism and Freudian psychoanalysis. Not only is a critique of Freudianism a common grounding to both Bloch and Voloshinov's respective programmes, despite clear difference in their Freud-readings, but so too do their respective Marxisms share a well-documented neo-Kantian inheritance, which acts as a further and definite conduit through which they can encounter each other on the question of language. Making such an encounter is the task below.

Despite these points of contact no comparison of Bloch and Voloshinov exists to date. That said, Ivan Boldyrev has intimated the significance of such a comparison. He does so, however, with reference to aesthetic debates that took place between Bloch and Lukács, which, he suggests, echo Mikhail Bakhtin's ideas. We are told that in a context characterised by neo-Kantianism and philosophy of life, Bakhtin's 'aesthetics of verbal creation' develop 'the conception of *outsidedness* ... and opposes the aesthetic *givenness* with ethical or religious *positedness*, the complete being of the hero to the "not-yet-being" of the human, who contemplates his own life from within himself'.[10] Given that Bloch did not develop a sustained account of language, the omission of a broader engagement with the two on the question of language is comprehensible. My aim below is to expand on Boldyrev's intimation.

Above and beyond these rare intimations, loose connections, and common intellectual inheritances and critiques, there is one final reason for why there is substance in comparing Bloch and Voloshinov, and it concerns the issue of syntax. As I have already noted in Chapter 2, focusing on syntax as an important linguistic phenomenon for the philosophy of language is controversial, at least to analytical philosophy of language. I have also noted that Bloch's oeuvre is scant of syntax's mention, bar his one essay on the anacoluthon. By dint of its marginality the figure stood up as something crucial: Bloch taught us to *follow the small things*. Voloshinov, too, was concerned with syntax, particularly with its marginality. Both Voloshinov and his collaborator Mikhail Bakhtin held the desire to step away from rational abstractness and to dive into the unique

---

8   See Voloshinov 1973, p. 17. Cf. p. 24: 'The category of mechanical causality in explanations of ideological phenomena can most easily be surmounted on the grounds of philosophy of language'.
9   See Brandist 2002a, p. 22.
10   Boldyrev 2014, pp. 57–8.

concreteness of the immediate material world.[11] For Voloshinov, a focus on syntax was one way to achieve this: 'problems of syntax', he writes, 'have immense importance for the proper understanding of language and its generative process'.[12] 'In point of fact', Voloshinov goes on, 'of all the forms of language, *the syntactic forms are the ones closest to the concrete forms of utterance*'.[13] More concrete than phonetic or morphological forms, syntactic forms 'are more closely associated with the real conditions of discourse'.[14] Voloshinov's philosophy of language will seek to show that, hitherto, the real conditions of discourse have been marginal to linguistics. What is the nature of this marginality? Strangely, insofar as 'the utterance as a whole', or, better, 'a whole utterance', has said to hitherto elude the linguist, so then syntax, in taking us to what is most concrete about discourse, brings us to 'the peripheries of speech', since syntax presents us with 'a whole linguistic entity', which Voloshinov will also call '*the verbal whole*'.[15] As seems to be the case with Bloch, then, it is the syntax's very *boundary-status* which ensures its relation to totality. The marginal is the concrete, and the concrete takes us far for it leads us towards totality. In Voloshinov's 1927/28 plan for the book on Marxism and language, a passage exists which does seem to problematise this supposed importance of syntax, however:

> The relations and connections between whole utterances [N.B. namely, those relations between persons or, better, between classes, which define the multiaccentuality of the word] are profoundly and essentially different from the connections and relations (morphological and syntactical) between the elements within utterances. The connections between rejoinders are profoundly and as a matter of principle different from the connections between the syntactical elements within a rejoinder.[16]

But Voloshinov then goes on to supplement this view with the following:

> The lack of understanding of these particular forms of connections between the elements of discursive interaction (i.e. between whole utter-

---

11   See Holquist 1990, pp. xv, xx–xxii, xxxvi and xxxviii. More will be said later on in the
      chapter concerning the relation for Bakhtin of the concrete to consummation.
12   Voloshinov 1973, p. 110.
13   Voloshinov 1973, p. 110.
14   Ibid.
15   Ibid.
16   Voloshinov 2004, p. 246.

ances oriented towards one another) has also had an effect on the study of connections within utterances: what has still not been understood is everything within the utterance that *leads beyond its limits*, everything within it that points towards another utterance (rejoinder). Connections between certain major elements within the utterance (for example, almost always between paragraphs, separated by a break line) are analogous in type to the connections between whole, independent utterances (rejoinders in a dialogue), but cannot be compared with paratactic and hypotactic connections within a complex sentence.[17]

If syntax is that marginally treated connection within an utterance which linguistics has ignored, then an outline of everything within syntax which leads that utterance to its (social) limits must necessarily include the anacoluthon, that figure of everyday speech which exemplifies the very moment an utterance finds its limit outside itself.

As perhaps one can glean from the above, relationality holds a significant position in Voloshinov's philosophy of language. The word is perceived by him as a relation, a 'border zone'.[18] The basic argument I wish to make here is that once Voloshinov's work is read alongside Bloch, one can begin to see that linguistic relationality simply cannot be reduced, as Voloshinov argues, to the socio-economic relations between living persons, as crucial as those are. Relationality within loquacity also has to be conceived of as a relationality between past and possible futures – Bloch's notion of non-contemporaneity being key here. This theme will enable me to elaborate the manner in which the figure of the anacoluthon embodies just such a type of relationality oriented forward (*nach vorn*). Bloch and Voloshinov's respective, albeit contrastive, inheritances of neo-Kantianism and Freudianism will allow me to mark this difference more clearly.

I argue, then, that the 'unrealised potential' of Voloshinov's philosophy of language[19] can be engaged with by critically reassessing it through the prism of Bloch's work. In the spirit in which Craig Brandist has recently called for,[20] one can more readily bring forth – or better, supplement – 'the incipient realism'[21] of Voloshinov's work by extending Marxist philosophy of language into a new terrain, namely, into the 'warm stream' of Blochian philosophy. Bloch once

---

17   Ibid.
18   Voloshinov 1973, p. 86.
19   Brandist 2002a, p. 177.
20   See Brandist 2002a, p. 5. Cf. p. 26.
21   Brandist 2002a, p. 87.

quipped: what is a realism that does not realise anything? A realism is desolate
that is not attuned to 'the tendency of what is actually real, to the objectively
real possibility to which tendency is assigned'.[22] Bloch's philosophy, which,
as Lucien Pelletier notes, was from its inception born of a close connection
between an epistemological realism and a utopian ontology,[23] allows us to re-
conceive Voloshinov's realist concept of the *refraction* of being as the refraction
not only of present socio-economic being, but of what is not-yet.

1   Voloshinov and Relationality

Voloshinov's intervention into the philosophy of language is structured along
the lines of a conceptual relationality. Voloshinov took to dialectically overcome 'two basic trends' in general linguistics at the time of his intervention,
namely 'abstract objectivism' and 'individualistic subjectivism'.[24] These trends
map onto a broad relationality within language, the poles of which are *stable
systematicity* and *creativity* respectively. Voloshinov's overarching and self-
stated task in *Marxism and the Philosophy of Language* is to answer questions concerning 'the true centre of linguistic reality', language's 'real mode of
existence'; he frames this concern by asking whether the true centre of language can be taken as 'the individual speech act – the utterance – or the system of language'; indeed he queries whether the 'real mode of existence of
language' is 'unceasing creative generation' – as subjectivist linguists hold –
'or inert immutability of self-identical norms' – as objectivist linguists see
things.[25] Voloshinov considered that if each position were left pure unto itself
the true core of language, as he set out to discover it, would withdraw from
view.

Unlike Saussure's structuralism Voloshinov saw the importance of creativity
and historicity in the core life of language. For the structural objectivist there
is 'a special kind of *discontinuity between the history of language and the system
of language*'.[26] This split of a logical systematicity and an a-logical historicity

---

22   Bloch 1986, p. 145.
23   Pelletier 2018, p. 29.
24   Voloshinov 1973, pp. 47–8.
25   Voloshinov 1973, p. 63. See Lecercle 2006, pp. 111–13. Utopianism plays out a similar dis-
        tinction between an *archistic* utopia of perfect order and an *anarchistic* utopia of perfect
        freedom (see Saage 2016).
26   Voloshinov 1973, p. 54.

is most apparent in Saussure's abandonment of the concrete utterance, *parole*, as a legitimate concern for linguistics. The system of language is most crucial to Saussure. Voloshinov, however, evades the pitfall of objectivism's assertion of an incontestable system of language which only ever expresses normative identity by moving this creativity of historicity away from an individualist bent and into a class-framework. If Voloshinov's objections to abstract objectivism lie in its exclusion of history and the multiaccentuality of the sign (the contestedness of linguistic norms), then it is not individuals as such but classes who act as the sites from which linguistic creativity arises. As Voloshinov states, the abstract objectivist can never countenance ' "tragedies" in language', since for her there can be no counter-ideological thrust to linguistic life, that is, no creative generation of a particular sort – in this case, of that sort stemming from class struggle.[27] For Voloshinov, language does not exist above the fray of historical becoming because it is 'grounded in ideological motives' of a class nature.[28]

In emphasising class as a vector for linguistic creativity Voloshinov therefore equally pushes back against psychologism, or individualistic subjectivism.[29] In emphasising the importance of the open production of a novelty of meaning[30] in the 'borderzone of continuous interaction',[31] prizing and not downplaying the importance of linguistic creativity which is the ground of the multiaccentuality of the sign, the sign's application to ever-new contexts, Voloshinov nevertheless avoids reducing this creativity to an abstract notion of human psyche or individual consciousness, a notion which for him, as for Marx, could only ever be legitimately seen in any case as a 'socioideological fact'.[32] Individualistic subjectivism is the reverse pole of a binding normativity and systematicity of the abstract objectivist,[33] being instead an emphasis on the continuous stream of creativity such as is emblematic of Humboldt's notion of language as actualisation (*energeia*). For Voloshinov, this insight into linguistic creativity had to be rendered Marxist.[34] The so-called voluntarism of individual psychology

---

27   Voloshinov 1973, p. 56, see also p. 57.

28   Voloshinov 1973, p. 57.

29   See Brandist 2002, p. 80.

30   Morris 1994, pp. 5 and 10.

31   Morris 1994, p. 12.

32   Voloshinov 1973, p. 25. Cf. Cassirer, who paints the picture of an extreme case of the notion of creativity, the '*spontaneity* of the spirit' (Cassirer 1980, p. 141), which underpins the sort of psychologism meant by Voloshinov. This freedom ultimately places the accent on stylistics, which exposes the impossibility of any universal grammar.

33   See Voloshinov 1973, p. 53.

34   See Voloshinov 1973, pp. 48–9. For Humboldt, language is not a completed work (*ergon*),

and its emphasis in linguistics on *expression* as the 'individual creative act of speech'[35] – *Sprache als Rede*, language as art and as 'aesthetic activity'[36] – was assigned a class role, then. Individualistic subjectivism's 'stylistic individual-isation of language' ensures that style precedes grammar, just as expression precedes system. In being rendered along class lines, this meant that the system of language was subject to struggle and was therefore a site of class conflict.[37]

In sum, abstract objectivism views language as a pure givenness, while individualistic subjectivism views language as pure positedness.[38] If abstract objectivism grasps the importance of the givenness of totality, it loses sense of the historical becoming of totality and of the place of the new (positedness), especially along the class-lines which Voloshinov interpolates this positedness with. On the other hand, if individualistic subjectivism grasps the significance of the non-repeatable and the creative counter-position to system (posited-ness), it loses a sense of the location of the non-repeatable, creative counter-position both outside and against, but also *within*, totality (the given). Indeed, as will be shown, for Bloch, the givenness of socio-economic conditions of being do not exhaust givenness as such. Instead there is a depth of being (a givenness as lack) which remains to be posited.

With regards to my reading of the anacoluthon in the previous chapter, it can be noted that the figure dialectically unites the subjectivist and objectivist trends. The a-syntactic nature of the figure, precisely to be a-syntactic, presup-poses the existence of the systematicity and normativity of language, through which it potentially breaks through. The anacoluthon thereby also points to the linguistic creative generation of subjectivism by potentially constituting the point of a linguistic break with such objectivism. The anacoluthon is the site of a possible prising open of the pervading linguistic norms for their entrance into novelty. The class nature of the anacoluthon is, however, a supplementa-tion that Voloshinov's thought gives to Bloch.

Unlike abstract objectivism, Voloshinov does not conceive of the utterance as adhering to 'linguistic laws of connection between linguistic signs within a given, closed linguistic system';[39] that is, as Voloshinov puts it, the utterance

---

but following Fichte's prioritisation of action as a condition for the possibility of experi-ence, language is seen as an action prior to facts. Here the reader should recall Nietzsche's notion of language as a creative medium (see Forster 2011, p. 92).

35   Voloshinov 1973, pp. 48 and 52.
36   Voloshinov 1973, p. 48.
37   Voloshinov 1973, p. 51.
38   See Beasley-Murray 2007, p. 91.
39   Voloshinov 1973, p. 57.

does not observe neo-classicism's 'cult of autonomous, rational, fixed form'.[40] For Voloshinov, objectivism's 'stationary rainbow arched over that stream'[41] of singular speech acts is in truth none other than concrete dialogue. It is class-based concrete dialogue which accounts for the historically shifting 'normative identity of linguistic form', and thus this normative identity of linguistic form is subject to change.[42] Additionally, then, the anacoluthic rupture of such normativity within language is not derived from singular acts of speech, as Bloch's essay would seem to suggest, but instead acts of speech in dialogue. What Voloshinov helps a Blochian philosophy of language to grasp is that the anacoluthon is a feature of dialogue, a 'discursive embodiment of intersubjectivity' – it cannot be reduced to the genius of an artist or the prophetic speech act of a charismatic leader.[43] The 'not-following' of the anacoluthon in speech is a rupture within dialogue, between interlocutors, occurring right now, and so the anacoluthon concerns rupture within social relations. Following Voloshinov it could be argued that the anacoluthon's existence exemplifies the variability that marks the life of a linguistic sign. It is the zero-point of the word's multiaccentuality, so long as this variability does not expunge the possibility of real realisation (always a hangover question for Voloshinov). In fact, the very manner in which Voloshinov deduces his programme maps onto the problematic at the heart of Marx's *Brumaire* passage, which is read in depth in the next chapter. There, the new revolutionary content is said to transcend the phrase and thus needs to be communicated by the revolutionary class with a new tongue (a new collective positedness), a creative generation of an almost non-repeatable or at least hitherto unheard-of speech act. I will return to Marx's *Brumaire* passage.

For Voloshinov, language *is* relationality on a number of different though connected levels, some of which will serve as points of comparison with Bloch's philosophy later on. These can be outlined as follows. Firstly, language presupposes and is the ongoing result of a relation between persons, as noted above. While this might seem like an obvious point, the key strength of Voloshinov's work in language, when we look to supplement the nascent work of language surrounding the anacoluthon in Bloch's work, is this dialogic conception of language:

40   Voloshinov 1973, p. 57n19. Bloch was equally repelled by classicism, its aesthetic of 'solidification' and 'calm', an opposition which plays itself out in the Expressionism debate (see Bloch 1991, pp. 199–200 and Bloch 1992).
41   Voloshinov 1973, p. 52.
42   Voloshinov 1973, p. 53.
43   Brandist 2002, p. 81.

> In order to come close to the actual life of a language one must achieve a much broader and more fundamental grasp of its immediate givenness. This givenness is ... the social event of the discursive interaction of a least two utterances. Only in dialogue is language real.[44]

This type of relationality is decisive for Voloshinov's philosophy of language and in fact for his collaborator Bakhtin, who is said to have been a 'constant mediator on the meaning of borders', i.e. on language as a being-between-two.[45] Voloshinov viewed the word as a bridge, too. This dialogic conception of language did not just mean that one speaker relates via language to another, but also that it is through language that I relate to *myself as another*; it also concerns the relation of my language to a 'concrete situation' and indeed to the wider *objective social conditions of my being* which pervades my existence: that is, 'the extra-verbal situation' of the utterance, which includes both 'the immediate situation and through it the broader one'.[46] All of these levels of relationality – person to person, person to herself, person to person within both an immediate context and within the broader condition of social being – cannot be abstracted out of being inherently bound together. And because language plays such a key intermediary, relational role on these levels, Voloshinov will say that language does not simply *reflect* these conditions of social being, but *refracts* them. Relationality is not simply defined by mimicry.

To show how Bloch and Voloshinov differ on the question of refraction, the latter two levels of relationality – the word as a relation of inner and outer life, and the relation of the word to broader socio-economic being – will serve as my points of comparison with Bloch's categories. My claim is that Bloch can help supplement Voloshinov's account of the utterance with a broader notion of the being that the word refracts, while, as has been indicated above, Voloshinov helps to supplement Bloch's nascent linguistic ideas surrounding the anacoluthon with a more dialogic account of the figure.

As Voloshinov writes in a plan to *Marxism and the Philosophy of Language*, what we often experience as the 'immediate givenness of language', namely phonemes, morphemes, the 'physical phenomenon of the sound' of a word as well as the 'physiological process of its production', do not in fact exhaust what the immediate givenness of language is.[47] This is because language's immediate givenness relates to nature, and not history. Only in the 'system of history' can

---

44   Voloshinov 2004, p. 246.
45   Holquist 1990, p. xix.
46   Voloshinov 2004, p. 247.
47   Voloshinov 2004, pp. 243–4.

the 'fullness of the social sense and significance of discourse' be revealed.[48] My argument is that the fullness of the social sense and significance of language turns out to be a restricted fullness in Voloshinov's philosophy of language because its account of language occludes from this fullness the possibility of arrival, *the possibility of fullness*, as it were.

As the first chapter showed, Bloch develops a utopian notion of relationality, one in which present material existence is traversed by its own incompletion and relates to a possible Novum that would be its fulfilment. It is this fundamental relationality at the heart of material existence – and so at the core of linguistic materiality – which touches on Bloch's notion of the 'warm stream' of Marxist critique. And it is this notion, grasped through the prism of Voloshinov's concept of 'refraction', which I will argue enriches Marxist philosophy of language.

As has been discussed above, Voloshinov sought to dialectically overcome the dualistic opposition of objectivism and subjectivism as it had played itself out in linguistics. What is of note is that the innovative dimensions that are found Voloshinov's work surrounding the notion of language-as-relationality emerge when he further unpacks these two opposing linguistic tendencies as 'transcendental validity' and 'concrete actuality'. He does so more specifically with two key concepts: 'refraction' and 'inner speech'. With the aim of developing a comparison between Bloch and Voloshinov, it is to these two concepts that I now turn.

2   Refraction

Voloshinov's attempt to steer a course between objectivist and subjectivist trends in linguistics was in part tied to his reception of neo-Kantian sources. This can be gleaned by turning to an early plan of *Marxism and the Philosophy of Language*, where Voloshinov writes the following of Cassirer's work, and which again stresses the significance of borders and the state of being-between for Voloshinov's concept of language:

> ... 'the word' becomes a *partition* between transcendental validity and concrete actuality, a 'third realm', as it were, lying between the cognising psycho-physical subject and the empirical actuality surrounding him on the one hand, and the world of a priori, formal being on the other ... It is

---

48   Voloshinov 2004, p. 244.

precisely on the ground of the philosophy of language that the Marburg School's scientism and logicism and the Freiburg School's abstract ethicism are presently being overcome.[49]

Voloshinov will attempt to render this 'partition' in his own, Marxian direction as class-based and dialogic, one which maintains in its own unique way both the 'transcendental validity' and 'concrete actuality' of the utterance. Voloshinov will therefore speak of language as being '*a semi-transcendental form*':[50]

> *... what is important for the speaker about a linguistic form is not that it is a stable and always self-equivalent signal, but that it is an always changeable and adoptable sign.* That is the speaker's point of view. ... the understander, belonging to the same language community also is attuned to the linguistic form not as a fixed, self-identical signal, but as a changeable and adaptable sign. ... Thus the constituent factor for the linguistic form, as for the sign, is not at all its self-identity as signal but its specific variability; and the constituent factor for understanding the linguistic form is not recognition of 'the same thing', but understanding in the proper sense of the word, i.e., orientation in the particular, given context and in the particular, given situation – orientation in the dynamic process of becoming and not 'orientation' in some inert state.[51]

In the same plan for *Marxism and the Philosophy of Language* Voloshinov speaks of the 'refraction of being in the word'.[52] Refraction refers to the above reference whereby the sign is taken as being related, not as representation of, but as a creative force within, a given situation (the immediate vicinity of a dialogue), and a given context (the broader social totality). The word is always a refraction of the given socio-economic being in which it is spoken: 'Voloshinov

---

49 Voloshinov quoted in Brandist 2002, p. 75. 'It is precisely on the ground of the philosophy of language that at the present time the scientism and logicism of the Marburg School and the abstract ethicism of the Freiburg School are being overcome. By means of the *inner form of language* (*as a semi-transcendental form*) movement and historical becoming is being introduced into the petrified realm of transcendental-logical forms. It is also on this basis that an attempt to re-establish the idealist dialectic is being made'. (Voloshinov quoted in Brandist 2002, pp. 106–7). On Cassirer's influence on Bakhtin, see Brandist 2001.

50 Voloshinov quoted in Brandist 2002a, p. 106.

51 Voloshinov 1973, pp. 68–9.

52 Voloshinov 2004, p. 226.

holds fast to the notion that the sign "refracts" something that is given to consciousness rather than producing a totally detached world of culture'.[53] Language, then, is a *response* to socio-economic givenness, the latter of which stands in for that 'transcendental validity' which Voloshinov had appropriated from neo-Kantian sources. However, language is not merely a representational response to that givenness, simply reflecting what it 'sees'. Instead, the word is taken as 'that medium which is the most sensitive and at the same time the most complicated refraction of the socioeconomic governance'. Wherein does this sensitivity and complicatedness lay? As Voloshinov will write in *Marxism and the Philosophy of Language*:

> Signs ... are particular, material things ... A sign does not simply exist as a part of a reality – it reflects and refracts another reality. Therefore, it may distort that reality or be true to it, or may perceive it from a special point of view, and so forth. ... Every ideological sign is not only a reflection, a shadow, of reality, but is also itself a material segment of that very reality. Every phenomenon functioning as an ideological sign has some kind of material embodiment, whether in sound, physical mass, color, movements of the body, or the like.[54]

The key premise of refraction is therefore that language does not passively *reflect* the given social conditions of being which make language possible and to which language is a response. Language refracts that being, playing an active part, as a 'material segment of that reality', in the reproduction of social being. As Lecercle writes of this, language 'is *in* the world and *of* the world'.[55] Therefore language likewise possesses the scope to *contribute* towards transforming social life.[56] The word is a materially active part of the 'transcendental validity' within which and of which it finds itself – the given socio-economic governance. Does language help change social life on its own account? By no means. Importantly for the concept of refraction, the word's role in the reproduction of social being and in its possibility of change relates to class struggle as the axis of refraction:

> How is this refraction of existence in the ideological sign determined? By an intersecting of differently oriented social interests within one and

---

53   Brandist 2009, pp. 202–3.
54   Voloshinov 1973, pp. 10–11.
55   Lecercle 2006, p. 113.
56   See Voloshinov 2012, p. 142.

the same sign community, i.e. *by the class struggle.* ... This social *multiaccentuality* of the ideological sign is a very crucial aspect. By and large, it is thanks to this intersecting of accents that a sign maintains its vitality and dynamism and the capacity for further development. A sign that has been withdrawn from the pressures of the social struggle – which, so to speak, crosses beyond the pale of the class struggle – inevitably loses force, degenerating into allegory and becoming the object not of live social intelligibility but of philological comprehension.[57]

Language is '*a semi-transcendental form*'[58] since this 'transcendental validity' as the socio-economic conditions of being gives rise to the 'concrete actuality' of class struggle. The flow of this interactional generation of meaning is not conceived of in a Leibnizian continuity of movement in which the production of meaning makes no leaps: this would be far too akin to the rationalism of a Saussure. The creativity of new meaning is premised instead on the 'concrete actuality' of oppositional interaction, moments of fracture in which a word 'provokes its "counter" word'.[59]

As Lecercle notes, for Voloshinov the concept of sign calls-up an active process of productive interaction which contains within it social *agon*. Language is not cut off from the world, framing from afar the utterances to be found within it, but is instead an active, intervening, transformative materiality, but only insofar as the subject of this change is a class.[60] This dialectical relation of 'transcendental validity' and 'concrete actuality' affects how meaning is grasped by Voloshinov: 'there is no reason for saying that meaning belongs to a word as such. In essence, meaning belongs to a word in its position between two speakers'.[61] As the basic unit of language, the word (or sign) represents a fully-fledged relationality because meaning is relative to the agonistic struggle between class interests, with all the potential consequences Marx attributed to this epochal struggle. If it is the case that '[o]nly the current of verbal intercourse endows a word with the light of meaning',[62] then it follows, from Voloshinov's position, that this is a class current in which the speaker and listener occupy class positions in the process of their linguistic intercourse. In this light, it can be argued

---

57   Voloshinov 1973, p. 23.
58   Voloshinov quoted in Brandist 2002a, p. 106.
59   Morris 1994, p. 12.
60   Lecercle 2006, pp. 106–7 and 110–11.
61   Voloshinov 1973, p. 102.
62   Voloshinov 1973, p. 103.

that the 'meaning' of the anacoluthon resides in indicating that there is now taking place an 'in-between' of interlocutors, it is, to paraphrase Voloshinov, 'the effect of interaction between speaker and listener produced via the material of a particular sound-complex'.[63] The anacoluthon is a semi-transcendental form.

Given this outline of the refraction of the prevailing conditions of social existence in Voloshinov's philosophy of language, a potential critical assessment can be levelled against it from within Bloch's philosophical perspective. If in Voloshinov's 'dynamic and oppositional theory of language'[64] the structuralism of an already achieved Hegelian arrival of meaning (a stability achieved) is rejected in a manner akin to his rejection of outright structuralism, it can be argued that in place of this Voloshinov stands in favour of a (neo-)Kantian openness of history, spread across the incomplete arc of an 'unfinal-izability',[65] as fundamentally defining the givenness which the word refracts. This is because the movement of word and counter-word which is the interactional basis of meaning generation, indeed the very constitution of the word, is forever without end for Voloshinov. It is 'a continuous process' subject to 'constant variation', as Lecercle says,[66] with 'no beginning and no end'.[67] Here there is not so much the impossibility of a termination to givenness as such (that is very much possible for language), but the impossibility of a termination of constant becoming without arrival:

> The first and last words, the beginning and end points of real-life utterance – that is what already constitutes the problem of the whole. The process of speech, broadly understood as the process of inner and outer verbal life, goes on continuously. It knows neither beginning nor end. The outwardly actualized utterance is an island rising from the boundless sea of inner speech ...[68]

---

63   Voloshinov 1973, pp. 102–3, original emphasis removed.
64   Morris 1994, p. 14.
65   Morris 1994, p. 7, see also p. 13. As Peter Ives notes, the Bakhtin Circle derived a substantial philosophical influence from neo-Kantianism (Ives 2004, p. 59).
66   Lecercle 2006, p. 114.
67   Lecercle 2006, p. 116.
68   Voloshinov 1973, p. 96. See Morris 1994, p. 15. Cf. Côté's (2000, p. 32) sketch of Bakhtin's position: '"universal history", as the ultimate locus of the totalisation of meaning for the understanding of expression, remains "open" – or, rather, "infinite"; it always expresses for Bakhtin the situation of organization and experience of the space and time relations of human experience'.

Here one might recall Bloch's criticism of Kant's 'approximative infinity of reason' which 'makes of the world an ocean without a shore'.[69] One indeed might ponder why the metaphor of an island rising from and returning to the boundless potentiality of the sea is employed by Voloshinov – but the point is that the possibility of a shore in Bloch's sense of that word is missing here. The relation of possibility to real realisation is severed and lacking is the possibility of arrival. Brandist describes Bakhtin's dialogism in much the same terms, albeit, unlike Voloshinov, Bakhtin emphasises the personal responsibility of the utterer in the immediate moment of speech. Dialogism is 'the logic of relations between juridical persons in the never-ending task of the co-creation of the shared image of the world'.[70] As Voloshinov writes in the 1927/28 plan for the Marxism book:

> Any utterance, however significant and complete in itself, is only a moment of uninterrupted discursive intercourse (pertaining to life, literary, cognitive, political). But this uninterrupted discursive intercourse is itself in turn but a moment of the uninterrupted all-round becoming of a given social collective.[71]

In his study on Gramsci's work on language, Ives has indicated how this neo-Kantian understanding of meaning, extended to an infinite openness through the dialogic exchange, makes of this open dialogic an inherent and a-historical essence of language.[72] This essentialism of dialogic openness amplified to infinity paradoxically severs language, together with the social being from which it arises and refracts, from a *real openness*, that is, to the realness of being susceptible to possible fulfilment. As was outlined in Chapter 1 with regards to Bloch's Kant-Hegel reading, it is this possibility which determines the proper being of matter according to Bloch's materialism.[73] It is a possible realisation which appears obscurely in Marx's *Brumaire* passage of the necessity of moving into the new, as will be shown in Chapter 4, and it can be traced back to Marx's letter to Ruge.[74]

---

69   Bloch 2000a, p. 178.
70   Brandist 2001, p. 220.
71   Voloshinov 2004, p. 247.
72   See Ives 2004b, p. 76.
73   See Barron 2021.
74   While 'unification' does not equate to 'arrival' in Bloch's utopian sense of the term, the notion of consummation in language has political consequences of course. The issue turns on concepts of totality and unity: 'Bakhtin and Vološinov rejected unified national languages as necessarily "monologic" and as supressing heteroglossia'. (Ives 2004a, p. 54).

In this light, if one were to act in the spirit which Brandist has recently called for,[75] namely to more readily bring forth 'the incipient realism'[76] of Voloshinov's philosophy of language, then my claim here is that Bloch's work is one possible site to visit to engage with Voloshinov's ideas, opening up their 'unrealised potential'[77] via critical reassessments. This is because from its inception Bloch's philosophy was the combination of an epistemological realism and a utopian ontology.[78] Bloch's philosophy therefore grants one a space to constructively re-conceive Voloshinov's realist concept of the *refraction* of being. With Bloch, the refraction of giveness need not only concern socio-economic being, but also what is not-yet in the broader sweep of being: the very deeper sense of being that Bloch sought to open up Lukács's eyes to (see Chapter 4).

It can be argued that from a Blochian materialist perspective the problem with Voloshinov's philosophy of language resides, then, not in the manner in which it distinguishes between 'the event of communication' and its 'broader ... social connections',[79] that is, the distinction between the 'concrete actuality' of speech and its 'transcendental validity', but the manner in which this 'transcendental validity', the broader validity of speech, is narrowed to the socio-economic alone. It is this project of Bloch's which of course has a bearing on his assessment of fascism – Bloch's notion of a 'warm stream' within Marxism belongs here, then. As Voloshinov writes:

> ... every concrete utterance always reflects the *immediate* small social event – the event of communication, of exchange of words between persons – out of which it directly arose. .... what interests us here is not the immediate context of the utterance but the broader, more enduring and

---

Gramsci, on the other hand, drew out a more nuanced approach to unification. Opposed to the passive unification process of the Risorgimento (and indeed, despite Gramsci not stating as such, Stalinism – the latter being a greater concern for members of the Bakhtin Circle), Gramsci saw the emancipatory potential of processes of (linguistic) unification along the lines of a democratic centralism (see Ives 2004a, p. 57). A progressive, in contradistinction to a regressive, process of unification is thus possible in the context of language (see Ives 2004, pp. 58–9 and 82–3). While the Bakhtin Circle were determined to theoretically counter 'Stalin's centralization of everything involving culture and language', Gramsci was engaged with re-constructing a fractured working-class movement that had been devastatingly defeated by fascism (Ives 2004, pp. 72–3; cf. Brandist 2002a, p. 2).

75   See Brandist 2002a, p. 5. Cf. p. 26.
76   Brandist 2002a, p. 87.
77   Brandist 2002a, p. 177.
78   Pelletier 2018, p. 29.
79   Voloshinov 2012, p. 139.

steadfast social connections out of whose dynamics are generated all elements of the form and content of our inner and outer speech, the whole repertoire of value judgements, points of view, approaches, and so on with the help of which we illuminate for ourselves and for others our actions, desires, feelings, and sensations.[80]

The 'whole repertoire' of these 'value judgements, points of view, approaches and so on' never, however, are conceived of by Voloshinov as being pervaded by any possibility of fulfilment, and how such a possibility and desire for fulfilment interpolates speech acts as a moment of their broader condition of being. A reconstructed Blochian critique of Voloshinov here is therefore located in the narrow conception of totality – as we will see is the case with Lukács – with which Voloshinov works. However, the 'whole repertoire of value judgements, points of view, approaches and so on' which allow us to 'illuminate for ourselves and for others our actions, desires, feelings, and sensations' work within an expanded notion of totality in Bloch's utopian materialism, within a new depth relation to being.

The claim that Voloshinov restricted the givenness which language refracts to a Kantian infinity can be buttressed by briefly considering the manner in which his collaborator, Mikhail Bakhtin, a thinker also steeped in the neo-Kantian tradition, particularly the work of Hermann Cohen, approached the question of consummation. This small digression is all the more significant to make because in rejecting Cohen's idealism of an all-encompassing oneness, *Allheit*,[81] the question of completeness for Bakhtin – which is by him, however, always treated in an aesthetic sense – bears close parallels with Bloch's category of the darkness of the just lived moment. This is because the question of consummation for Bakhtin orbits his notion of perception, his focus on perception being allied to his quest to reach the immediacy of the material world.[82]

Regarding the question of consummation in Bakhtin, then, he will speak of an 'excess of vision'. This excess of perception constitutes an individual and names the incompleteness of that individual's vision of the world: 'whatever is perceived can be perceived only from a uniquely situated place in the overall structure of possible points of view'.[83] As Holquist notes of this key idea in Bakhtin:

---

80   Voloshinov 2012, pp. 139–40.

81   See Holquist 1990, pp. xii–xvi, xxviii, xxxiii and xxxv.

82   See Holquist 1990, p. xxii.

83   Holquist 1990, p. xxiv.

The a priori from which the rest of Bakhtin's thought flows is the assumption that each of us occupies a situation in existence that, for the time we occupy such space, is ours and ours alone: what I see is not the same as what anyone else sees. Perception, how I 'see' the world, is always refracted, as it were, through the optic of my uniqueness. Bakhtin calls this uniqueness of vision my 'excess of seeing' insofar as it is defined by the ability I have to see things others do not.[84]

It is already noteworthy that Bloch renders this 'excess of seeing' a mode of being insofar as the present relates to the future as a surplus of itself, whereas Bakhtin, focused on the immediacy of situatedness in the material world and on a juridically understood individual (a Robinson Crusoe), foregoes 'any presupposition of an underlying stratum of Being'.[85] As Bakhtin writes:

> When I contemplate a whole human being who is situated outside and over against me, our concrete, actually experienced horizons do not coincide. For at each given moment, regardless of the position and the proximity to me of this other human being whom I am contemplating, I shall always see and know something that he, from his place outside and over against me, cannot see himself: parts of his body that are inaccessible to his own gaze (his head, his face and its expression), the world behind his back, and a whole series of objects and relations, which in any of our mutual relations are accessible to me but not to him. As we gaze at each other, two different worlds are reflected in the pupils of our eyes. It is possible, upon assuming an appropriate position, to reduce this difference of horizons to a minimum, but in order to annihilate this difference completely, it would be necessary to merge into one, to become one and the same person. This ever-present *excess* of my seeing, knowing, and possessing in relation to any other human being is founded in the uniqueness and irreplaceability of my place in the world.[86]

The 'aesthetics of verbal creation'[87] – Bakhtin's main concern in his earlier texts – is only possible because 'two noncoinciding consciousnesses' relate to one another.[88] Verbal creation exists because 'my own exterior is not part of

---

84   Holquist 1990, p. xxv.
85   Holquist 1990, p. xxxviii.
86   Bakhtin 1990, pp. 22–3.
87   Bakhtin 1990, p. 11.
88   Bakhtin 1990, p. 22.

the concrete, actual horizon of my seeing'[89] and because, like the other human being that stands against me, I 'do not encounter my own outward expressedness in being as an outwardly unitary object among other objects'.[90] While drawing close to Bloch's notion of the darkness of the just lived moment, it can be said that for Bloch each definite *historical moment* – and not just each historical individual abstracted from a broader historical era – is refracted by its own excess of seeing (another translation of the Russian Bakhtin employs, *izbytok*, would be indeed 'surplus'). But while having bounded this excess of seeing to the level of an individual so as to bolster the irreplaceability of what is unique, Bakhtin's merit lays in relating this excess of seeing to novelty: 'The excess of my seeing is the bud in which slumbers form, and whence form unfolds like a blossom'.[91] In placing this 'surplus' of seeing into being itself, into the wider conditions of being that language refracts, Bloch will name this 'excess of seeing' the utopian call, the utopian demand within being and so then within verbal creation, even if this verbal creation also tends towards or is framed in his work in an aesthetic direction.

Finally, on the score of this lack within one's vision Bloch shares with Bakhtin the idea that it is only through a 'We' that this lack becomes evident. Marx's reference to the presence of community in the scientist's work touches on the same idea. My excess always relates to another's deficiency of seeing, for Bakhtin.[92] But like Kant, the question of consummation is posed but then denied as a possibility: 'we are fated ... fated to need the other if we are to consummate our selves'.[93] Like Voloshinov, Bakhtin detains this possibility of consummation to a Kantian regulativeness. Since perception in Bakhtin is radically rooted in its situatedness, no matter how far the 'We' extends in its scope, all claims to oneness must be discarded; one person's situated perception is both the excess of another's perception and therefore the condition for that other's lack, and vice versa.[94] No finalisation or consummation is possible and thus the disavowal of this possibility is made into an a priori by Bakhtin – an '*Urdifferenz*' structures the components of what could be the basis for consummation, an original difference between individuals' perceptions, which can never be 'connatural',[95] and which renders consummation a task without end.[96]

---

89   Bakhtin 1990, p. 27.
90   Bakhtin 1990, p. 28.
91   Bakhtin 1990, p. 24.
92   See Holquist 1990, pp. xli and xliv.
93   Holquist 1990, p. xxv.
94   See Holquist 1990, p. xxvi.
95   Bakhtin 1990, p. 28.
96   Holquist 1990, p. xxviii.

In sum, then, while Bakhtin gives an advance on Voloshinov's apparent disregard for this question of completeness by at least further broaching the importance of consummation as a question, locating this tendency to consummate in perception, since 'least of all are we ourselves able or competent to perceive in ourselves the given whole of our own personality',[97] he nevertheless, like Voloshinov, restricts this tendency of consummation to a postulate in the Kantian sense of it being a regulative as opposed to a constitutive possibility.[98] Bakhtin will speak of value of the human being (*werthaft*) as being 'axiologically yet-to-be'[99] (*predstojashchij*, German *bevorstehen*). But he will curtail this 'yet-to-be' to a permanent non-coincidence with ourselves, an always 'yet-to-be'.[100] Thus it would be better to speak of this 'surplus' – as indeed Bakhtin himself does – as an '*empty* seeing', an ultimately empty verbal creativity.[101]

3   Neo-Kantianism

Voloshinov's 'realist predilections',[102] which translate into his concept of language as refraction of being, partly lie in his creative inheritance of neo-Kantian sources. This sounds counter-intuitive given neo-Kantianism's trenchant idealism. Spending a little time on this point though will add substance to the Blochian inflection of this notion of 'refraction' that I have argued for above. Firstly, this is because an exploration of the philosophical sources of Voloshinov's philosophy of language helps to provide greater insight into the stakes of Voloshinov's overall theoretical standpoint, including what critical reassessments are required to prolong this programme into new, unchartered territory.[103] Secondly, because Bloch's own take-up of neo-Kantian categories, placed in comparison with Voloshinov's, can shed further light on Bloch's difference with Voloshinov on the score of 'refraction'. And finally, because rich work has been conducted in a similar vein. Konstantinos Kavoulakos, for instance, has sought to explore the neo-Kantian predisposition of Lukács's early Marxism, particularly on how neo-Kantian ideas are 'reflected in the central position which the problem of otherness occupies in his' – Lukács's – 'thought'.[104] Galin

---

97   Bakhtin 1990, p. 5.
98   See Holquist 1990, p. xxxi.
99   Bakhtin 1990, p. 13.
100   See Bakhtin 1990, p. 16.
101   Bakhtin 1990, p. 31.
102   Brandist 2002b, p. 537.
103   Brandist 2002a, p. 15.
104   See Kavoulakos 2018.

Tihanov has also realised a similar intention in comparing the neo-Kantian and *Lebensphilosophische* inheritances at work in Mikhail Bakhtin and Lukács's respective outputs.[105] And one should note in passing that Gillian Rose has also spoken of the neo-Kantian provenance of Lukács's and Adorno's respective Hegel and Marx receptions,[106] not to mention Cat Moir's recent research into the Nietzschean and Expressionist provenance of Bloch's philosophy of language, touched on in the Introduction, which also draws passing attention to the importance of neo-Kantian philosophy of culture (such as with the work of Heinrich Rickert and Georg Simmel) as a central intellectual context in which Bloch forges his implicit, largely unstated approach to the language question.[107] The neo-Kantian inheritance is, then, a real thread which Bloch and Voloshinov both share. It serves as a valid reason for their comparison.

The first point to note is that neither Bloch nor Voloshinov reduced their receptions of Kantianism to 'mere "Kant-philology"', what Ernst Cassirer, an important figure for Voloshinov,[108] opposed to Hermann Cohen's engagement with Kant.[109] 'None of the neo-Kantians takes Kant dogmatically; they are all interested in seeking the correct path for philosophical problems'.[110] The common ground concerning neo-Kantianism more or less ends there for Bloch and Voloshinov, since both read similar sources but in distinct ways. I have already covered how Bloch enacted this with his assertion that Kant ought to 'burn' through Hegel. The assertion signalled an intent on Bloch's part to re-think the two classical German philosophers in a utopian direction. For the time being I will therefore focus on Voloshinov's inheritance.

Besides the much noted Marxian import of Voloshinov's work (primarily via Bukharin and Marr), commentators have located and tend to invest importance in the philosophical influences on the Bakhtin Circle during the period 1927–29. Commentators speak of the philosophy of language developed by the Circle as a product of original combinations of the neo-Kantianism of the Marburg School, the *Lebensphilosophie* of Georg Simmel, and the phenomenological works of Edmund Husserl and Max Scheler, all significant figures in

---

105   See Tihanov 2000. Cf. Löwy 1979, pp. 86, 96–8, 125, 130–2, 141–2, Kavoulakos 2018, pp. 13–
        34. The neo-Kantian inheritances of critical theorists seems to be an under-studied area.
        Gillian Rose (2017, p. 177), for instance, has noted the lack of study into Walter Benjamin's
        relation to neo-Kantianism. Cf. Rose 2009, p. 24.
106   See Rose 2009, pp. 26–39. Bloch too is spoken of as a dissatisfied graduate of 'the schools
        of neo-Kantianism' (Rose 2009, p. 31).
107   See Moir 2019b, p. 314.
108   See Brandist 2002a, p. 14.
109   Cassirer 2015, p. 221.
110   Kagan 2004, p. 197. M.I. Kagan was a pupil of Cohen's and member of the Bakhtin Circle.

Bloch's own philosophical development.[111] Brandist also asserts the influence of Lukács's writings on Voloshinov's philosophy; crucially, he does not fully specify in what way this influence is characterised.[112]

What is essential for my argument is that, somewhat counter-intuitively, Voloshinov's neo-Kantian roots are of a more realist than idealist derivation. While Marburg School neo-Kantianism represents an extreme idealism in its attempts to accomplish an entire elimination of the Kantian thing-in-itself, Voloshinov sought to take advantage of different neo-Kantian resources available to him to theorise language as a realist refraction of social being.[113] In mining Voloshinov's intellectual sources Brandist has shown that neo-Kantianism's emphasis on non-realist categories of thought does not influence Voloshinov as much as has often been stated. Brandist points to the largely overlooked moorings of Voloshinov's philosophy of language which rest in Anton Marty and other philosophers of language of a Brentanian outlook, including Cassirer's philosophy of symbolic forms.[114] It is this realist trajectory of Voloshinov's philosophy of language which ties into Bloch's realest refunctions of similar intellectual sources developed in an environment in which neo-Kantianism was a key port of call for German philosophy.

In this regard Brandist identifies Karl Bühler's theory of language use as significant for Voloshinov.[115] Voloshinov would go on to translate into Russian the now lost 1922 work of Bühler's 1922 on syntax, 'Vom Wesen der Syntax'.[116] Being

---

111   See Pelletier 2018 on Bloch's neo-Kantian inheritance. See Brandist 2002a, pp. 12–14 and
        Tihanov 2000, pp. 83–4 on Voloshinov's writings in the late 1920s, which, as Brand-
        ist writes, 'reflect an attempt to integrate Marxism into a perspective framed by neo-
        Kantianism, life-philosophy, and phenomenology'. (Brandist 2002a, p. 25). Voloshinov's
        Marxism and the Philosophy of Language is said to contain 'fascinating palimpsests of
        Lebensphilosophie and neo-Kantianism' (Tihanov 1998, p. 600). The neo-Kantian or philo-
        sophy-of-life thinkers which Tihanov mentions are Hermann Cohen, Georg Simmel and
        Ernst Cassirer (cf. pp. 604 and 607–9 for a discussion on Voloshinov and Simmel). We
        hear of the 'neo-Kantian ground of ... Vološinov's philosophizing' (Tihanov 1998, p. 616),
        of Voloshinov's attempt to 'unify Marxist sociology with neo-Kantianism' (Brandist 2002a,
        p. 62, cf. p. 75), and of the 'triple clef of Marxism, *Lebensphilosophie*, and neo-Kantianism'
        at work in Voloshinov's philosophy of language (Tihanov 2000, p. 84).
112   See Brandist 2009, p. 193.
113   Hermann Cohen headed the Marburg School and emphasised the regulative (read: limit-
        ing), not constitutive nature of this concept. The 'thing-in-itself' is said to be the produc-
        tion of the transcendental subject alone (see Beiser 2014, p. 490).
114   See Brandist 2002a, pp. 14 and 55.
115   See Brandist 2002a, pp. 63 and 76. Brandist speaks of Voloshinov's serious engagement
        with Bühler's ideas as demonstrated by the fact that Voloshinov translated into Russian
        Bühler's essay on syntax (see Brandist 2009, p. 194).
116   See Brandist 2004, p. 102.

situated within the Brentano tradition, Bühler would adopt 'an Aristotelian and anti-Kantian epistemology in which the mind "feeds" on objects that it encounters and derives formal categories from this encounter rather than imposing those categories a priori'.[117] Bühler himself stood in Marty's line of influence[118] and it is to this more realist push-back within the context of neo-Kantianism that I wish to briefly consider.

Brandist's claim is that Voloshinov's refunctioning of Bühler's work on the utterance provided the scope for Voloshinov to materialise Bakhtin's original, abstract claim that the utterance names 'the co-participation of the I and the other in the "event of being"'.[119] There also exists a suspicion that Bühler's critical reception of Freud in his work titled *The Crisis of Psychology* (1927) was influential for Voloshinov's own sharp confrontation with Freudianism, which is to be touched on below. Voloshinov's materialisation of this Bakhtinian event of being will transliterate into the utterance's 'extraverbal context', namely, its socio-economic conditions of being,[120] what Marx had called the 'actual life-process',[121] the non-verbal-situatedness of the utterance in dialogue.

The reason for why Voloshinov's inheritance of Bühler is important to look at when differentiating Voloshinov's philosophy of language from Bloch's nascent philosophy of the same, is because Bühler's model of the utterance (*Sprechakt*) foregrounds the significance of *anticipation* in the production of utterances. Brandist shows how Bühler's model is developed by Voloshinov for his own Marxist concerns in this respect. The anticipation of the utterance was in part encapsulated for Bühler by an anticipation of the response of one's interlocutor in dialogue, that 'counter-word' which Voloshinov took to be the proper existence of the sign's multiaccentuality. As Brandist writes, Bühler's

> ... model of the utterance as a goal-oriented structure (*Zweckgebilde*) requires three corresponding 'relational foundations': a sender (whose inner states are intimated); a receiver (whose reaction is triggered); and the things or state of affairs represented. ... As well as binding the three

---

117   Brandist 2009, p. 194.

118   See Dewalque et al. 2021, pp. 2–3.

119   Brandist 2002a, p. 65. Walter Benjamin (2002) discusses Bühler's theory in his essay 'Problems in the Sociology of Language: An Overview', published in 1934 in the *Zeitschrift für Socialforschung* (see Beasley-Murray 2007, pp. 97–8). It is not clear if Bloch ever read this overview or if Bloch ever benefited from Benjamin's closer, though still cursory, association with Russian culture, not to mention Benjamin's unlikely encounter of the Bakhtin Circle (see Beasley-Murray 2007, p. 5).

120   Brandist 2002a, p. 65.

121   Marx and Engels 1976a, p. 36.

moments of communication into a relation of 'three-way multilateral dependence', Bühler amended Marty's account of 'triggering' to argue that what was anticipated were not always certain mental processes in the receiver, but often the actions he or she may perform. ... In 1927 Bühler characterises language as, above all, a form oriented towards 'communicating some existentially significant surplus of perception that one member of the group might be in possession of in the context of shared actions embedded in shared times and spaces'.[122]

Not only then does Bühler suggest anticipation is inherent in language insofar as an utterance anticipates the minds and actions of others, but – and here one cannot deny the utopian ring of this – language is also anticipatory because it contains within itself a surplus of perception. This intimation (*Kundgabe*, later reformulated as *Ausdruck*, expression), triggering (*Auslösung*, later termed *Appell*, or appeal), and representation (*Darstellung*) form a unity (*Gestalt*), which together form the *Sprechakt*.[123] The important broader notions of the symbol-field (*Symbolfeld*) and the deictic-field (*Zeigfeld*) also belong to the speech act. While the former refers to the 'verbal context of the utterance', that is, to the word, the phoneme, the sentence and the paragraph, the latter – the *Zeigfeld* – refers to 'the spatial-temporal situation' in which language-users and their utterances are to be found, that is, the non-verbal situatedness of language.[124] As Brandist notes of this inheritance, Voloshinov 'recasts the familiar dichotomy between art and life in terms of Bühler's "two-field" theory: meaning in life is more heavily dependent on the deictic field',[125] that is, on the spatial-temporal situatedness of utterances (an accentuation which relates to Voloshinov's ultimate rejection of Russian Formalism).

As I have asserted earlier on in this chapter, the 'deictic-field', which takes on great prominence in Voloshinov's philosophy of language, is a 'non-verbal situatedness' that is largely restricted by socio-economic coordinates of being, but drawn-out across an unfinalizability. The 'existentially significant surplus of perception' that Brandist refers to above as key to Bühler's model of the utterance – or model of the 'speech event (*Sprechereignis*)'[126] – is a much more expansive surplus for Bloch than for Voloshinov since it is one containing the possibility of arrival. This claim can be fleshed out by once more briefly con-

---

122   Brandist 2004, pp. 104–6.
123   See Brandist 2004, p. 104.
124   See Brandist 2002a, pp. 63–4.
125   Brandist 2002a, p. 64.
126   Brandist 2009, p. 200.

sidering one feature of Bloch's own inheritance of neo-Kantianism, despite Habermas's assertion that Bloch simply 'skipped Kant ... with a pre-critical approach'.[127] Bloch's thought was imbued with a clear encounter with neo-Kantian philosophers. Like Voloshinov, Bloch's thought contains a 'profound legacy of Kant and neo-Kantianism'.[128] Not only did neo-Kantianism influence Bloch's work,[129] it played a pivotal role in Bloch developing his utopian conception of ontology.[130] This neo-Kantian strain within Bloch's philosophy could be located in the (anti-capitalist) sociologist of culture Georg Simmel, Bloch's and Lukács's teacher in Berlin,[131] who 'metaphysicalised' in a tragic vein Marx's critique of commodity fetishism and alienation, applying that critique more broadly to culture as such – along the lines of the Heidelberg School's neo-Kantianism, e.g. Rickert and Lask.[132]

In his *Philosophy of Money* (1900) Simmel states the book's intention as one of constructing 'a new storey beneath historical materialism' in which 'economic forms themselves are recognized as the result of more profound valuations and currents of psychological or even metaphysical pre-conditions'.[133] While Bloch was certainly not Simmelian to the ground, Simmel's formulation here at least has the benefit of allowing the difference between Voloshinov and Bloch to be pinpointed further. Bloch certainly will want to conceive of totality and its access via the 'now' as consisting of depths that go beyond economic life alone, as his dispute with Lukács demonstrated, but any 'takeover' of this Simmelian project on Bloch's part[134] had far less a tragic character than its original stamp in Simmel's philosophy of culture. This is because it is the 'warm stream' of hope, rather than a Weberian-style despair, that Bloch sought to disclose to Marxism as its own proper heritage. In *The Spirit of Utopia* Bloch will speak of 'the necessity of a fundamental metaphysical rethinking neglected by

---

127   Habermas 1970, p. 325.
128   Moir 2019, p. 80. In 1909 Bloch (see 1978) wrote his doctoral dissertation on the leading figure of the Baden Southwestern School of neo-Kantianism, Heinrich Rickert (see Rickert 2015), which he dedicated to Hermann Cohen, leader of the Marburgian neo-Kantian school (see Mendes-Flohr 1983, pp. 637–8).
129   See Gadamer 1976 p. 75 and Lambrianou 2005, p. 86.
130   See Moir 2019a, pp. 10, 13, 19, 79, 89–96. Bloch's refunction of neo-Kantianism was 'very complex and differentiated' to be sure (see Boldyrev 2014, p. 4). This is especially so if one takes into account that Bloch held a large portion of responsibility for drawing Lukács away from neo-Kantianism, towards Hegelianism (see Boldyrev 2012, p. 39).
131   See Löwy 1979, p. 43 and Karádi 2010, p. 500.
132   See Löwy 1979, pp. 44 and 66.
133   Simmel 2011, p. 56. See Löwy 1979, pp. 45–6 for a note Simmel's correspondence with Engels. Cf. Rose 2009, p. 29. For Simmel's influence on Bakhtin, see Brandist 2001.
134   See Karádi 2010, p. 501.

Marx', and this on the score of 'the relationship between "subjective" Will and "objective" Idea'[135] – that is, as we saw in an earlier chapter, between that utopian space staked out between Kant and Hegel, and, as we saw via Voloshinov himself, between transcendental validity and concrete actuality. For Bloch, this 'objective Idea' was nothing other than 'the What for' of society, which, to disclose it, required 'placing Marx into the higher space', 'of bringing the usually all too truncated construal of society back into Weitling's, Baader's, Tolstoy's utopianly superior world of love'.[136]

A similar logic is at play in Bloch's appropriation of neo-Kantian sources in an earlier account he produced of this intentionality behind the depth that remains a 'storey beneath' – or a social life beyond current – economic life. Writing his dissertation on Rickert, Bloch had sought to criticise the latter's ideographic approach to historiography, which, akin to Bakhtin's focus on the non-repeatable individuality of the utterance, neglected the broader being of which an historical event takes place. Bloch thought that the ideographic treatment of isolated historical events, while positive insofar as it avoided a mechanical application of abstract law, led nevertheless to relativism, unless, that is, it were supplemented with a notion of utopian transcendence.[137] The ideographic approach to history chimes with individualistic subjectivism, as outlined by Voloshinov himself, in the sense that the individual utterance is treated solely in its creative unrepeatability with no idea of its relation to a whole. In this vein Bloch speaks of 'the happy-difference [*die Glücksdifferenz*]' that accompanies each and every historical present (each and every historical utterance) which is unable to make peace with the current conditions of its being: there is the 'the uneasy certainty [*die unglückliche Gewißheit*]' that results from this discontent with the contemporary shape of things, a discontent the content of which Bloch does not simply reduce to the coordinates of the contemporary shape of things.[138] For Bloch, this almost inherent discontent with the present state of things would lapse into the relativism of historicism were it not for the (ontological) upholding of 'a pervasive utopian call [*eine beherrschende utopische Foderung*]' which relates the discontented present to a positive notion of itself, however incomplete that notion itself remains:[139]

135 Bloch 2000a, p. 242.
136 Bloch 2000, p. 245.
137 See Mendes-Flohr 1983, pp. 637–8.
138 Bloch 1978, p. 74.
139 Ibid.

> The entirety of historical this-sidedness [*Das ganze historische Diesseits*] is still so insufficiently illuminated that the idea of the brighter and value-accented [*wertbetonten*] future can scarcely fade away. Since the path [*Weg*] over history certainly can never be bypassed [*umgehen*] so then will the worth [*die Geltung*] of historical conditions not be decided [*entscheiden sein*] again merely from an historically conditioned perch. Hence it is absolutely inadmissible to conceptually break off the relations [*die Beziehungen*] between the historical and utopian materials [*Gegenstände*].[140]

While Voloshinov's appropriation of Bühler's 'surplus of perception' – of language being outside itself – is tied to a line of thought which leads to a neo-Kantian infinity of regulation (an infinity of surplus), Bloch's appropriation of a similar idea, albeit via a different route, will lead to an intentionality that is open to the possibility of its full realisation. We could therefore say that, for Bloch, there is a dialogue between historical this-sidedness and its purpose, the material of hope in this-sidedness, which, here, read through but also against Voloshinov, can be said to articulate itself through language and its utterances. In sum, this dialogue between the present and its purpose is not defined by a Kantian transcendental restrictedness on the possibility of an arrival at purpose. It is therefore a process of '*transcending in this-sidedness* [*Transzendierens ins Diesseits*]'.[141]

Within Voloshinov's philosophical influences one does witness a linguistic relationality to something anticipated, then, as well as to a goal-orientation of sense (*Sinn*).[142] For Voloshinov, Bühler's notion of 'triggering' (*Auslösung*), later termed 'release', is an anticipatory triggering related to one's interlocutors, but it is, however, solely garbed by the spatial-temporal situatedness of the contemporary 'now' and its pervading socio-economic present. For Bloch, arguably this anticipatory triggering expands to the whole situatedness of contemporary utterances as such, including their hopes, which he terms a 'new depth relation to being' and which, as not-yet being, could constitute a new realist pull within the utterance.[143] This could act as a potential answer to Brandist's

---

140   Ibid.
141   Bloch quoted in Haug 2012, p. 251.
142   See Brandist 2004, p. 107.
143   Bühler's (2011, p. 149) notion of 'imagination-oriented deixis' (*Deixis am Phantasma*) deals with a temporal as opposed to a spatial pointing, with echoes in Bloch's category of the not-yet conscious. Bühler's notion of 'imagination-oriented deixis' has the benefit of being focused not on night-dream states but on daydreams.

call[144] for a more realist phenomenological underpinning to the otherwise 'ambivalent realism'[145] of the Voloshinov-project. If 'refraction' asserts, then, that something not only is given to language but also that the utterance is a part of and a response to that givenness, an internal relation to it, then Bloch's materialist categories allow us to view that givenness more broadly than Voloshinov permits.

Indeed, in *The Spirit of Utopia* Bloch will refer to 'the simple fact *of the commonality of willing*'.[146] As Bloch writes: 'no social order, however successful, can do without this final link in the correlative series between the We and the final problem of the What For'.[147] One could therefore speak of Voloshinov's relationality as a 'closed-openness' (the infinity of the utterance's counter-word) and Bloch's as a 'real-openness' (an acknowledgement of the Kantian gap intersected with an Hegelian possibility of arrival). This relationality *of* the We-problem concerned Bloch deeply of course, but by all intents and purposes it did not seem to explicitly concern Voloshinov. The 'We-apprehension [*Wirer-fassung*]'[148] is not, for Bloch, solely ascertained by the co-ordinates of present socio-economic being, nor simply by 'what can appear in respectively determined historical-materialist conditions', to recall one side of his definition of matter as possibility.[149] It is rather ultimately related to the question of 'the correlate of objective-real-possibility, or pure beingness',[150] namely, the interwoven possibility of arrival, '*the founded expectation of attainability itself*'.[151] Voloshinov only knows this – to paraphrase Bloch here – as 'unrelatedness [*Beziehungslosigkeit*]'.[152] While, then Voloshinov never succumbs to the positivistic attachment to present meaning, for to do so would be to forgo the multiaccentuality of the sign, he nevertheless subscribes to the positivistic rejection of utopian surplus, that is, of the 'real undisclosed We-mystery [*real unenthüllten Wirgeheimnis*]' which Bloch associates with the utopian within present actuality.[153] As Cat Moir very insightfully writes of this in the context of Bloch's review of Lukács's *History and Class Consciousness*, 'this within was also a without for

---

144   See Brandist 2004, pp. 123–4. See Brandist 2001, pp. 220–5 for a similar call with regards to Bakhtin's work.
145   Brandist 2002a, p. 76.
146   Bloch 2000a, p. 241.
147   Bloch 2000a, p. 246.
148   Bloch 1969, p. 614.
149   Bloch 1970a, p. 233.
150   Ibid.
151   Bloch 1986, p. 207.
152   Bloch 1969, p. 615.
153   Bloch 1969, p. 621.

Bloch to the extent that he understood the darkness of the lived moment – the "now" – as the interface that connects consciousness to the in-itself'.[154] A Blochian philosophy of language would contain the same. If, for Voloshinov, the orientation of a speaker is one in which language is not 'a system of invariant rules with which he must comply but ... a field of possibilities which he is to utilize in concrete utterances in particular social contexts',[155] then the field of possibilities referred to here is confined to a strange mix of infinite excessiveness and restricted contemporaneousness. If the work done in Chapter 1 is recalled: for Bloch this field of possibilities always includes the possibility of full realisation.

Bloch and Voloshinov, then, have this much in common: both object to the closed totality with which Lukács and Saussure work within.[156] The meaning of any given word is not merely constituted by its difference to other words within a system of language, but through anticipated responses with other interlocutors, which means: other interlocutors situated within the possibilities which the current normative system of language affords, possibilities arising from the being which conditions those consciousnesses. As Bakhtin wrote of Dostoevsky's poetics: 'In every voice he could hear two contending voices, in every expression a crack'.[157] Historically emerging social conditions which continue to be subject to historical becoming afford the language-user 'material' for their utterance and these conditions set 'constraints on the utterance's possibilities'.[158] Voloshinov has therefore restricted the utterance's possibilities to 'what is in accordance with given material conditions' (see Chapter 1). If Voloshinov's critique of Saussure moves his philosophy of language away from a closed totality within language, opening language up to its social referent, the manner in which this social referent is conceived is one of another type of closure, narrow in its unrestricted openness: *the Kantian infinity of (a) never arriving (referent)*. The 'polysemanticity of the word',[159] that is, the word's constitutive susceptibility to a multiplicity of contextual determinations, correctly embedded in the class struggle, is however framed within such a negative self-relation of the *totality with itself*, such that, while it is born from a retrieval of the social referential life *of* language – language's social relationality – this recuperation of

---

154   Moir 2020, p. 8. Cf. Boldyrev 2014, p. 126.
155   Bennett 2003, p. 61.
156   Ibid.
157   Bakhtin 1994, pp. 91–2. For Bakhtin this is why, in comparison to Tolstoy, Dostoevsky depicts his characters' lives 'on the threshold', not as finalised consciousnesses, but their 'crises and turning points' (Bakhtin 1994, p. 96).
158   Voloshinov 2012, p. 127.
159   Bennett 2003, p. 65.

the social life of language, the social being of the utterance, is circumscribed and prejudged within a certain vision of what, for that life, is and is not possible.

4   Freudianism

The question of relationality in Voloshinov and in Bloch should not, and cannot, be divorced from exotopy, that is, put briefly, from a state of being outside oneself. Language itself can be seen as exotopic insofar as it is refractive. That is, it constitutes a human mode of response to that which the human both is and is outside of: the given conditions of its being. Voloshinov explored this idea further via a critical engagement with Freud's theory of the unconscious. Bloch critically encountered Freudian psychoanalysis, too, in his own manner. Both sought to assess Freudianism's 'discovery of a whole new world', one 'extraordinarily close to us' and yet 'ready at any moment to erupt through the crust of our consciousness and find reflection in our utterances'.[160] While their reasons for initiating a critique of Freud are akin, and while the content of their respective critiques bear some close correspondence, Bloch and Voloshinov's respective critiques of Freud nevertheless move in distinct directions, which, as was the case with their own concepts of 'totality', do not strictly coincide. Freudianism therefore serves as another site for a productive engagement between Bloch and Voloshinov.

Indeed, Voloshinov's Freudianism: A Marxist Critique was published before his Marxism and language book, but the work contains a discernible line of continuity with that book since Voloshinov's critique of Freudianism anticipates later conceptual developments in his philosophy of language.[161] Bloch's critique of Freud, on the other hand, is primarily located in an early section of The Principle of Hope, and it is not explicitly tied to a discussion of language. However, it does concern itself directly with a construction of a utopian conception of consciousness ('Not-Yet-Conscious'), prefigured, for Bloch, in the daydream. The question of consciousness was key for Voloshinov in grasping the core essence of language, as will be outlined below, and so Bloch's discussion of a new theory of consciousness is arguably apt for a linguistic appraisal. It facilitates the development of an identifiable philosophy language in his work.

---

160   Voloshinov 2012, p. 40.
161   See Lecercle 2006, p. 116.

As I will argue, while Voloshinov knows 'tendency' in consciousness, namely, the historical becoming of the drivers of social existence (class forces), he misses 'latency': the 'what for?' of these drives, or at least he does so in Bloch's sense of that term. This was the case with Voloshinov's working notion of 'total-ity'. The same point applies to consciousness. Bloch sees things differently: 'real realism ... is fully attuned to the tendency of what is actually real, to the object-ively real possibility to which this tendency is assigned, and consequently to the properties of reality which are themselves utopian, i.e. contain future'.[162] For Bloch, consciousness is also in tune with the future, with a sense of what is coming up, of what is around the corner, as it were, in Bloch's sense of the 'music of reason'. As I try to show below, despite building a Marxist account of the Freu-dian unconscious as really constituted by an 'unofficial conscious', Voloshinov is unable to root this 'unofficial conscious' in the real, material possibility of future fulfilment. Bloch's category of 'Not-Yet-Conscious' accomplishes this needed extension of Freudianism, and acts to supplement Voloshinov's pro-ject.

Like Marx, Voloshinov considers the very existence of a word to imply a social relation. Voloshinov's notion of the 'utterance' captures this social con-dition of possibility for the emergence and existence of language. Just as Marx the scientist works alone but draws on and implies the whole fruit of social production and intercourse, so then does the single utterance, for Voloshinov, imply and rely on the whole social connections of speech acts from which it emerges and to which it is a response. But Voloshinov goes further to dispel any residue of psychologism. The relationality of language is not merely con-fined to one between classed social beings, nor between an individual and the 'nonverbal situatedness' of their utterances. The relationality of language also concerns the inside and outside of an individual. Here, the old question of the possibility of a private language emerges. Indeed, what of monologues, which surely are linguistic phenomena – the monologue being that proper speech-form of the psychoanalytic therapy session, after all? Are they not a-social types of utterances which disrupt Voloshinov's model of a radically socially determ-ined concept of language? But for Voloshinov, as Bruss notes, even 'autistic uses of language' are said to be 'variations' on the utterance's 'essentially social nature'.[163] Seemingly autistic uses of language are merely processes in which 'the idea of an audience is abstracted out of situations in which actual audi-ences are present and retained for those in which audiences are not'.[164] To

162   Bloch 1986, p. 145.
163   Bruss 2012, p. 236.
164   Bruss 2012, p. 237.

show this one must engage with Voloshinov's concept of 'inner speech' and his broader assessment of Freudianism.[165]

Voloshinov rightly notes that Freudianism far exceeded its 1893 inception in psychiatry and therapeutic method alone,[166] and moved towards 'elaborating its own philosophy of culture'[167] by extending and expounding its discovery of the unconscious for areas of human life such as religion, art, and politics. Voloshinov's critique of Freudianism and his notion of 'inner speech' circle this philosophy of culture, Freudianism's 'basic ideological motif'.[168] Voloshinov has two broad points of contention with Freudianism.

Voloshinov's first point of contention with the Freudian theory of the unconscious is that, to his mind, it is conceptualised a-historically, an old leitmotif of the ideological life of any ruling class which, in periods of its developmental crisis and decline,[169] is representative of its pending fear of history.[170] Freudianism articulates this ideological reflex of a ruling class in decline with its focus on 'the vicissitudes of ... sexual instinct',[171] in which the sexuality of the individual human organism becomes 'a surrogate of history'.[172] As Voloshinov writes, in Freudianism '[t]hat which in man is nonsocial and nonhistorical is abstracted and advanced to the position of the ultimate measure and criterion for all that is social and historical'.[173] For Voloshinov, the unconscious just as much as the conscious is subject to history.

Bloch shares Voloshinov's suspicion of Freud's reduction of the drive (*Trieb*) – man's motivation – to a sexual character.[174] For Bloch, it is '[t]he stomach' and not the genitals which 'is the first lamp into which oil must be poured'.[175] The Freudian libido – whether as pleasure or as death-drive – wholly

---

165   Voloshinov's exactingly critical stance towards psychoanalysis is in some respects a question of timing – any utterance is marked by its specific situatedness. Marxism only begins to engage with Freud and Freud's inheritors proper after the Second World War, since at that point Marxism undergoes a serious attempt 'to theorize its own crisis and political defeat' through adopting 'the interlocutory position of the analysand'. (Roberts 2011, p. 125).

166   See Voloshinov 2012, pp. 5–6.
167   Voloshinov 2012, p. 4, emphasis removed.
168   Voloshinov 2012, p. 7.
169   See Voloshinov 2012, p. 10.
170   See Voloshinov 2012, pp. 11 and 16.
171   Voloshinov 2012, p. 8.
172   Voloshinov 2012, p. 10.
173   Voloshinov 2012, p. 11.
174   See Bloch 1986, p. 51.
175   Bloch 1986, p. 65.

governing life both in its 'time and content'[176] is substituted by Bloch with the drive of hunger, the longing of which is 'precise' and 'unavoidable' as to be ultimately irrepressible.[177] The drive of hunger, always omitted from psychoanalysis,[178] has the added benefit of being subject to historical becoming in both its form and in the matter that bears it.[179] For Bloch, the tendency to the new which hunger carries within itself constitutes it trigger-status for revolution.[180] Hunger is a drive to which socio-historical layers are added, and thus is open and extends beyond 'what has already been drawn and allotted to the self'.[181] This hunger-drive thus ventures beyond the material conditions – contains a 'surplus' – which had initially given rise to it. It negates not only the immediacy of an empty stomach but expands out to the wider context of that immediacy's origination. It works on nature and thus reworks itself.

Voloshinov's second point of objection, very much tied to the first and one that is again shared by Bloch, lies in Freudianism's subjectivism.[182] Rehearsing his discussion of objective and subjective psychology which maps onto the dialectical argument developed in the later *Marxism and the Philosophy of Language* concerning abstract objectivism and individualistic subjectivism,[183] Voloshinov asserts that 'Freudianism transferred into its constructs all the fundamental defects of the subjective psychology of the time'.[184] The unconscious thereby mimics all those categories of mental phenomena with which subjective psychologists characterised the psyche: the 'subjectivist bricks'[185] of 'Will (desires, drives), Feeling (emotions, affects), and Mind (sensations, presentations, thoughts)'.[186] Freudianism is never able to capture the conflicts of these components of the psyche with reference to the objectively material basis, to '[w]hatever real, objective forces might underlie that conflict', and it is thus incapable of seeing subjective psychology as merely a *projection* of

---

176   Bloch 1986, p. 51.
177   Bloch 1986, p. 65.
178   Bloch 1986, p. 64, emphasis removed.
179   Bloch 1986, p. 67.
180   See Bloch 1986, p. 75.
181   Bloch 1986, p. 69.
182   Bloch (1986, p. 84) speaks of Freud's 'pure psychologism ... without regard to the social environment'.
183   Voloshinov's *Freudianism* was published prior to Freud's *Civilization and Its Discontents*. Voloshinov can be somewhat faulted, then, for not having incorporated Freud's later insights into the social implications of psychanalysis (see Bruss 2012, pp. 242–52).
184   Voloshinov 2012, p. 107, original emphasis removed.
185   Voloshinov 2012, p. 110.
186   Voloshinov 2012, p. 108.

social forces *into* subjectivity.[187] There is thus a 'rift' between the spheres of inner-subjectivity and the material world to which that subjectivity belongs. Voloshinov includes the bodily organism as part of this material world, alongside 'any kind of material environment'.[188] This contention of Voloshinov's relates to the central importance of language and the utterance in Freudianism:

> Freud's whole psychological construct is based fundamentally on human verbal utterances; it is nothing but a special kind of interpretation of utterances. All these utterances are, of course, constructed in the *conscious sphere of the psyche*. To be sure, Freud distrusts the surface motives of consciousness; he tries instead to penetrate to deeper levels of the psychical realm. Nevertheless, Freud does not take utterances in their objective aspect, does not seek out their physiological or social roots; instead he attempts to find the true motives of behaviour in the utterances themselves – the patient is himself supposed to provide him information about the depths of the 'unconscious'.[189]

Freud is praised for treating the analysand's utterance as non-transparent to the utterer. Indeed Freud's merit lies in perceiving '*strife*', '*chaos*', and 'the *adversity* of our psychical life' as entering into and in fact constituting the utterance. But Freud is equally admonished for his *formalist* confinement of the source of the utterance – the source of this strife – to subjectivity. The utterance stands alone bereft of its actual objective conditions. Much like Russian Formalism's restriction of defamiliarisation to literary texts (see below), this centring of conflict at the heart of the psyche is only ever restricted to subjective consciousness alone in Freud's account of it.[190] Voloshinov, however, transposes the conflictual dynamics of the psyche into a '*social dynamics*'.[191] The conflict of the verbal utterance of the analysand must instead be sought in its 'objective roots'.[192] As Voloshinov writes: '[n]ot a single instance of verbal utterance can be reckoned exclusively to its utterer's account', for the meaning of an utterance always

---

187   Voloshinov 2012, p. 110.
188   Voloshinov 2012, pp. 111–14, emphasis removed.
189   Voloshinov 2012, p. 122.
190   Freud's account thus has the benefit of avoiding subjectivist psychology for which mental life is 'from birth to death a smooth, straight path of steady and purposive progress' in the stages of mental development (Voloshinov 2012, p. 120). Freud avoids this '*psychological optimism*' (Voloshinov 2012, p. 120).
191   Voloshinov 2012, p. 128.
192   Voloshinov 2012, p. 124.

arises through the concrete and class-ridden nature of the exchanges of dia-logue.[193] Hence, 'any product of the activity of human discourse – from the simplest utterance in everyday life to elaborate works of literary art – derives shape and meaning in all its most essential aspects ... from the social situation in which the utterance appears'.[194] Once again, within the deep recesses of the unconscious, here we encounter the 'non-verbal situatedness' of the utterance which Bühler had termed the speech act's *Zeigfeld*.

Despite its a-historicity and purported subjectivism, then, Voloshinov sees in Freudianism the benefit of revealing the conflictual nature of the uncon-scious and its veiled utterances. Voloshinov proceeds to embed this struggle of the psyche into objective material by connecting it to class struggle, which pertains to the objective conditions of the life of the unconscious. In sum, by asserting the social, objectively derived nature of the utterance Voloshinov argues for the social nature of the unconscious and its motives. Recalling that for Marx '[c]onsciousness [*das Bewusstsein*] can never be anything else than conscious being [*das bewusste Sein*]',[195] for Voloshinov any notion of an uncon-scious is equally *das Unbewusste Sein* – unconscious being. Voloshinov is there-fore led to affirm that the distinction between consciousness and the uncon-scious is not a distinction of being but of *ideological content*. Each deals with given objective conditions differently: 'in this sense Freud's unconscious can be called the "unofficial conscious" in distinction from the ordinary "official con-scious"'.[196]

In light of Bloch's category of 'not-yet conscious', and with Bloch's notion of 'totality', my argument is that Voloshinov can be seen to be espousing a narrow vision of the ideological content contained in the class opposition found in the 'unofficial unconscious'. Voloshinov here is developing a cold-stream critique and conception of ideology in language: 'in the strict sense', ideology is 'the expression of class consciousness', 'no ideology', however, 'whether of person or class, can be taken at its face value or its word'.[197] Combining Freud's insist-ence on the non-transparent nature of the utterance with a socially dynamic vision of the utterance's origins, Voloshinov asserts that '[a]n ideology will lead anyone astray who is incapable of penetrating beyond it into the hidden play of objective material forces that underlies it'.[198] Thus the Marxist must bring to

---

193   Voloshinov 2012, p. 126.
194   Voloshinov 2012, pp. 126–7.
195   Marx and Engels 1976a, p. 36.
196   Voloshinov 2012, pp. 138.
197   Voloshinov 2012, p. 124.
198   Ibid.

light the 'real economic and social conditions' from which any ideology, and, by dint of that, any utterance, necessarily arises from, even the 'inner speech' of the unconscious:[199]

> Those areas of behavioural ideology that correspond to Freud's official, 'censored' conscious express the most steadfast and the governing factors of class consciousness. They lie close to the formulated, fully fledged ideology of the class in question, its law, its morality, its world outlook. On these levels of behavioural ideology, inner speech comes easily to order and freely turns into outward speech or, in any case, has no fear of becoming outward speech.[200]

While Voloshinov will often imply that the official conscious is the purview of a ruling class, in the above quotation the notion that *any class* possesses its own 'official' and 'unofficial' conscious is pressed for. Despite this slippage Voloshinov proposes that '[o]ther levels' which correspond to the Freudian unconscious 'lie at a great distance ... from the stable system of the ruling ideology'.[201] This 'unofficial' ideological content, which sometimes 'bear[s] an incidental character' and is itself, like the official conscious, 'conditioned by historical time and class', indicates 'the disintegration' of the otherwise stable official conscious of a (ruling) class or sections of it; it thereby constitutes a sign of 'the vulnerability of the usual ideological motivations'.[202] As Voloshinov writes:

> The wider and deeper the breach between the official and the unofficial conscious, the more difficult it becomes for motives of inner speech to turn into outward speech (oral or written or printed, in a circumscribed or broad social milieu) wherein they might acquire formulation, clarity, and rigor. Motives under these conditions begin to fail, to lose their verbal countenance, and little by little really do turn into a 'foreign body' in the psyche. Whole sets of organic manifestations come, in this way, to be excluded from the zone of verbalized behaviour and may become asocial. Thereby, the sphere of the 'animalian' in man enlarges.[203]

---

199   Ibid. Cf. p. 140.
200   Voloshinov 2012, p. 144.
201   Voloshinov 2012, p. 144.
202   Voloshinov 2012, pp. 144–5.
203   Voloshinov 2012, p. 146.

Here, Voloshinov indicates the potential weakness of the Blochian reading of the anacoluthon, which, in its logic of discontinuity, could be read as this moment of breach between official and unofficial conscious, but which, being conceived of by Bloch – at least explicitly – without a social force behind it, potentially leads to the Expressionist individualism which, losing its 'ideological formulatedness',[204] becomes alienated from the life activity of the masses:

> Of course, not every area of human behavior is subject to so complete a divorce from verbal ideological formulation. After all, neither is it true that every motive in contradiction with official ideology must degenerate into indistinct inner speech and then die out – it might well engage in a struggle with that official ideology. If such a motive *is founded on the economic being of the whole group*, if it is not merely the motive of a déclassé loner, then it has a chance for a future and perhaps a victorious future.[205]

If Voloshinov helps shine a light on the possible formalism of Bloch's reading of the anacoluthon, then it is Bloch who arguably develops not only a broader notion of the 'nonverbal situatedness' of the utterance, but also a broader notion of the significance of all ideological content in its relation to the unofficial conscious. This is because Bloch's engagement with psychoanalysis points more towards a serious encounter with the dream (or better, the daydream) in Freud's work, which according to Bloch Freud merely collapses into the nocturnal dream, or serves only as a stepping stone towards it.[206] Besides the broader notion of the non-situatedness of the utterance it generates, Bloch's reading of Freud also yields another advance on the terrain that Voloshinov's work has brought into view and which concerns the 'frontlike anticipatory content'[207] of the daydream – the dream of an open eye,[208] as opposed to the 'No-Longer-Conscious' – the repressed old conscious material – of the night-dream.[209]

For Voloshinov, the Freudian unconscious lacked a clear comprehension of how seemingly solipsistic utterances are stamped by objective conditions of being and are intended for audiences beyond the analyst – it did not compre-

204   Ibid.
205   Ibid.
206   See Bloch 1986, pp. 86–7.
207   Bloch 1986, p. 87.
208   See Bloch 1986, pp. 77–8.
209   Bloch 1986, p. 116.

hend that even 'autistic uses of language' are utterances of a social nature in Voloshinov's sense.[210] But this state of affairs is even more acute with Freud's theory of dreams, which Voloshinov himself neglects in developing his concept of the 'unofficial conscious'. In the *New Introductory Lectures on Psychoanalysis* (1932–33), Freud writes the following:

> Let us suppose ... that ... a patient in analysis ... tells us one of his dreams. We shall assume that in this way he is making us one of the communications to which he had pledged himself by the fact of having started an analytic treatment. It is, to be sure, a communication made by inappropriate means, for dreams are not in themselves social utterances, not a means of giving information. Nor, indeed, do we understand what the dreamer was trying to say to us, and he himself is equally in the dark.[211]

On the score of the dream Voloshinov's analysis of Freud is charged with a drawback. As Bruss writes:

> In his lengthy presentation of psychanalytic theory, Voloshinov very explicitly discusses those concepts that pertain to the psychical construct he finds so invalid: the unconscious, free association, the Oedipus complex, censorship, resistance, and others. Yet in his discussion of dream formation, the concepts of condensation and displacement notably lack the type of foregrounding that others receive in his argumentation. At best, the two are submerged within the general discussion, indistinguishable from their many superficial and theoretically secondary manifestations. At worst, Voloshinov may not have recognized the significance of the two concepts at all.[212]

It is the dream-related concepts of condensation and displacement which in their own manner allow the latent dream thought, or the otherwise censored wish, 'to be partially expressed'.[213] Voloshinov therefore allegedly misses the semiotic strand of these two dream-related concepts:

> The fundamental nature of condensation and displacement was confirmed as Freud extended the dream analysis to the larger semiotic realm,

210   See Bruss 2012, pp. 236–8.
211   Freud 1964, pp. 8–9.
212   Bruss 2012, p. 203.
213   Ibid.

including pathological symptoms, 'psychopathologies of everyday life' such as slips of the tongue and jokes, and myths, religious rituals, and works of verbal and plastic art.[214]

Freud's 'free associationism' is 'the means of retracing paths of condensation and displacement, of establishing deductive links between underlying messages and superficial symptoms'[215] and ties in with a logic of 'not-following' which the analyst must follow should she seek to undercover the repression-material. In *The Interpretation of Dreams* (1900), Freud draws attention to the relationship between the small things and the things that do not follow:

> It may be that free play of ideas with a fortuitous chain of associations is to be found in destructive organic cerebral processes; what is regarded as such in the psycho-neuroses can always be explained as an effect of the censorship's influence upon a train of thought which has been pushed into the foreground by purposive ideas that have remained hidden. It has been regarded as an unfailing sign of an association being uninfluenced by purposive ideas if the associations (or images) in question seem to be interrelated, in what is described as a 'superficial' manner – by assonance, verbal ambiguity, temporal coincidence without connection in meaning, or by any association of the kind that we allow in jokes or in play upon words. ... [W]e have seen instances of this – not without astonishment – in many dream analyses. No connection was too loose, no joke too bad, to serve as a bridge from one thought to another. But the true explanation of this easy-going state of things is soon found. *Whenever one psychical element is linked with another by an objectionable or superficial association, there is also a legitimate and deeper link between them which is subjected to the resistance of the censorship.*[216]

And as Bruss notes, in Freud's earlier work, prior to *Die Traumdeutung* of 1900, he had also regarded physical symptoms as signs for repressed-material: 'What were regarded as merely physical, nonrational processes would henceforth be seen as signs'.[217] And so, in light of this 'significative nature'[218] of the symptom, such as a slip of the tongue, in which, not in the meaning by which it mani-

---

214   Bruss 2012, pp. 204–5.
215   Bruss 2012, p. 216.
216   Freud 2010, pp. 523–3.
217   Bruss 2012, p. 218.
218   Ibid.

fests, but in the structure through which the meaning comes, we have to ask ourselves: what is the apparent non-rational pause or break of the anacoluthon a sign of, and how does it relate to Volsohinov's notion of the 'unofficial conscious'? 'For Voloshinov, Freud's unexpected belief that meaning in psychoanalysis was *not* to be found in consciousness but rather in the structure would be particularly appealing – but not without a social definition of structure'.[219] If the anacoluthon is a sign in its structure of breakage and rupture, then it is a sign of something social, but what?

As a general principle Bloch, like Voloshinov, also sees Freud as putting into the consciousness what in fact pertains to the objective world – namely, struggle. Freud's assertion that we are possessed by uncontrollable forces is thereby merely a subjectivisation, 'made into the libido-id', of 'the alien domination of the capitalist mode of production'.[220] Like Voloshinov, Bloch merits in his own manner Freud's aspiration to bring these conflictual forces to the light of rationality – 'to step over the threshold of consciousness',[221] but identifies Freud's drawback as confining analysis 'within the private libido'.[222] What Freud never countenanced was the libido being *a variable of socio-economic conditions*.[223] Besides, Bloch writes, the analysand is rarely if ever a worker, and, as Voloshinov indicates, psychoanalysis is ascribable to the middle-class *déclassé*.[224]

The dream, which, as Bloch rightly says, in Freud's view protects against wish-fulfilment ('fictitious fulfilments of an unconscious wishful fantasy'),[225] is stripped of social content by Freud. Just as with the unconscious the dream is perceived as entirely meaningless. Freud connects this a-social dream material to its opaqueness: it remains dark both to the analysand who dreamt it and the analyst who hears it. But the dream is precisely that node of Freudianism that is most ripe for a utopian appraisal, according to Bloch. And it is not hard to see why: the dream in some sense relates to the more expanded sense of 'surplus' which defines what I have constructed as Bloch's account of the 'non-verbal situatedness of the utterance'. But it is for Bloch the *daydream* that is key as a form of Not-Yet-Conscious material, 'the psychological birthplace of the New' – a type of anticipatory consciousness of what has not yet been and

219   Bruss 2012, pp. 232–3.
220   Bloch 1986, p. 53.
221   Bloch 1986, p. 54.
222   Ibid.
223   Bloch 1986, p. 64.
224   See Bloch 1986, pp. 65–6. Cf. Voloshinov 2012, pp. 144–9.
225   See Bloch 1986, p. 78.

whose correlate is what is 'objectively emerging in the world'.[226] The daydream is 'frontal' consciousness.[227] While, then, Bloch takes the question of unconscious desire to be crucial, his response moves in a different direction to the psychoanalytic desire of, say, a Jacques Lacan, for whom real desire is bathed in 'the impossibility of the sexual relationship as full enjoyment' and for whom this impossible desire 'alone supports all speaking'.[228]

Bloch asserts that the daydream contains four properties: although external circumstances can certainly act as an obstacle to fulfilment, the day dreamer, unlike the oppressive censorship of the night-dream, maintains a degree of voluntary and carefree exploration of what is wished-for; moreover, the waking dreamer remains unaltered, consciously preserved, and stably him or herself, in fact the daydream potentially strengthens the individual by way of revealing what they *could be*, it gives them an uprightness, unlike with the deadened trance of a night-dream in which one's consciousness becomes misty; the day dream also seeks to become outward and public (truly 'refractive') and thereby potentially conjoins the dreamer to embrace others in collaboration, while the night dreamer remains alone; finally, the daydream contains a desire to want to be fulfilled in a world-improving arrival and thus has a tendency within it to journey to the end, while the night dreamer has bad conscience of his or her night-longings and, in any case, once awake, the reality woken to once more seems immutable.[229]

All this means that for Bloch a daydream pre-figures plans for a better life and can act as a lever on objective conditions. The daydream is said to derive from an existent and felt lack, which while not inherently mediated with objective conditions in their manner of imagining this lack's overcoming, can nevertheless tend towards the real-possibility that is nestled in their conditions of emergence.[230] The merit of the daydream, for Bloch, is that even in its worst escapist trappings and in its least mediated relation to objective conditions, the contents of this daydream contain that unrepressed element of wish-fulfilment, 'the fringe of futurity'[231] that, for Bloch, helps found consciousness. As Bloch writes: 'The amount of venturing beyond that takes place in daydreams ... indicates nothing repressed, even psychologically, nothing that has simply sunk

---

226   See Bloch 1986, p. 116.
227   See Bloch 1986, p. 127.
228   Bosteels 2019, p. 8. Cf. pp. 48–9.
229   See Bloch 1986, pp. 88–99.
230   Bloch 1986, p. 76.
231   Pelletier 2018, p. 37.

down out of consciousness that already existed'.[232] The daydream concerns what is not-yet. As Pelletier writes, '[t]he experience of the Not-Yet-Conscious is precisely an act of meaning and of anticipative perception of a destination that would be the fulfilment required by the negativity of the obscure instant'.[233]

If Voloshinov's objective grasp of 'inner speech' and 'unofficial unconscious' has the merit of allowing one to draw out the *social implications* of the otherwise opaque, seemingly a-social dream content, Voloshinov nevertheless fails to fulfil this interpretative possibility that he opens up. This is despite Voloshinov himself striking at the main point of contention that Bloch holds against the spirit of Freudianism concerning its interpretation of dreams: 'the socioeconomic paradise of political utopias ... clearly display [for Freudianism] unmistakable signs of their origin from that urge to return to the intrauterine life that all men once experienced';[234] indeed such collective, socialised dream contents (normal formations) *'have as their basis a vague, unconscious memory of a paradise that really did exist, ... their truth belongs not to the future but to every man's past'.*[235] But Voloshinov's notion of the 'unofficial unconscious' apparently failed to properly take hold of the true import of the dream in Freud and the future-matter which, for Bloch, daydreams participate in.

Voloshinov develops an assiduously objective grasp of all supposed subjective content,[236] including 'hazy' content, which contains the same objective material underpinning that pertaining to all ideological content. 'The haziest content of consciousness of the primitive savage and the most sophisticated cultural monument are only extreme links in the single chain of ideological creativity'.[237] Voloshinov would therefore dismiss, it seems, Lukács's own rejection of utopianism as a purely subjective, and thus ideologically retrograde, content (see Chapter 4): 'Dreams, myth, joke, witticism, and all the verbal components of the pathological formations reflect the struggle of various ideological tendencies and trends that take place within *behavioral ideology*',[238] that is, both within 'inner' and 'outer' speech.[239] This would seem to suggest that even erroneous utopian content cannot be confined to a status of mere detritus when

---

232   Bloch 1986, p. 77.
233   Pelletier 2018, p. 39.
234   Voloshinov 2012, p. 99.
235   Voloshinov 2012, pp. 99–100.
236   See Voloshinov 2012, p. 141.
237   Ibid.
238   Voloshinov 2012, p. 144.
239   See Voloshinov 2012, p. 143.

the goal is emancipation. In the shape of daydreams, as not-yet conscious anticipations, they occupy the 'unofficial conscious' at a level Voloshinov intimated but did not know. Bloch makes a similar point, but he does so in the context of his category of a general anticipatory consciousness, to which the daydream is assigned: 'future-oriented intentions, that of expectant emotions and that of expectant ideas ... extend into a Not-Yet-Conscious, that is, into a class of consciousness which is itself to be designated as not filled, but as anticipatory'.[240] The Not-Yet-Conscious arguably instantiates what Voloshinov termed the 'unofficial conscious',[241] and does so in the interruption of a 'not following' in the course of official ideology.

One final drawback of Voloshinov's treatment of the 'unofficial conscious' is that insofar as it misses the 'not-yet conscious' dimension of the 'unofficial unconscious', so then it overlooks the real purport of the rupture that 'unofficial conscious' is said to contain. By missing the site of real rupture in this respect, Voloshinov omits the importance of *error* in the utterance. Voloshinov's line of critique of psychoanalysis renders his philosophy of language bereft of the import of error for grasping the core life of language. As Roberts writes, 'implicative and culpable language of errors is internal to the very dynamic of psychoanalytic theory'.[242] Indeed, 'psychoanalysis is the domain where the error, the mistake, the lapse, have flourished as explicitly productive concepts', a discipline in which the error is 'no longer the detritus to be expunged ... but the thing to be cherished, noted, embraced'.[243] But Voloshinov makes no real claim to the error, just as he fails to make a claim to the dream, compounding the narrowness of Voloshinov's notion of the real. How are the two – the daydream and the error – connected, if at all?

Bloch shares with the psychoanalyst an attentiveness to the small things, the psychoanalyst's watchfulness of the analysand's errors. Both Bloch and the psychoanalyst exude the mark of a detective.[244] This is because 'psychoanalysis *is the science of a speech that does not know itself*, and as such reflects on objects that are unknown (and cannot be fully known) to the analysand'.[245] As Roberts writes, 'the subject in speaking or not speaking *always says more, far more, than he or she means to say*. Hence the error becomes the medium of

240   Bloch 1986, p. 113.
241   See Bloch 1986, pp. 115–16.
242   Roberts 2011, p. 109.
243   Roberts 2011, p. 111.
244   See Roberts 2011, p. 114.
245   Roberts 2011, p. 123.

that which speaks more than it does'.[246] Even more importantly, 'the prospect of error, the arrival of error, of speech acts that betray the "stability" of language as correspondence, is something ... that is indivisible from language as a trace of ideological struggles and affective force'.[247]

What is key here is that the surplus of the error, just as for Bühler's model which sees in the utterance a 'surplus of perception', contains the affective-ideological force of anticipation of the future. As Lacan writes, through the mistake 'the subject signifies something other – *aliud* – than what he means'.[248] The 'other' given by the error manifests primarily, for Lacan, through the slip of the tongue, which for him is 'fundamental', 'since it is the radical facet of the non-meaning which all meaning possesses'.[249] The 'surplus of the erroneous utterance' does not point to a surplus of transcendent meaning but to the lack or incompleteness of meaning as such, to the hole in that hypothesised transcendent truth – the referent that hangs everything together. Importantly, the error for Lacan is also thereby the site of the Novum, for the slip is 'a point where meaning emerges, and is created'.[250] While for Lacan the joke is a calculated slip, 'a calculated irruption of non-sense into a discourse which seems to make sense',[251] it can be argued that akin to the daydream an *uncalculated* anacoluthon is an eruption of anticipation into the 'official conscious' of ruling ideologies, which nestle themselves in the 'inner speech' of an individual class subject:

> In analysis, truth emerges in the most clearcut representative of the mistake – the slip, the action which one, improperly, calls *manquée* [missed, failed, abortive].[252]

Admittedly, Lacan is not the most appropriate figure to draw on here despite his efforts to foreground the importance of error for psychoanalysis: 'the paths of truth are in essence the paths of error';[253] 'psychoanalytic paths of truth are wayward, in so far as error speaks the truth and truth speaks of error'.[254] Not the most appropriate because Lacan will see it as impossible that syntactical

---

246   Roberts 2011, p. 119. Roberts is discussing the error in Lacanianism.
247   Roberts 2011, p. 151.
248   Lacan 1988, p. 260.
249   Lacan 1988, p. 280.
250   Lacan 1988, p. 280.
251   Ibid. Recall the intentional use of the anacoluthon.
252   Lacan 1988, p. 265.
253   Lacan 1988, p. 263.
254   Roberts 2011, p. 119.

error – syntax being 'a sequence of directed signs'[255] – could be uncalculated or unexpected. *Manquée*, 'that which is missing', for Lacan, has no relation to or bearing on syntax nor mistakes in syntax, which 'are only accidents',[256] in stark contrast to Voloshinov, for whom syntax takes us closest to the concreteness of dialogue, a concreteness which includes for Bloch that 'new depth of being'. As Lacan says:

> What are we faced with when the human subject addresses himself to us? His discourse is an impure discourse. *Impure* – is it so because of mistakes in syntax? No, of course not. The whole of psychoanalysis is quite rightly founded on the fact that getting something meaningful out of human discourse isn't a matter of logic. We look behind this discourse, which has its own meaning, for its meaning, in another meaning, and precisely in the symbolic function which is manifested through it.[257]

For Lacan, syntax is merely a pre-ordering activity, a scansion. He therefore distinguishes 'truth immanent to errors from the mere breakdown in syntax, the glitches of computer programmes, or the malfunctioning of machines'; these malfunctions of syntactic machines, as Roberts writes, 'infer the breakdown or omission of pre-given actions or units of information'.[258] Indeed by a machine Lacan does not mean 'a little box', but rather, a *directed activity*, a pre-given movement to subscribe to, an invariant of direction: 'when I am writing on paper, when I go through the transformations of the little 1s and 0s, that is also directed activity'.[259] As pre-given order so then 'nothing unexpected comes out of the machine', 'it stops just where we have determined that it would stop'.[260] But the anacoluthon arguably is not a pre-prepared decision before the moment, nor as tendency is its activity directed to what is pre-given, rather it is directed to what is not-yet, but latent. And as an anacoluthic expression within consciousness and within the utterance, the daydream and its directed activity can be put to political work.

---

255   Lacan 1991, p. 305.
256   Lacan 1991, pp. 305–6.
257   Lacan 1991, pp. 305–6.
258   Roberts 2011, p. 120.
259   Lacan 1991, p. 305. Lacan is discussing cybernetics. 'Cybernetics is a science of syntax, and it is in a good position to help us perceive that the exact sciences do nothing other than tie the real to a syntax'. (Lacan 1991, p. 305).
260   Ibid.

CHAPTER 4

Bloch and Fascism

... the characteristically uncompleted being: Man, was established.
Man alone ... is here the latest and yet the firstborn creature; only
he broke through, exceeded the genus fixed for so long among the
animals. Under pain of destruction, he became the tool-making,
detour-making animal; thus he could also not get by with inborn
reflexes, earlier signals. With time he becomes only more dependent
on deliberate planning, in the building of nests and related activit-
ies: absolutely artificial, and yet right on the front.

BLOCH, *The Spirit of Utopia*[1]

∴

To make detours is to live on the Front of becoming; it is to transgress givenness, dispensing with the straight line. To detour is what makes the human
being an historical animal. Detours mark the voice, too. Anacolutha punctuate
the utterance, and not merely the poetically formed utterance. Such punctuation of the spoken utterance has been shown to possess within the framework of Bloch's materialism both the tendency and latency of matter, both
process and possible goal, both becoming and the possibility of fulfilment.
And with the help of Voloshinov, the anacoluthon can be seen to contain class
struggle and the unconscious as an ideological refraction of being. Labour
and discontinuity combine and indeed this detouring animal speaks in devi-
ations, and the very social history it creates is pervaded by detours of time,
non-contemporaneous layers of time. The non-contemporaneity of the present
marks the spoken word. In *Marxism and Literature*, Raymond Williams suggested that a 'definition of language is always, implicitly or explicitly, a definition
of human beings in the world'.[2] A definition of language entwines itself with
questions of what and who we are, where we are going and what can be hoped
for.

---

1 Bloch 2000a, p. 234.
2 Williams 1977, p. 21.

Marx was a thinker, as Bloch says, 'concerned with the actuality of the future as the future of actuality'.[3] Bloch endeavoured to raise to attention what he considered had been lost to Marxism despite its proper heritage: 'Not only political economy but the tendency toward and the latency of an ultimate'.[4] As was noted in the first chapter of this book, for Bloch this ultimate actuality, as a possibility in the world-stock itself, can only be a Novum, for in no historical moment has it yet come to pass. The notion of relationality to this not-yet ultimate reality, worked out and honed in on in Bloch's thought, helps us, I argue, to think the future of actuality as co-present in the loquacity of human beings. I take seriously Bloch's suggestion that the goal of Marxist philosophy is 'to penetrate ever wider and deeper domains of being',[5] to extend Marx beyond himself. Bloch helps us move Marxism into the domain of linguistic being in a novel way. The previous chapters have aimed to be preliminary steps in that direction.

In keeping with the overarching conviction laid out by Raymond Williams, I have sought to demonstrate how Bloch's utopian philosophy gives rise, at least in outline, to a certain approach to language, and thus to a certain approach to human beings in (their relation to) the world. The incompleteness, and yet the real possibility for a not-yet fullness of being, constitutes human beings in the world and their relation to it. This is an axiomatic premise of Bloch's philosophical outlook, one which must imbue any given Blochian philosophy of language. This condition of becoming to that which is not-yet is therefore inscribed in the very loquacity that defines the human being's creative relation and inhabitancy of the world. The figure of the anacoluthon, I argued, captures this dynamic in its very a-logical structure. Its treatment appears as a rare instance in Bloch's work where the issue of language is dealt with head-on.

There is, however, another clear instance in Bloch's collected writings where treatment of language is given a sustained focus. It is an instance where Bloch discusses language and fascism. The task in this final chapter, then, is to outline what Bloch says in this other moment given to language speculation, and to connect what he says there to what has thus far been argued above. Through the anacoluthon it has been shown that linguistic being possesses both tendency and latency. Here in this chapter the role of latency within linguistic being will be further determined both through a discussion of Lukács and Bloch's

---

3   Bloch 2018, p. 12.
4   Bloch 2018, p. 171.
5   Bloch 2018, p. 124.

dispute over German Expressionism, Marx's opening passage to the *Eighteenth Brumaire*, and how the preceding discussion relates to the question of language and fascism.

1   Marx's *Incipit*

What is surprising about the omission within previous Marxian attempts at language speculation of the well-known linguistic-oriented passage within the opening of Marx's *Eighteenth Brumaire of Louis Bonaparte* – from Gramsci to Rossi-Landi, from Voloshinov to Lecercle – is that here Marx noticeably draws on the topic of language in a period of potential revolutionary upheaval. The context is language at a time of potential social transformation, language during a moment of rupture, during a *volte face*, an event of revolt.[6] In this text, Marx draws our attention to the temporal relationality of language during the possibility of revolution – in Bloch's parlance, during the possibility of a Novum. Indeed, for this very reason, according to Bloch the text in question captures the significance of the darkness of the just lived moment.[7]

To grasp the significance of Marx's opening passage in the *Brumaire* one would need to understand those other moments in which Marx touches on the issue of language. Human labour power is a commodity but one that cannot be reduced to the same condition as the existence of every other commodity. The potentially rebellious commodity of human labour power is also a power that *speaks*, produces utterances: 'we are dealing with a *talking commodity*'.[8] All the fragments that Marx had to say of this human being as *loquens* can be termed Marx's *incipit* – his beginning for a Marxist philosophy of language (even if Voloshinov never refers to these fragments for his own project).[9]

Lecercle follows Althusser in positing a cut – an epistemological break – in the body of Marx's works, dividing Marx between the younger ideological-Hegelian and the mature scientist of *Capital*.[10] Lecercle applies this same epistemological break to the numerous language fragments of Marx's *incipit*. There is the Marx of 'an abstract, grandiloquent humanism' and a Marx who

---

6   The exception to this rule is Anthony G. Smith, for whom Marx's passage intimates 'language as a privileged field within which we humans move and act and think' (Smith 2010, p. 105). In this context Smith focuses on Stalin's work on language and the national question.

7   See Bloch 1986, p. 294.

8   Rossi-Landi 1992, p. 258.

9   See Holborow 2006.

10   See Althusser 2005.

is Marxist in the proper, Althusserian sense of that term,[11] for whom reference to language – already a marginal concern at the commencement of his writings – fades in frequency comparable to his earlier output.[12] It bears repeating that Bloch's iteration of Marxism was of a more humanist variety,[13] a *'creative humanism'*,[14] which for Bloch could not be 'confined to the young Marx' alone but stretches across Marx's developments.[15] Bloch's inheritance of Marx was to see Marxism *in fieri*, rather than as a *factum*.[16]

Be that as it may, Lecercle notes two connected theses on language which shine through in Marx's *incipit*: seeing language as *materiality* and seeing language as *social praxis*.[17] However, none of the passages in Marx's work that Lecercle brings up for discussion include the *Eighteenth Brumaire* passage that I want to primarily focus on here; in fact, this text is not mentioned at all. Before reading the *Eighteenth Brumaire* passage, we can summarily outline those passages in Marx's work which serve as material for Lecercle's Marxist philosophy of language, as the latest, explicit attempt to pose and respond to the language question for Marxism. They will serve the reading of the *Brumaire* passage which I develop later on.

In the *Economic and Philosophical Manuscripts of 1844*, Marx thinks over the *social* essence of language. It is contrary to the Expressionist position outlined in the Introduction:

> But also when I am active *scientifically*, etc. – an activity which I can seldom perform in direct community with others – then my activity is *social*, because I perform it as a *man*. Not only is the material of my activity given to me as a social product (as is even the language in which the thinker is active): my *own* existence *is* social activity, and therefore that which I make myself, I make of myself for society and with the consciousness of myself as a social being.[18]

The anti-methodological individualism enlists Hegel's position in the *Phenomenology of Spirit* that '[t]he *labour* of the individual for his own needs is just as much a satisfaction of the needs of others as of his own', and thus

---

11   Lecercle 2006, p. 91.
12   See Lecercle 2006, p. 92.
13   Bloch 2018, p. 23.
14   Bloch 2018, p. 138.
15   Bloch 2018, p. 22, see also p. 76. Cf. Löwy1979, pp. 181–4 and 191, on Lukács's humanism.
16   See Haug 2012, pp. 247–8.
17   See Lecercle 2006, p. 93.
18   Marx 1987a, p. 298.

'the individual in his *individual* work already *unconsciously* performs a *universal* work'.[19] In the immediacy of an utterance – what Hegel would call the '[mere] being'[20] of the individual's linguistic production – must be recognised as really an outcome of the mediation – 'the double movement'[21] – of always more than one consciousness. This is of course Voloshinov's basic premise. An individual being, 'an immediate being on its own account', is 'such only through this mediation' with the other.[22] My activity of speaking is both mine and non-reducible to me, since to speak as, in Marx's example, a scientist, entails 'a collective and ongoing system of knowledge production'.[23] Of course, this recognition can be and indeed has been and remains 'one-sided and unequal',[24] given the economic order which pertains behind any utterance as the latter's condition of being. The utterance is of course mediated by such inconcinnity. Marx, then, is aware of the Hegelian 'supraconsciousness',[25] but not as Hegel imagines it as determined on a purely national level. As Voloshinov writes, '*The verbal component of behaviour is determined in all the fundamentals and essentials of its content by objective-social factors*'.[26] Thus, when Marx speaks in the shoes of a scientist, we can join Voloshinov in asserting that 'the verbal is not his property but the property of his *social group* (his social milieu)'.[27] And, to compare once more with Voloshinov, Bloch will write:

> For Marx ... the fundamental subject is never mind but man, economic and social. Nor is this the same abstract man, man as a mere species being, as in Feuerbach, but man as a totality of social relationships, changing through history – and, in the last analysis, *a being as yet undiscovered and unemancipated*.[28]

As such, Marx will disparage the self-creative egoism of Max Stirner in *The German Ideology*:

---

19   Hegel 1977b, p. 213.
20   Hegel 1977b, p. 113.
21   Hegel 1977b, p. 112.
22   Hegel 1977b, p. 112.
23   Roberts 2011, p. 80.
24   Hegel 1977b, p. 116.
25   Roberts 2011, p. 80.
26   Vološinov 2012, pp. 139.
27   Vološinov 2012, p. 139.
28   Bloch 2018, p. 111, my emphasis.

Far from it being true that 'out of nothing' I make myself, for example, a 'speaker', the nothing which forms the basis here is a very manifold something, the real individual, his speech organs, a definite stage of physical development, an existing language and dialects, ears capable of hearing and a human environment from which it is possible to hear something, etc., etc. Therefore, in the development of a property something is created by something out of something, and by no means comes, as in Hegel's *Logik*, from nothing, through nothing to nothing.[29]

All speech acts have as their condition of possibility not only an individual's bio-physical being – the tongue, the vocal chords etc. – but an already extant language (an already extant sensuous expression of conscious being), and so also the existence of other human beings (those 'ears capable of hearing'). Contra Stirner, for Marx all language comes not from and to nothing (the pure creativity of an individual), but from and to this multiple something as precondition to speak.

There are other instances in Marx's work in which this social character of language is clearly discernible – including the *Grundrisse*[30] and *The German Ideology*.[31] In the *Grundrisse* Marx states that the very possibility for someone to be able to perceive their language production as *their* loquacity in the first place is precisely the precondition of a society: 'As regards the individual, it is clear e.g. that he relates even to language itself *as his own* only as the natural member of a human community. Language as the product of an individual is an impossibility. But the same holds for property'.[32] In the *Economic and Philosophical Manuscripts*, Marx gives a keener sense of how this social dimension of language is tied to the materiality of language: 'The element of thought itself – the element of thought's living expression – *language* – is of a sensuous nature'.[33] The sensuousness of thought arrives in the shape of language, thought's living expression. The presence of language is the co-presence of at least two human beings, and language demonstrates in a unique way, along with labour, the materiality of that co-belonging of two. In *The German Ideology*, Marx and Engels write the following with analogical reference to language (analogy being important for the *Brumaire* passage I read later on):

---

29   Marx and Engels 1976a, p. 150.
30   See Marx 1993, pp. 490 and 492.
31   See Marx and Engels 1976a, pp. 43–4.
32   Marx 1993, p. 490.
33   Marx 1987a, p. 304.

The production of ideas, of conceptions, of consciousness, is at first directly interwoven with the material activity and the material intercourse
of men – the language of real life. Conceiving, thinking, the mental intercourse of men at this stage still appear as the direct efflux of their material
behaviour. The same applies to mental production as expressed in the
language of the politics, laws, morality, religion, metaphysics, etc., of a
people. Men are the producers of their conceptions, ideas, etc., that is,
real, active men, as they are conditioned by a definite development of
their productive forces and of the intercourse corresponding to these,
up to its furthest forms. Consciousness [*das Bewusstsein*] can never be
anything else than conscious being [*das bewusste Sein*], and the being of
men is their actual life-process. If in all ideology men and their relations
appear upside-down as in a *camera obscura*, this phenomenon arises just
as much from their historical life-process as the inversion of objects on
the retina does from their physical life-process.[34]

If language is the material expression of consciousness, then consciousness
is always 'conscious being', that is, a consciousness which belongs to a definite 'actual life-process'. *Language is therefore the living expression of conscious
being, of being that is at a certain moment of its historical becoming.* Bloch will
stress that the being to which consciousness belongs, and of which therefore
it is an expression, is always a definite being (a definite 'actual life-process')
which possesses *the horizon of the future and indeed the possibility of fulfilment.* The being that we are conscious of and of which language refracts, is
a being with definite conditions (certain circumscribed possibilities) but also
an indefinite possibility for realisation (an Ultimum). This future-matter as a
being that consciousness is conscious of can be related to a passage in *The
Germany Ideology* where the reader is told that consciousness (language precisely as a sensuous expression of consciousness) is never 'pure', indeed the
'"mind" is from the outset afflicted with the curse of being "burdened" with
matter, which here makes its appearance in the form of agitated layers of air,
sounds, in short, of language'.[35] The idea here points towards Bloch's oft-quoted
reference to Marx's own deployment of Jakob Böhme's concept of matter as *tension*. The agitation of language is the unrest of the tension in matter. As Marx
writes:

---

34   Marx and Engels 1976a, p. 36.
35   Marx and Engels 1976a, pp. 43–4.

> Among the qualities inherent in *matter, motion* is the first and foremost,
> ... in the form of an *impulse*, a *vital spirit, a tension* – a '*Qual*', to use a term
> of Jakob Böhme's – of matter.[36]

Marx points not only to the social and material nature of language, but also to
its ideological dimension (the *camera obscura* reference above already indicated this). In *The German Ideology* Marx speaks of the contradictions and
abstractions which define the being of which language is the sensuous expression. He writes of German philosophy and its misconception of the liberation
of man as being tied to the *mental acts* of philosophy and not residing in an
historical act given appropriate conditions. Trivial economic development in
Germany gave rise to highly abstract notions of liberation,[37] much like the utopian socialists are said to have taken flight from the present by developing
cookbook recipes for the '*model society* of the future' without historical conditions being ripe for their realisation.[38] Philosophy tends to undercook its social
conditionedness, much as does language. Marx writes, however, that 'Language
is the language of re[ality]'.[39] That is, even if language takes flight from the
actual life-process and intercommunication of human beings – as philosophy
is said to do – such abstract departures capture certain truths about the material activity that grounds the sensuousness of language nonetheless. They are
(refracted) expressions of real material life in its own distortion:

> One of the most difficult tasks confronting philosophers is to descend
> from the world of thought to the actual world. *Language* is the imme-
> diate actuality of thought. Just as philosophers have given thought an
> independent existence, so they were bound to make language into an
> independent realm. This is the secret of philosophical language, in which
> thoughts in the form of words have their own content. The problem of
> descending from the world of thoughts to the actual world is turned into
> the problem of descending from language to life. ... The philosophers have
> only to dissolve their language into the ordinary language, from which it is
> abstracted, in order to recognise it as the distorted language of the actual
> world, and to realise that neither thoughts nor language in themselves
> form a realm of their own, that they are only *manifestations* of actual
> life.[40]

---

36   Marx and Engels 1975c, p. 128.
37   Marx 1987c, p. 180.
38   Marx 1988, p. 394.
39   Marx and Engels 1976a, p. 38.
40   Marx and Engels 1976a, pp. 446–7.

Of course, this 'actual life' of which language is a (often distorted) manifestation is not fully actual in the sense of being realised, but is rather pervaded
by the possibility of being otherwise than it presently is. Utopias convey this
'being otherwise' of actual life, often in the guise of abstractions. In *Capital*
Marx alludes to the tendency of language to escape this, its socio-material
condition of being, and yet it is this very escaping of its socio-material conditions of being that captures the real co-ordinates of that being from which it
escapes:

> Men do not therefore bring the products of their labour into relation
> with each other as values because they see these objects merely as the
> material integuments of homogenous human labour. The reverse is true:
> by equating their different products to each other in exchange as values,
> they equate their different kinds of labour as human labour. They do this
> without being aware of it. Value, therefore, does not have its description
> branded on its forehead; it rather transforms every product of labour into
> a social hieroglyphic. Later on, men try to decipher the hieroglyphic, to get
> behind the secret of their own social product: for the characteristic which
> objects of utility have of being values is as much men's social product as
> is their language.[41]

Just as value becomes a social hieroglyph which distorts the reality of its existence, so then, Marx seems to say, language as a social product also distorts
its social basis. Behind language is a social being as a condition of relation.
And so material relationality is the proper being of the social and thus the
proper being of language. This comment can be tied to the question of utopianism if we turn to the *Grundrisse*, where Marx gives voice to the notion
that speech acts move not only *from* and *to* their present social condition
of being, but *to* (as a movement forward) *the new as a dimension of that
being*:

> Not only do the objective conditions change in the act of reproduction,
> e.g. the village becomes a town, the wilderness a cleared field etc., but the
> producers change, too, in that they bring out new qualities in themselves,
> in that they bring new powers and ideas, new modes of intercourse, new
> needs and new language.[42]

------

41   Marx 1990, pp. 166–7. Cf. Lecercle 2006, p. 95.
42   Marx 1993, p. 494.

These, then, are the instances in Marx's works where the otherwise marginal question of language is hinted at. As Lecercle light-heartedly notes: 'For fragmentary notations, that is not bad'.[43] But most commentators, including Lecercle himself, tend to overlook an essential language fragment that arises at an important juncture in Marx's corpus, and which inserts into the relationality of social being, of which language is an expression: *futurity* – precisely a more substantial *'new'* that was highlighted by Marx in the quotation above. Marx's opening passage to the *Eighteenth Brumaire*, a text connected to the question of fascism in later debates within Marxism, speaks to this co-belonging of conditionedness and openness within language as a refraction of social being. It is a significant passage precisely because it combines the future-dimension of language with its present socio-material actuality.

2   *The Eighteenth Brumaire*

> Criticism has torn up the imaginary flowers from the chain not so that man shall wear the unadorned, bleak chain but so that he will shake off the chain and pluck the living flower.[44]

The semiotician Rossi-Landi suggested that there is no more radical definition of the human being – *radix*, that which goes to the root – than that which includes the capacity of the human to produce material and linguistic artefacts.[45] Behind such production, both of speech and of those objects worked to satisfy historically changing human need, there is desire. When Pasolini writes in his 1965 essay 'From the Laboratory (Notes *en poète* for a Marxist Linguistics)' that '[m]y language doesn't ... consist of a stable structure, but lives this restlessness in motion, the need of metamorphosis of a structure that wants to be *another* structure',[46] the question ought to be posed of why desire arises in language at all, and how it is connected to the social being which it refracts? Wherein is the desire of the material-actuality which language is an expression of? It is interesting to note that Lecercle describes Pasolini's position above in an Heideggerian register, in which language is perceived as an unstable structure due to anxiety: language is 'a process in constant variation,

---

43   Lecercle 2006, p. 96.
44   Marx 1987c, p. 176.
45   Rossi-Landi 1992, p. 193.
46   Pasolini 2005, p. 56.

a disequilibrium, an *anxiety*'.[47] But what if the expectant emotion that defines language's process (language's *lettre d'attente*, as it were) is not anxiety, but *hope*?[48]

The 'what for [*Wozu*]?' of material and loquacious production can be given greater attention here. Bloch's nascent philosophy of language provides a response to the question of the 'what for?' of speech production, and of the substance which speech production is a refraction of. By turning to consider another moment in Marx's corpus where reference to language is made – Marx's opening *Brumaire* passage – we can bear witness to the 'what for?' of loquacious production in Marx, too, and one that can be connected to Bloch.

The question of why Marx uses an analogy of language in his assessment of what hinders the revolution – the emergence of a new social content – has rarely been posed by Marxists working in language theory, at least to my knowledge. Taken together with the other language fragments in Marx's work that were noted above, this opening passage to the *Brumaire* constitutes an *inconspicuous* fragment, despite the influence of this text being comparable to Marx's other works, with some claiming that perhaps its influence even surpasses that of *Capital*.[49] Deploying it as a centrepiece around which to develop a Blochian-informed Marxist philosophy of language activates Bloch's method of *following the small things*. It applies that axiom of perception to Marx's corpus itself. As Geoghegan has intimated, albeit with a different focus than what is at stake here, the *Brumaire* text offers a clear and decisive connection between Marx and Bloch. I will argue that it does so on the score of language and utopia. This is because the notion of a temporal relationality *within loquacity* is present and at work within the opening passage of Marx's text. Marx's famous passage, rarely assigned a role in discussions of language by Marxists, will fulfil the task of anchoring the thematic analysis of relationality that has been developed earlier in the book. The passage is selected somewhat arbitrarily, and yet, as was the case with the anacoluthon, such a selection will take us far: 'What is slight and odd often leads the furthest'.[50] It is one of the best-known of Marx's and is quoted at length:

---

47   Lecercle 2006, p. 85, my emphasis.
48   Lecercle's focus on anxiety could have something to do with his reading of Pasolini's position on spoken language as one embedded in mythic, primitivist origins (see Lecercle 2006, pp. 85–6).
49   Walker 2019, p. 33.
50   Bloch 2006, p. 5.

Men make their own history, but do not of their own free will; not under circumstances they themselves have chosen but under the given and inherited circumstances with which they are directly confronted. The tradition of the dead generation weighs like a nightmare on the minds of the living. And, just when they appear to be engaged in the revolutionary transformation of themselves and their material surroundings, in the creation of something which does not yet exist, precisely in such epochs of revolutionary crisis they timidly conjure up the spirits of the past to help them; they borrow their names, slogans and costumes so as to stage the new world-historical scene in this venerable disguise and borrowed language. Luther put on the mask of the apostle Paul; the Revolution of 1789–1814 draped itself alternately as the Roman republic and the Roman empire; and the revolution of 1848 knew no better than to parody at some points 1789 and at others the revolutionary traditions of 1793–5. In the same way, the beginner who has learnt a new language always retranslates it into his mother tongue: he can only be said to have appropriated the spirit of the new language and to be able to express himself in it freely when he can manipulate it without reference to the old, and when he forgets his original language while using the new one.[51]

Voloshinov gives us the conceptual tools with which to initially grasp this passage with regards to its importance for a philosophy of language. Voloshinov distinguishes between, but dialectically relates, what he calls 'signalization' and 'semioticity'. Using these notions, it can be argued that Marx's dispute with the so-called revolutionaries was that they reduced the content of the revolution to 'signality':

> ... the factors of signalization and its correlative, recognition ... are not constituents of language as such. They are dialectically effaced by the new quality of the sign (i.e., of language as such). In the speaker's native language, i.e., for the linguistic consciousness of a member of a particular language community, signal-recognition is certainly dialectically effaced. In the process of mastering a foreign language, signality and recognition still make themselves felt, so to speak, and still remain to be surmounted, the language not yet fully having become language. The ideal of mastering a language is adsorption of signality by pure semioticity and of recognition by pure understanding.[52]

---

51   Marx 2019, pp. 480–1.
52   Voloshinov 1973, p. 69.

This reversion backwards of the revolution is a being dogged down in signality, in the inert state of the passive reception of a signal which thus miscarries the movement towards the not-yet. This tendency, for Voloshinov, is inextricably related to the past, since it mirrors the removal of the ideological thrust of language, that is, the class struggle of the present: 'if we reify linguistic form divorced from ideological impletion, ... then we end up dealing with a signal and not with a sign of language-speech'.[53] What the ruling classes desire is that signality obtain between their ideological messages and the workers, that the otherwise 'multiaccentual' dialogism of the social life of language be reduced to uniaccentual linguistic life.[54] But in dissolving this 'multiaccentual' essence of the sign to a signality, the revolutionaries not only themselves strip out the class struggle from their language, but arguably, at the same time, gloss over the sign's permeation by the 'invariant of direction' that, using Bloch's materialist categories, has been shown to shape language. The revolutionary attempt in question was not ideological enough for Marx, which marked its borrowed language.

In fact, what the revolutionaries serve to do in borrowing language of the past as if it were a 'system of normatively identical forms' is to echo the birth of European linguistics and the latter's 'practical and theoretical' preoccupation with 'the study of defunct, alien languages preserved in written monuments'.[55] As Voloshinov writes:

> This philological orientation has determined the whole course of linguistic thinking in the European world to a very considerable degree ... European linguistic thought formed and matured over concern with the cadavers of written languages; almost all of its basic categories, its basic approaches and techniques were worked out in the process of reviving these cadavers.[56]

This 'philological need' is the very tendency of return that Marx describes in the passage – the revolutionaries resuscitate the cadavers of language.[57] This philological need is tightly tied to the uniaccentual, or signality, for Voloshinov: 'Guided by the philological need, linguistics has always taken as its point of departure the finished monologic utterance – the ancient written monument,

53   Voloshinov 1973, p. 71.
54   See Ives 2004a, pp. 80–1.
55   Voloshinov 1973, p. 71, emphasis removed.
56   Ibid.
57   Ibid, emphasis removed.

considering it the ultimate realium'.[58] Here the study of language, and, by the extension of Marx's passage the present life of language during a revolutionary phase, are determined by a relation, indeed by a relationality which is thoroughly steered backwards towards the past so as to deny its real fulfilment in moving into the new. In both cases what is deemed primary is a reality, an ultimate realium, which has already been achieved, or has already been marked on the historical script of the human species. The revolutionaries become philologists:

> The philologist-linguistic tears the monumental out of that real domain [the ideological domain, N.B.] and views it as if it were a self-sufficient, isolated entity. He brings to bear on it not an active ideological understanding but a completely passive kind of understanding, in which there is not a flicker of response, as there would be in any authentic kind of understanding. The philologist takes the isolated monument as a document of language and places it in relation with other monuments on the general plane of the language in question.[59]

Despite this initial insight Voloshinov provides for reading Marx's passage, once again he is found wanting on the question of the 'what for?' of linguistic production:

> The dead language the linguist studies is, of course, an alien language. Therefore, the system of linguistic categories is least of all a product of cognitive reflection on the part of the linguistic consciousness of a speaker of that language. Here reflection does not involve a native speaker's feeling for his own language. No, this kind of reflection is that of a mind striking out into, break trails through, the unfamiliar world of an alien language.[60]

Voloshinov is right insofar as he draws attention to this philologistic need of linguistics, but he is wrong insofar as he falsely dismisses the unfamiliar in the life of language as wholly tied to the signality of a defunct language. For in Marx it is surely precisely this unfamiliarity – not of the philological kind, but of the new, of the not-yet – that the revolutionary is meant to enter into with both action and speech.

---

58   Voloshinov 1973, p. 72.
59   Voloshinov 1973, p. 73.
60   Ibid.

Grasping the outlines of the context in which Marx penned this text is important in discerning the meaning of the analogy Marx uses. In reading Marx's *Eighteenth Brumaire* passage as consisting of 'a theory of history in which historical protagonists necessarily blind themselves to the social content of their own deeds by dramatically imitating long-dead events',[61] Hartley shows how, in comparison to journalistic censorship, a broader historical censorship is the concern of Marx in this text, one in which a class unconsciously denies its desire as a class in what, as such, constitutes a contrived awakening or phony realisation of a new social form.[62] And as Walker writes, Marx here is attempting to push back against 'the warped mimetic operations of the historical process' and to this end treats the 'gap' between ideological appearance and material reality as his object of analysis.[63] The notion of a 'gap' is crucial to Marx's analysis.

The text, then, concerns precisely an 'anacoluthic juncture' between two fundamental moments of social being, between the old and the possible new. The *Eighteenth Brumaire* is a text in which, as Étienne Balibar writes, Marx 'had tried to account for the paradoxical coexistence of imminent revolution and triumphant counterrevolution in the same conjuncture'.[64] The text is therefore a conjunctural analysis penned in the midst of counter-revolution in Europe. It arises under and is stamped by 'the immediate pressure of events',[65] as Marx says of it, cast in the shadow of defeat for the workers and the pending prospect of a proto-fascist attempt to (always impossibly) resolve the contradictions of capital. The text therefore contains a deep relevance to the contemporary conjuncture,[66] but also to the break in flow that defines the figure of the anacoluthon.

The issue of non-contemporaneity pervades the text. Marx opens it by articulating his notion of active sensuousness, and thus he recapitulates his decisive break with Feuerbach and the Young Hegelians, reiterating the spirit of those other language fragments that have been briefly explored in the previous section: language as collective materiality. While the material object determines the human subject, an object which for Marx consists of an ensemble of social relations, and not a *Gegenstand*, Marx equally resists an otherwise likely dis-

---

61   Hartley 2016, p. 43.
62   Hartley 2016, p. 44.
63   Walker 2019, p. 35.
64   Balibar 2009, p. 63.
65   Marx 2019, p. 477.
66   See Walker 2019, p. 39. Not coincidentally, Walker highlights Bloch's *Heritage of Our Times* as an important Marxist text influenced by the *Eighteenth Brumaire*, see p. 35.

position of materialism to go too far on the scale of such determinism; for collectively human subjects also determine their own history as active agents of their lives, they refract their conditions of existence. Human subjects therefore make their own history, but 'not of their own free will; not under circumstances they themselves have chosen but under the given and inherited circumstances with which they are directly confronted'.[67] Not only does Marx reject an economic determinism, but also pure opportunism. And yet Marx wants to shake the past and move into the not-yet. In this he shares a commonality with the spirit of Expressionism, minus the latter's individualism.

Indeed, the text undergoes a dramatic shift when Marx takes up the matter of revolution. Marx analyses a potentially revolutionary event that nevertheless denies itself, turning to inherited, already tried ideological dispositions to announce and articulate itself. Marx considers a revolutionary moment in social life which refuses its own potentiality to create and move into new historical territory, turning instead to what has been transmitted from the past, which re-orients a movement that otherwise should be forwards backwards on itself. Indeed, just at that moment when 'the revolutionary transformation of themselves and their material surroundings' emerges on the horizon and 'the creation of something which does not yet exist' pre-appears, 'the spirits of the past' are conjured up to reach this new stage in history, the names, the slogans, the attire, which are deployed 'to stage the new world-historical scene in this venerable disguise and borrowed language'.[68] In formulating the revolutionary event in this way, Marx produces a curious analogy:

> ... the beginner who has learnt a new language always retranslates it into his mother tongue: he can only be said to have appropriated the spirit of the new language and to be able to express himself in it freely when he can manipulate it without reference to the old, and when he forgets his original language while using the new one.[69]

Past forms of linguistic becoming are impotent in their capacity to capture the foreseeable proletarian revolution because unlike previous social revolutionary classes, the proletarian revolution does not secure its own way of life but abolishes it, overcoming all class determined forms of living. The content transgresses the phrase precisely because the proletariat's 'true interest lies beyond

---

67   Marx 2019, p. 480.
68   Ibid.
69   Marx 2019, pp. 480–1.

its current way of life'.[70] This concerns what Bloch calls 'the ultimate of total liberation' which 'it is necessary to find anew through magnification and imagination'.[71] Such new and anticipatory desire is barely expressible in language of the past, in 'heroic illusion',[72] as Bloch says. It entails errors and not mimicry.

Webb has rightfully addressed the broad connection of this text with socialist utopianism, although he does not draw specific attention to Marx's deployment of the analogy concerning language. There are, however, two shortcomings with Webb's discussion of this relation between the text and utopia which deserve attention. Marx's immanent critique *within* utopianism is often revoked by those who argued and struggled in his name,[73] despite it not being Marx's aim to destroy or abrogate utopianism, but perfect and fulfil it. There is a certain paradox in Marx's *Brumaire* (1852) text on the score of utopia, however, the 'ahead' of praxis. If in that text Marx scathes the petty-bourgeois democratic forces of 1848–51 precisely for their 'inactive glorification of the anticipated future',[74] as he does the Parisian proletariat – the 'June insurgents'[75] – for their vacuous frontal manoeuvre, described by Marx as 'utopian humbug',[76] how then is one to explain the opening passage of the *Brumaire*, in which a radical break with present social relations, with the absolutisation of the positivity of the present, is proposed as necessary? There Marx announces the need to fully step into the future and leave the past behind; he announces the need to move beyond that 'thought pattern of givenness and facticity', as Bloch says, for which 'the emergent new ... [remains] an embarrassment'.[77] The first shortcoming of Webb's reading of the implicit critique of utopianism within Marx's *Brumaire* text then, relates to the above point insofar as it carries on this tradition of conflating *utopian projections* with what was Marx's proper focus of critique, namely, the revolutionaries' philological reliance on *past images* in conveying upcoming revolutionary content. As Webb writes:

> ... Marx offers a brief historical analysis of the role played by utopian imagery in the process of social and political transformation. The principal conclusion reached by Marx is that utopian phrases have played a

70   See Kavoulakos 2018, p. 186.
71   Bloch 2018, p. 51.
72   Ibid.
73   See Abensour 2016, p. 20.
74   Marx 2019, p. 485. Cf. p. 496.
75   Marx 2019, p. 489.
76   Marx 2019, p. 488.
77   Bloch 2018, p. 100.

compensatory role, serving to disguise the lack of radical emancipatory content in the historical and political movements they have been called upon to justify.[78]

But articulating one's actions in 'clothes borrowed from the past'[79] hardly amounts to a utopian disguise if by utopian is meant a new desire for a better life that has not yet been. Webb, then, ignores 'the cardinal distinction ... between utopias that are inventive, creative, in many respects revolutionary, and those that are repetitive, reproductive of bourgeois society', particularly insofar as the latter disguise the cracks in a society through which the new can be born.[80] And if one follows this distinction between 'a utopia that is only the shadow cast by existing society' and one 'that offers the imaginative expression of a new world',[81] then during the very same historical period with which the *Brumaire* text deals, Marx is placed in the latter camp:

> In the years 1830 to 1848, one can observe in France the constitution of what Michel Foucault called a history of limits precisely in the form of a critique of utopia written very often from a 'pathological' perspective and from the points of view of the existing order. From the elder Blanqui (Adolphe) to Adolphe Thiers, there is a transition from a liberal critique to an openly counterrevolutionary one. The bourgeoisie and its publicists, after having admitted, for the first time, dialogue or confrontation – in the salons of the 1830s it was still good form to speak of utopia and one could support it without renouncing the liberal credo that was so often detrimental to it; a little utopia, provided that it was concrete or realistic, could be useful – soon after threw utopia out on the street among the barbarians and even into the psychiatric asylums, and showed those who would be tempted to take utopias seriously that the bourgeoisie also had a solution to the social question, namely, grapeshot. In the course of the Revolution of 1848, the division is taken to a point of no return and produces the totally reified opposition between reality and utopia. Its consequence is utopia's expulsion from bourgeois society. Utopia, in all its forms, becomes that over which the dominant class exercises its censorship. It will not be surprising that this often obscure

---

78 Webb 2002, p. 246.
79 Ibid.
80 Abensour 2016, p. 22.
81 Ibid. Indeed 'the new utopian spirit gives utopia the freedom Roland Barthes attributes to speech'. (Abensour 2016, p. 42).

discourse had been forgotten. Characteristic of this kind of history is the necessary forgetting, the deepest possible burial of the memory of one class.[82]

Marx's call for the 'dead to bury their dead', for the revolution to unshackle itself from the ideals of the past *was* utopian insofar as it seeks to rupture the ruling tendency of the time to assert the impossibility of utopias. Marx and Engels 'articulate not the point of view of reality, or that of adaptation to the real, but the point of view of the subversion of existing reality, of the revolution that is to disrupt all social spheres'.[83] Far from being anti-utopian, Marx was articulating an intension to smash 'a history of limits',[84] and in doing so he occupied a site *within* utopia, *against* the camp of bourgeois positivism, only then to subject utopia to his own manner of critique.[85] The anti-historicist thrust to Marx here, then, strikes the same chord as the anti-historicist break between past and future which characterises Bloch's conceptualisation of a utopian temporality.[86] Marx's tendency is one of, as Bloch writes, tearing 'itself loose from the superannuated' and reaching 'out to new shores, with the night behind it and the day ahead'.[87] For Bloch, Marx was moved by an 'objective optimism',[88] echoing the early nineteenth century utopianism which was marked, as Abensour says, by 'a fundamental wish to affirmation',[89] by 'a new relation of desire to things that escapes the trap of representation'.[90]

'The trap of representation'. This phrase concerns the second shortcoming of Webb's (post-modernist) tendency to read Marx's position as a form of Wittgensteinian apophaticism: 'the content of the social revolution of the nineteenth century transcends all attempts to phrase it';[91] the revolution is a 'phrase-defying content',[92] and so on. In response to this one could say the following: while Marx was certainly laconic on the content of communism, he never remained *silent* on the matter,[93] nor does he demand the revolutionar-

82   Abensour 2016, p. 18.
83   Abensour 2016, p. 19.
84   Ibid.
85   See Abensour 2016, p. 20. Cf. Rose 2009, pp. 230–1.
86   Beck 2019, p. 97.
87   Bloch 2018, p. 51.
88   Bloch 2018, p. 12.
89   Abensour 2016, p. 27.
90   Abensour 2016, p. 28.
91   Webb 2002, p. 251. See p. 247.
92   Webb 2002, p. 248.
93   See Hudis 2012.

ies to. If it were the case that all new objective content were inexpressible then there would be no language change whatsoever, since language would be incapable of registering and refracting these new objective transformations, of social daydreams. Marx does not ask the revolution to remain silent, but to speak anew without reliance on the past.

What are the effects of all of this for a Marxist philosophy of language? What does the analogy tell us about Marx's view of language during a period of potential revolution? It could be said that Marx identifies a proto-Freudian or 'pre-psychoanalytic'[94] death drive to repetition in the revolutionaries' philological acts – a 'necromancy',[95] or 'a contraction of the present into the past' within, among other domains, linguistic being.[96] We have already seen that Bloch's reading of Freudianism closes in on the otherwise neglected daydream as a manifestation of hunger for transformation: Marx seems to call for the move to a daydream rather than the retrograde shift to the night-dream. Taken on its own terms, Marx's opening passage might lead to a situation which Roberts rallies against:

> ... although emancipation is necessarily tied to the release of speech acts from their prevailing conditions of class restraint, it is impossible to imagine emancipation as directly tied to the release of speech acts *from the process of subjectivication as such* – as if there was an emancipatory speech waiting on the other side of this process of subjectivication.[97]

But the point here is more that Marx deploys a reference to language within a context in which he criticises supposed transformative social forces for their *contemplativeness*. We have here, to paraphrase Bloch, 'the power of ... antique contemplative theory' at the heart of a social force, which keeps that force 'not only in a contemplative miasma, but fixed *in a relationship to what was past* – a relationship built into all contemplation'.[98] Marx demands that this 'spirit of *anamnesis*',[99] 'this granite having-beenness of a matter'[100] be dispensed with, and instead the unfulfilled dream of something that pervades the past of social struggle, and which imprints itself within language, be brought home into a

---

94   Roberts 2011, p. 158.
95   Marx 2019, p. 481.
96   Roberts 2011, p. 135.
97   Roberts 2011, p. 153.
98   Bloch 2018, p. 101.
99   Ibid.
100   Bloch 2018, p. 102.

new social intercourse. In its place there ought to step forth a theoretical attitude which is imbued with real praxis toward the future and 'the unfinished
matter which it illuminates'.[101] As Bloch writes:

> Only so long as humans direct their interest – in an observing contem-
> plative way – towards the past *or* future, both become petrified into a
> foreign being, and between subject and object the unsurpassable 'dead
> space' of the present is stored. As soon, however, as the itself responsive,
> itself dialectical concept is capable of grasping the present as becoming,
> and recognises it in its tendencies out of whose dialectical contradiction
> it is capable of *creating* the future, the present becomes *its* present, at the
> moment of the deepest, widest-branched mediation, at the moment of
> the decision, the birth of the new.[102]

The spirit of Marx's opening passage to the *Brumaire* apparently moves against
the grain of Marx's letter to Ruge, so important for Bloch, which asserts that
'the world has long dreamed of possessing something of which it has only to
be conscious in order to possess it in reality'.[103] Very few thinkers interested
in Bloch's utopianism discuss the *Brumaire* text in relation to his work, and
indeed it is true that Bloch himself has little to say of it. Vincent Geoghegan
is unique in this regard in attempting to address Bloch and the text together
with the aim of illuminating the stakes of a contemporary move towards post-
secularism.[104] Despite this not being my theme here, Geoghegan makes some
useful observations, and briefly touches on Marx's language-analogy without
however espousing or touching on a (Marxian nor Blochian) philosophy of
language.[105] Firstly, Geoghegan notes that Marx's pronouncement for a radical break with the past, ironically captured in Marx's debt to the Bible with
his reference to 'let the dead bury their dead', connects with what Bloch calls
Jesus's 'morality of an advent world'.[106] Turning then to Derrida, Geoghegan
notes that Marx's text teaches that the spectre of the future can also haunt the
present just as can the past.[107] And finally, he makes the related point that the
non-contemporaneity at the heart of Marx's text – its opening passage being

---

101   Bloch 2018, p. 103.
102   Bloch in Moir 2020, p. 18.
103   Marx 1987b, p. 144.
104   See Geoghegan 2002.
105   Geoghegan 2002, p. 9.
106   Bloch 1986, p. 1263. See Geoghegan 2002, pp. 7 and 11.
107   Geoghegan 2002, p. 10.

'a meditation on the complex modalities of the past in the present' – relates to Bloch's key category of *Ungleichzeitigkeit*,[108] decisive in Bloch's analysis of fascism. And as Walker writes, Marx's text

> ... is an intervention into our received and dominant way of thinking the relationship between the past and the present, an intervention that emphasizes, above all else, the presence of the past, not as the past, but as social forms that we inherit in the present: characters, narratives, modes of creating oppositions and complementarities, linguistic forms for our social reality, and forms of thought through which ideology intersects with material interest.[109]

Marx, then, inserts non-contemporaneity into the active sensuousness that defines the object as a social relationality. As such, this social relationality is not entirely with itself, but not only because the social is riven with 'the history of class struggles'[110] (Marx's cold stream). Rather, the social totality does not form a unified whole also because its present moments are strewn with the temporality of the past as well as with future possibilities. As Howard notes, Marx's acknowledgment of the existence of non-contemporary contradictions, non-reducible to the present mode of production, is really only taken up by *Bloch* as a Marxist, who seriously extends this obscure tendency of a 'polyrhythmic Now' within Marx.[111] Not only is society riven with class contradictions, but the present moment in which that composition of class relations finds itself is a contradiction of times, and therefore the now is dark to itself. This latter point goes to the heart of Bloch's objection to Lukács, which I will return to later on.

This can be tied back to my earlier criticism of Webb. This is because, during the same period in which the events that are covered by the *Brumaire* were playing themselves out in real time, in the *Communist Manifesto* (1848) Marx and Engels assert that the fundamental coordinates of the relationality between conditionedness and openness are expressive of two radically different types of social being: 'In bourgeois society ... the past dominates the present; in Communist society, the present dominates the past'.[112] In other words, it is not in the case of language past linguistic forms which hold sway over the objective content of the present, but the objective content of the

---

108   Geoghegan 2002, p. 14. Cf. Howard 2019.

109   Walker 2019, p. 34.

110   Marx and Engels 1976b, p. 482.

111   Howard 2019, p. 57.

112   Marx and Engels 1976b, p. 499.

present, and the ascending class power which owns that content, which holds sway over and which organises past linguistic forms to its own, *new* ends. Deploying the Jewish thinker Martin Buber, Marx's concern here could be initially named as one of a revolt against language's 'potential possession';[113] that is, as Buber writes, against the 'damned up basin of possession' of language:[114] 'The place of possession is the sum of what in a language, up to a certain period of time, has been spoken and written in all its forms of preservation'.[115] But it is a revolt against taking up this possession as if it were crafted of pure signality, and not itself semiotic.

What then did Bloch himself write of the *Eighteenth Brumaire* text? Geoghegan notes that for Bloch the *Brumaire* remained an unimportant text precisely because Bloch was not interested in burying the dead, and that, we are told, in his *Natural Law and Human Dignity*, Bloch 'seeks to draw teeth from the text', interpreting it very much against the grain of Marx's original intention to shirk the past.[116] Here the claim is that Bloch opted for Marx's letter to Ruge rather than the latter's analysis of Bonaparte. But are the two themes that different? Bloch demonstrates a quite different approach elsewhere, which Geoghegan fails to address in his treatment. In *The Principle of Hope* a clear connection is established by Bloch between the *Brumaire* text and the darkness of the lived moment: 'The situation-analyses of Marx and Engels give the most splendid example of *fathomed* presence of mind, headed by the "Eighteenth Brumaire"'.[117] Bloch's statement emerges in a section of *The Principle of Hope* which focuses on the darkness of the just lived moment, which is located in the larger part on 'Anticipatory Composition and its Poles: Dark Moment – Open Adequacy'. Arguably, then, for Bloch the *Eighteenth Brumaire* concerned the tendency and latency of material process on the front of possibility:

> If something is properly realized, life comes to the place where it has never been, that is, it comes home. In this possible realization of something still possible, however, two moments *ultimately* constitute source and outflow. The source is characterized by the *darkness of the Now*, in which realization rises, the outflow by the *openness of the object-based background*, towards which hope goes.[118]

---

113   Buber 1961, p. 353.
114   Buber 1961, p. 354.
115   Ibid.
116   Geoghegan 2002, p. 13.
117   Bloch 1986, p. 294.
118   Bloch 1986, pp. 288–9.

The structure of a relationality between *conditionedness* and *openness*, actuality and possibility, is at play in Marx's work, and his infamous opening passage to the *Brumaire* expresses this relation with reference to language. Marx provides an inception in language theorisation that concerns *the relationship between old and new language material*. It therefore concerns the relationship between old and new consciousness, and thus old and new social being. It concerns the question of 'a praxis that moves ahead'[119] as opposed to one that remains sealed in the coordinates of already-become actuality, in which, to paraphrase Lecercle, there is an ideological constraint on 'the production of utterances'.[120] But to return home for Bloch means to arrive at the new, and not to move back to one's native tongue.

For Bloch, Marx's communism is a form of social being in which possibility within the 'now' holds precedence over an encrusted actuality that otherwise would drag the 'now' back to a condition of repetition, that is, to a condition of pre-history. The revolutionary philosophy of communism prefigures and articulates a society in which '[t]he present dominates, *together with the horizon it contains*, which is the horizon of the future, that provides the flux of the present with its specific space – the space and scope of a new and practicable better present'.[121] Communism is a form of social being which 'opens ultimately at and in *the horizon of the future*; with the knowledge of the New, and with power to take the way to it'.[122] But what is the new here? Utopian thought is often said to constitute a negative ideal at odds with the reality (the possibilities within reality) of a current moment; 'a negative ideal ... opposed to empirical consciousness',[123] 'dwelling in a realm distinct from real social relations'.[124] 'It has no *presence* as the communal achievement (*Werk*) of existing individuals, and can only be represented as *beyond* real existence'.[125] But if the problem with utopia is that its content lacks real presence in the present, so then Bloch will locate it in presence as such, in the darkness of the present and its lived moment.

Marx's *Brumaire* passage, then, seems to be stamped with the notion of a linguistic utterance with Front. Revolution is always a moment on this linguistic Front into the open where a potential homecoming is intimated. Echo-

---

119   Bloch 2018, p. 89.
120   Lecercle 2008, p. 489.
121   Bloch 2018, p. 100.
122   Ibid.
123   Rose 2009, p. 74.
124   Rose 2009, p. 80.
125   Rose 2009, p. 80.

ing Pasolini's engagement with Gramsci on the language question, one could move between theory and the life of the thinker,[126] developing a biographical note to partially explain Marx's analogy as one that concerns this Front. It could communicate the integral relation of theory and praxis in Marx's work. Thrown into the life of agitation alongside the Parisian radicals, Marx began to speak French fluently. Exiled from Germany he fled to Paris – ('French was nearly a second mother tongue for Marx').[127] At the hands of the French authorities Marx subsequently moved to Brussels, a city at one remove from the hub of worker agitation, when during that period Dutch was spoken as the majority language (Marx having had no familiarity with Dutch despite his mother's origins).[128] Eventually Marx spoke English, having lived the last decades of his life in London writing *Capital*. But for a period English, industrial capitalism's homeland, 'still seemed quite exotic' to Marx; early on Marx would still quote Adam Smith from the French.[129] This life of agitation may well have taught Marx that a revolutionary existence transcends any one native tongue. The internationalist content of communist revolution transcends any given national phrase in a revolutionary culture.[130] It was, after all, this transgression of national boundaries which allowed Marx to discover land: the historical materialist terrain. Marx's very historical materialist conception of society was born of an *inter*nationalism of conceptual matrices which were acknowledged as unique to, and indexes of, given cultural territories. His growing familiarity and cross-conceptualisations of British economic thought (Ricardo, Smith), German philosophy (primarily Hegel), and French political theory were key of course.[131]

Marx's revolutionary-peripatetic life could have, then, given rise to a certain linguistic insight – 'many critical linguistic insights are generated from people who are considered out of place or are displaced'.[132] Perhaps Marx meant to imply by this analogy that proletarians must unite across their national borders, relinquish their attachments to their mother tongues and to their

---

126   See Mariniello 1994, pp. 113–17.

127   Liedman 2018, p. 158.

128   Liedman 2018, p. 167.

129   Liedman 2018, p. 158.

130   See Ali 2019, p. xii.

131   See Boothman 2010, p. 115 and Liedman 2018, p. 192. Cf. Ives 2004b, p. 112.

132   Heller and McElhinny 2017, p. 12. Bloch can be counted among such exiles, not only in the more literal sense – Bloch was exiled no fewer than three times – but also in the sense that he occupied intellectual positions which stood close to or outside of the 'traditional Marxist pale', as Martin Jay (1984, pp. 174–5) puts it.

national materialities, and renounce their national consciousness, forgoing the narrower social being of which that consciousness is an expression.[133] Marx, though, did not subscribe to the creation of a common, universal language, along the lines of an Esperanto.[134] 'Though we are educated to differ one from the other in the use of sounds as the natural means to express and communicate this inner feeling [of universal brotherhood] to each other', so Wilhelm Weitling said, as recounted by Engels – nevertheless, that feeling, despite these linguistic differences, 'cannot be extinguished'.[135] What is this inextinguishable element? What is this *logos* common to the working classes of each nation? Marx writes in the *Brumaire* that contrary to the bourgeois revolutions of the eighteenth century,

> Proletarian revolutions ... such as those of the nineteenth century, constantly engage in self-criticism, and in repeated interruptions of their own course. They return to what has apparently already been accomplished in order to begin the task again; with merciless thoroughness they mock the inadequate, the weak and wretched aspects of their first attempts; draw new strength from the earth and rise again and again before the indeterminate immensity of their own goals, until the situation is created in which any retreat is impossible, and the conditions themselves cry out: *Hic Rhodus, hic salta!* Here is the rose, dance here![136]

Proletarian revolutions are therefore anacoluthic, and we can say that the common *logos* that unites the working classes of all nations is the anacoluthon – what Bloch termed 'the music of reason'. The anacoluthon's musical rationality, in Bloch's sense of 'seeing around a corner', and Marx's reference to 'here is the rose, dance here', are, I would argue, of a piece. Marx's reference here is to Hegel's own in the Preface of the *Philosophy of Right*,[137] to Aesop's fable 'The Braggart', in which an otherwise unsuccessful and much mocked athlete departs his town only to return to boast of performing an unimaginable leap at Rhodes. Upon hearing the story a bystander exhorts: 'Here is Rhodes,

---

133   Cf. Poulantzas 2014, p. 118.
134   As Heller and McElhinny note, International Auxiliary Languages (IALS), although created or imagined within a strictly European context, at least initially, were 'one manifestation of a general liberal democratic movement of internationalism produced to regulate competition and conflict'. (Heller and McElhinny 2017, p. 128).
135   Engels 1976, p. 12.
136   Marx 2019, p. 484.
137   See Hegel 1991, pp. 21–2.

[jump here]'.[138] Hegel seems to have deployed the fable as an anti-utopian pun
to set the record straight on the task of philosophy:

> To comprehend *what is* is the task of philosophy, for *what is* is reason. As
> far as the individual is concerned, each individual is in any case a *child of
> his time*; thus philosophy, too, is *its own time comprehended in thoughts*. It
> is just as foolish to imagine that any philosophy can transcend its contem-
> porary world as that an individual can overleap his own time or leap over
> Rhodes. If his theory does indeed transcend his own time, if it builds itself
> a world *as it ought to be*, then it certainly has an existence, but only within
> his opinions – a pliant medium in which the imagination can construct
> anything it pleases.[139]

Hegel thus pours scorn on the idea that the peak of reason could be discerned
in any other time than the present, that reason could be located in an 'ought to
be' preoccupied with the future and fashioned in (wild) imagination. One must
'recognize reason as the rose in the cross of the present and thereby ... delight in
the present'; Hegel thereby puns both the double meaning of the Greek '*Rhodus*'
('Rhodes', 'rose') and the Latin '*salta*' ('jump', 'dance') in his altered translation:
'*Here* is the rose, dance *here*'.[140] The present and its labour of the negative – 'the
cross of the present' – is always the best place to begin, rather than with a jump
to a place that nowhere exists.[141] But does not Marx want us to forget the old
and to focus on the present precisely so as to enter the new, to move to what
has not-yet been? As Mieszkowski notes of Marx's reference to Hegel's 'here is
the rose, dance here':

> As it turns out, the Greek that Hegel presents as the 'original' quotation
> is actually a hybrid of the two existing Greek versions of Aesop's fable,
> the one translated by Erasmus together with a second in which the rel-
> evant line reads: 'Look – Rhodes, and leap off from (it)!' In creating his
> own Greek version of Aesop and then 'complementing' it with Erasmus's
> Latin translation of one of the two standard versions, Hegel juxtaposes
> two lines from two foreign languages as if the one were a translation of
> the other, when in fact it is not. By the time Hegel arrives at his rewrit-
> ing of the Latin in German as 'Here is the rose, here dance', it is virtually

---

138   See Hegel 1991, pp. 390–1n24–6 and Marx 2019, p. 484n19.
139   Hegel 1991, pp. 21–2.
140   Hegel 1991, p. 22.
141   For a discussion of utopia and translation in Bloch, see Moir and Siebers 2011.

impossible to determine what motivates his individual 'emendations'. ... Having called on the revolutionaries of the nineteenth century to go beyond the traditional play of living and dead languages, Marx punctuates his account of the linguistic mobilization of the proletariat by coming close to quoting Hegel's near-quotation, or misquotation, an exercise in misprision that spans three languages, living and dead. Although Hegel and Marx both claim to craft a discourse of the here and now, their use of such citations confounds the relationship between the putative proximity and contemporaneity of German and the then and there of the Greek and Latin. If Hegel 'quotes' Aesop, or some fabular hybrid of Aesop, in order to emphasize the importance of philosophy not attempting to exceed its own time, Marx's mobilization of Aesop, Erasmus, and Hegel reveals Hegel's citational practice to be a challenge to the possibility of ever knowing if the language one is speaking is one of the past, present, or future.[142]

Indeed this obscurity of language may signal its occupation of the darkness of the lived moment:

Having presented us with a Latin citation and its German 'translation', [Marx] simply begins a new paragraph and starts making some relatively mundane observations about the events of 1848. ... we have a single sentence presented in two languages, as if to suggest that the best slogans occur in a tongue we may not understand. Far from direct and immediate in substance and consequence, the revolutionary battle cry is an exhortation that must, like the Bible, be translated.[143]

Recent work on a theory of language in Gramsci's body of writings advances the idea that translation must be grasped metaphorically, not literally. Translation does not name the process of converting one natural language into another, but rather the process of conveying one set of 'national realities and experiences'[144] through another set. These realities and experiences cannot, for Gramsci, be divorced from the real life of a language. In the Fourth Congress of the Comintern in 1922, Lenin laments that 'We have not learnt how to present our Russian experience to foreigners'.[145] Of course the failure of the Russian Revolution to

---

142   Mieszkowski 2019, pp. 67–8.
143   Mieszkowski 2019, p. 66.
144   Boothman 2010, p. 114.
145   Lenin cited in Boothman 2010, p. 109.

translate beyond its initial borders ties the concept of translation to counter-revolution just as much as it does to revolution itself: 'what brings both the fascist and the Stalinist counter-revolution into the space of counter-revolution generally is the freezing up of working-class politics inside national and patriotic borders'.[146] Gramsci, for whom revolution and the concept of translation are deeply connected, translates Lenin's statement with a substitution of '*tradurre* [translate]' for the original 'present', thereby opening up a broader notion of translation in the context of revolution.[147] In this light Marx's passage, set alongside his own reference to Hegel's pun, would seem to demand that the revolutionary not simply translate their national reality and experiences into that of another language, for this simply reiterates the bourgeois notion of language as a transferral of information. The notion of translation that Mieszkowski suggests underpins Marx's comment that 'the indeterminate immensity' of the proletariat's goals makes 'any retreat ... impossible' and which 'the conditions themselves cry out' for,[148] is not a literal notion of translation:

> A transference of the October Revolution into Italy would look more like a re-enactment, a theatrical event, or a 'farce' – as Marx speaks of in the *Eighteenth Brumaire* – than a revolution that could completely alter the structure of Italian society. 'Revolution', then, does not signify a content that can be transmitted into a different context, a different society. It is itself a relational concept. Its referent is not a static object, state, idea, blue-print, or theory, but rather a dynamic relationship among elements within a society.[149]

The task of a translation, then, is one of loosening the revolution from translating itself backwards into the prior history of its own national political and

---

146   Roberts 2011, p. 180.

147   See Ives 2004b, pp. 100–3.

148   Marx 2019, p. 484.

149   Ives 2004b, p. 102. Ives's commentary on Gramsci does not directly discuss Marx's *Brumaire* analogy. This may be why Ives fails to critically consider the backward trajectory (the layers of past meaning) which praises in meaning's social mutability as retrograde (see Ives 2004b, pp. 101–2). As he writes: since 'language is historically produced and always contains past meanings, traces, and sediments, every sign always has possible multiple meanings, and moreover, there can be "future" new meanings. ... Language used without consciousness of its past – including its multiaccentuality, its non-parthenogenetic history, its metaphoricity – is severely limited in expressing the life of individuals, especially as that life changes and grows'. (Ives 2004b, p. 93).

cultural coordinates, to that element of society which is not-yet and which refracts itself in the loquacity of the proletariat. An act of translation in this sense does not consist of an act of transferring the inessential information of a revolutionary event beyond its national borders of emergence, but rather is an act of translating, as Ives puts it, a process of 'realization',[150] a processual relation of possibility to actuality. The possibility of the revolution's 'translatability'[151] is precisely a possibility, and possibility is always oriented towards a future realisation. If the revolution is not ready-made, if it is not handed down from the past, then nor is this the solely determining characteristic of a language that is required to articulate it. Language cannot be viewed as 'a ready-made artefact handed down from one generation to another'.[152] Marx demands anacoluthic language in the process of translation within this context:

> In German ... 'translation' ('*übersetzen*') does not have the same 'traitorous' resonances as in Latin or Italian. As opposed to the lateral direction of 'trans-', '*über*' is a preposition for 'up' and 'over' as well as 'across'. '*Setzen über*' is 'to leap' or 'to jump' over something. This vertical movement – coupled with the metaphor of height with the divine, the heavenly, progress, achievement, and a general positive sentiment – carries with it very different resonances than the English or Italian term for translation.[153]

The task is not one of translating backwards to old linguistic material, but forwards – the act of jumping forwards linguistically, with its material content. Not only does '*übersetzen*' imply a leap toward something better, but it relinquishes that common conception of translation which holds its purpose and essence as the mere transferal of an original (text, revolutionary event) into a different language: it implies a movement into something new. Marx wants to escape a backward trajectory of a production of utterances – what is to be done is *not* a mimesis of an origin-al – which otherwise burrows itself in human loquacity. Voloshinov was alert to the very same regressive, philological tendency,[154] but Mario Tronti is perhaps that Marxist who has most forcibly expressed this objection to a glance towards an original: 'The working-class point of view has

---

150   Ives 2004b, p. 102.
151   Ives 2004b, p. 103.
152   Voloshinov 1973, p. 77.
153   Ives 2004b, pp. 103–4. Cf. p. 106.
154   Voloshinov 1973, p. 80.

no interest in defining the upheavals of the past using the concept of "revolutions".[155] *Here is Rhodes, jump here.* Later in the *Brumaire* text, Marx will point in this direction:

> The social revolution of the nineteenth century can only create its poetry from the future, not from the past. It cannot begin its own work until it has sloughed off all its superstitious regard for the past. Earlier revolutions have needed world-historical reminiscences to deaden their awareness of their own content. In order to arrive at its own content the revolution of the nineteenth century must let the dead bury their dead. Previously the phrase transcended the content; here the content transcends the phrase.[156]

A content that transcends the phrase means that the phrase is refracted by a content language has never known before – the effect of this on language is the same stuttering as seen in the anacoluthon. New social material emerges which ought to be expressed – which ought to find its mouthpiece – to *aid* its coming. If the content transcends the phrase, that is, as Marx implies, if the actual conditions of social life break through their current linguistic refraction, so then, rather than, as Webb has suggested, the phrase is seen lagging behind the tendency-latency of material process in a state of inept silence, *the phrase must transcend itself.* In the *Grundrisse*, Marx develops a line of thought with reference to language that is of a similar nature to the analogy in the *Brumaire* passage:

> (To compare money with blood – the term circulation gave occasion for this – is about as correct as Menenius Agrippa's comparison between the patricians and the stomach.) (To compare money with language is not less erroneous. Language does not transform ideas, so that the peculiarity of ideas is dissolved and their social character runs alongside them as a separate entity, like prices alongside commodities. Ideas do not exist separately from language. Ideas which have first to be translated out of their mother tongue into a foreign language in order to circulate, in order to become exchangeable, offer a somewhat better analogy; but the analogy then lies not in language, but in the foreignness of language.)[157]

---

155   Tronti 2019, pp. 249–50. Cf. Hartley 2016, p. 3 on a Marxist poetics.
156   Marx 2019, p. 483.
157   Marx 1993, pp. 162–3. Cf. Berardi 2019, pp. 151–7, who does not find it erroneous.

This reference to the 'foreignness of language' could of course simply relate to that work which concerns the translator, converting English prose into, say, Italian or French. But could it also be the case that this 'foreignness of language' is within language itself, whatever the language may be? This would refer back to the inherent tendency of language to transcend its given socio-conditions of possibility, in doing so distorting the presentation of that reality through its refraction of it. As we have seen, Bloch places the darkness of the lived moment at the centre of his materialism. The 'foreignness of language' could be situated within the context of the incomplete being at the centre of all loquacious production, which draws language and the conscious being of which it expresses forward beyond the given coordinates of the 'now'. However, the radical break with the past that Marx seems to want jars with Bloch's notion that the 'invariant of direction' of material process, which Weitling himself refers to, is an inextinguishable element that is preserved and alive *both* in the past and the present. To Bloch's mind this 'invariant of direction' arises in Marx's famous letter to Arnold Ruge of 1843:

> It will then become evident that the world has long dreamed of possessing something of which it has only to be conscious in order to possess it in reality. It will become evident that it is not a question of drawing a great mental dividing line between past and future, but of *realising* the thoughts of the past. Lastly, it will become evident that mankind is not beginning a *new* work, but is consciously carrying into effect its old work.[158]

This is perhaps Bloch's most prized of Marx's writings, for 'it represents an absolutely original utterance' and a '*completely new* point of view in respect of the past'.[159] The letter demonstrates that 'Marxism never renounces … the primal intention: … the *dream of the Golden Age*'.[160] Rather it wants to be a vehicle through which 'a future unfulfilled in the past'[161] is fulfilled now in the present. How then to square Marx's radical modernist break with the past, implied in his *Brumaire* analogy, and which wants the utterance to speak from a non-verbal situatedness of a material present pointing towards the future, and Bloch's suggestion that the past itself contains unfulfilled hope of a better life, and which itself can be put into action for the new that is coming up?

---

158   Marx 1987b, p. 144.
159   Bloch 2018, p. 28.
160   Bloch 2018, p. 36.
161   Bloch 2018, p. 130.

3   The Expressionism Debate

From a Blochian perspective, Voloshinov's construal of the 'non-verbal situatedness' of the utterance misses the most crucial part of material being: its real
incompleteness. This real incompleteness stands as the We-mystery of social
life, which necessarily implies, for Bloch, the possibility of arrival, of a home
that we have not yet been to. If one were permitted to frame the issue in categories given by Bloch then it could be said that in Voloshinov's theory the
'non-verbal situatedness' of the utterance is far too much in the grip of tendency without, however, the latency within it. Despite, then, the realist trappings
at the heart of Voloshinov's philosophy of language (that materialist category
of tendency is certainly what defines the multiaccentuality of the sign), there
remains a neo-Kantian severance operating between the utterance and what
for Bloch is the realest dimension of material being's extra-linguistic reality.
There is a poverty of arrival.

    More light can be shed on this difference, between Bloch and Voloshinov,
concerning the non-verbal situatedness of the utterance, if we turn to Bloch's
dispute with Lukács on the score of utopia – a dispute which would later play
itself out in their Expressionism debate. The latter is directly tied to a similar aesthetic debate concerning Formalism that took place in Russia after the
revolution, in which Voloshinov and the wider Bakhtin Circle participated, and
one can gain a better sense of Bloch's relation to Voloshinov through a discussion which picks up the common threads of the German Expressionism
controversy and the debate which took place on Russian Formalism.

    Though Voloshinov had criticised the Russian Formalists for their separation
of form and content, and, therefore, following Medvedev's critique of Hermann
Cohen's aesthetics, the Formalists are said to be incapable of knowing what
the real material being is that determines the aesthetic work,[162] Voloshinov's
attempt to bring the two back together itself remains, from a Blochian view-
point, also formalistic. What is important here is that Voloshinov's critique
of Russian Formalism closely mirrors the Expressionism Debate which unfol-
ded between key Marxist thinkers during the course of the first half of the
twentieth century. In a sense, Voloshinov's position vis-à-vis relationality, outlined in the previous chapter, reflects the same tendency which Bloch imputes
to Lukács's *History and Class Consciousness* (1923) on the question of totality
and its relation to the not-yet. This dispute between Bloch and Lukács under-
writes and impresses upon their differences concerning the Expressionist aes-

---

162   See Brandist 2002a, pp. 66–7.

thetic, its 'cultural-political' heritage, as Bloch put it, which directly tied it to a debate concerning it associations with fascism, despite Hitler later denouncing Expressionism as degenerate art.[163] Broadly put, the Expressionist aesthetic 'rebel[s] against dominant assimilation' by revealing the diremption between meaning and configuration.[164] Bloch was taken to represent *the* philosopher of the German Expressionist movement, primarily due to his dislocatory Expressionist style,[165] but he is also associated with the movement because of his staunch defence of it against Lukács's assaults on it.

The connection between German Expressionism and Russian Formalism is not hard to establish. Beck has noted that the Expressionism debate reflected a wider dispute within socialist thinking concerning aesthetics and artistic style. The confrontational dialogue that was staged earlier between Bloch and Voloshinov is not therefore without real traction with a dispute that took place within Marxism itself during the first half of the twentieth century. Here, I will roughly outline the coordinates of the Expressionism debate and show how it relates to the preceding discussion concerning language. Bloch and Lukács (and other thinkers associated with Marxism, including Adorno and Brecht) took part in a protracted debate in an attempt to assess and decide over the political-cultural value of German Expressionism. Their quite different conclusions tie into their respective readings of utopia and fascism. These conclusions closely parallel the conceptions of relationality that Bloch and Voloshinov have each been shown to develop. Firstly, the fates of Russian Formalism and German Expressionism are closely bound together, as Humberto Beck highlights:

---

163 Bloch 1992, pp. 16–7.

164 Rose 2009, pp. 156–7. For a pertinent study on the historical context of German Expressionism, see Bushart's (1990) *Der Geist der Gotik und die expressionistische Kunst*, in which the tendencies of socialism, utopianism, expressionism and gothic revival (tendencies which are all discernible in Bloch's first book) are woven into an illuminating explication of the immediate post-First World War production of German art.

165 Steiner is well aware of this connection between Expressionism and Bloch's philosophical style of expression: 'Like few other masters of German, he has broken the generically ponderous, clotted norms of German syntax'. (Steiner 1985, p. 113). Adorno is also attuned to the rich, versatile and 'expressionist tempo' of Bloch's medium of delivery: 'Its intensity is that of something to be expressed, the breakthrough that, explicitly or implicitly, forms the theme of every sentence Bloch ever wrote, a breakthrough he tries to evoke through the figure of his speech'. (Adorno 2008, p. 216). Bloch's style of writing is not my concern here. For discussions of Bloch's style, see Richter 2000, p. 107, Geoghegen 1996, p. 30, Holz 1975, pp. 38–43 and Bense 1978, p. 71. For a comment on the general intellectual backdrop behind Bloch's renewed philosophical expression, see Gluck 1985, pp. 143–73.

The Expressionism Debate was one manifestation of a much larger discussion over the role of artistic style in socialism. In the Soviet Union the debate found a dramatic analogue in the anti-Formalist campaign of 1936–1939, launched amid show trials and intensified political repression of the Stalinist Great Purge.[166]

Bennett has made a parallel point. The Association of Revolutionary Proletarian Writers (BPRS) was a key site from which Soviet influence took place in German debates over aesthetics, so much so that 'the dispersal of the Formalist and Futurists coincided, in Germany, with the defeat of Expressionism within the affairs of the BPRS and the consolidation of "the Lukács line" '.[167] This line refers to Lukács's assessment of Expressionism which traces this movement directly to fascism, drawing evidence in particular from the prominent Expressionist poet Gottfried Benn's transition to National Socialism, a thesis forwarded in particular by Lukacs's protégé, Alfred Kurella.[168] In Lukács's reckoning, Expressionism represented a dissolution of aesthetic realism, since it abounded in rejections of the need to reflect objective reality and was instead preoccupied with portraying the experience of immediacy in a stage of social disintegration during the age of capitalist imperialism.[169] Expressionists were abstractly subjectivist, 'frozen in their own immediacy', since they remained incapable of progressing beyond this level of immediacy by relating their experience of discontinuity and disintegration to the wider objective conditions and social forces which generated such immediate experience.[170] 'When the surface of life is only experienced immediately, it remains opaque, fragmentary, chaotic and uncomprehended'.[171] Fragmentation is taken to represent social totality itself, but here the appearance is taken as the essence, and Expressionist art is thereby impotent in ideologically anticipating real social tendencies such as Voloshinov would have assigned to the unofficial conscious – realism for Lukács meant not simply taking a photograph that 'mirrors the original' but grasping its more submerged future tendencies as tendencies of real social being.[172] Realism portrays 'man in the whole range of his relations to the real world'.[173]

---

166   Beck 2019, p. 114.
167   Bennett 2003, p. 30.
168   See Taylor 1990, p. 9 and Bloch 1992, p. 16.
169   See Lukács 1992, pp. 29–34.
170   Lukács 1992, pp. 36–7.
171   Lukács 1992, p. 39.
172   Lukács 1992, pp. 46–8.
173   Lukács 1992, p. 48.

Lukács, then, did not deny that ideological productions at the level of the superstructure were able to anticipate future social tendencies; he did, however, reject the idea that Expressionism itself did or was capable of so prophetically grasping the future of social being. This was because, for him, Expressionism, in its subjectivism, was inheritor to a broader 'formalist modernism, bereft of content'; similar to Russian Formalism, Expressionism, for Lukács, only anticipated new *aesthetic movements* (e.g. Surrealism) and not genuine objective changes in the social totality.[174] This is why, besides Trotsky's more favourable but still distorting and contradictory treatment of the Russian Formalists, which precluded a serious engagement of Marxism with Formalism, it is Lukács's 'line' that curtailed a fruitful encounter between Marxism and Formalism.[175] An important issue at the root of these debates is the question of totality, and the way that totality is understood will have implications for the way the proper core of language is grasped.

Expressionism's supposed 'anti-realist bias'[176] was fundamentally no problem for Bloch. The crux of Bloch's retort to Lukács's critique of Expressionism turns on 'the problems of the dialectical-materialist theory of reflection (*Abbildlehre*)'.[177] Lukács's conceptual framework for negatively assessing the Expressionist aesthetic is clothed in an admiration for classicism, in an 'undiluted objective realism'.[178] It is a 'continuous [*ununterbrochene*] 'totality'' in which 'the subjective factor has no place'; an 'objectively-closed concept of reality' without 'interruption' which leads Lukács to evaluate Expressionism unfavourably.[179] The following extended quotation of Bloch's without doubt bears a marked similarity to Bloch's rejoinder to Lukács's rejection of utopianism. The passage thereby serves to demonstrate the close proximity that utopianism and Expressionism both shared for Bloch and for Lukács:

> Lukács's thought takes for granted a closed and integrated reality that does indeed exclude the subjectivity of idealism, but not the seamless 'totality' which has always thriven best in idealist systems ... Whether such a totality in fact constitutes reality, is open to question. If it does, then Expressionist experiments with disruptive and interpolative techniques are but an empty *jeu d'esprit*, as are the more recent experiments

---

174   Lukács 1992, pp. 48–9.
175   See Bennett 2003, pp. 23 and 30.
176   Lukács 1992, p. 51.
177   Bloch 1992, p. 22.
178   See Bloch 1992, pp. 18 and 21–2.
179   Bloch 1971b, pp. 157–8.

with montage and other devices of discontinuity. But what if Lukács's reality – a coherent, infinitely mediated totality – is not so objective after all? What if his conception of reality has failed to liberate itself completely from Classical systems? What if authentic reality is also discontinuity?[180]

For Bloch, to reflect (*abbilden*) reality is always to refract it in the form of a *fortbilden*, a forming-forwards. For Bloch Expressionism was such a forming-forwards at the level of the superstructure, an anticipatory movement[181] whose 'themes were almost exclusively human expressions of the incognito, the mystery of man'.[182] This is not to say that Bloch did not recognise (and accept Lukács's assessment of) the subjectivism within it, nor the vague, sometimes pacifist opposition to bourgeois culture which blunted any possibility of class struggle, nor indeed its 'lifeless categories' (non-concrete) of the human being.[183] But it was certainly not for Bloch bound to lead to fascism by necessity. It was art which strove 'to exploit the *real* fissures in surface inter-relations and to discover the new in their crevices'.[184]

This critical reading of Lukács's notion of totality is not without its detractors of course, and there is good evidence that Bloch slightly misplaced his target here.[185] Be that as it may, Bloch took Lukács's approach to Expressionism as exemplifying an Hegelian closure of totality on itself, and, for my purpose here, it is important to note that Lukács's construal of totality in *History and Class Consciousness* exemplifies the same attitude that Bloch sees as detrimental to Lukács's negative assessment of Expressionism. Significant here is that this time in this text Lukács aims his realist reflection theory against utopianism. Indeed, Lukács took Bloch's utopian attitude as entirely detrimental to the workers' cause. Lukacs's 'funeral oration on Expressionism',[186] his repudiation of its aesthetic, resonates strongly with his assertion of utopianism's impotence, as it is located in *History and Class Consciousness*. Below I will briefly outline Lukács's comments on utopianism in the *History and Class Consciousness* text as well as Bloch's 1923 review of Lukács's book, 'Actuality and Utopia'.

---

180   Bloch 1991, p. 22.
181   See Bloch 1992, p. 20.
182   Bloch 1992, p. 24.
183   See Bloch 1992, pp. 19 and 24. Cf. Lukács 1992, p. 51.
184   Bloch 1992, p. 22. For Lukács (1992, p. 55) Expressionism's emphasis on rupture was just as un-dialectical as Reformism's emphasis on continuity: both sides of social process had to be grasped dialectically as forming a unity.
185   For a critique of this reading of Lukács, see Kavoulakos 2018, pp. 84–5.
186   Bloch 1992, p. 17.

It must be borne in mind that throughout the text Lukács's references to 'utopia' are always implicitly references to Bloch. The retrospective 1967 Preface to the new edition of *History and Class Consciousness* is a good place to start. Lukács emphasises that this text constitutes 'the summation' of a 'period of development' in which his 'messianic utopianism' lessened its 'grip' on his theoretical work,[187] and he then goes on clearly to distinguish the 'messianic utopianism of the Communist left', on the one hand, and the 'authentic Marxist doctrine', on the other.[188] He describes his earlier utopian phase (largely defined by his interest in aesthetics) as nothing but 'idealism'.[189] Recall that it was Lukács's subscription to a classicist-realist notion of totality without the (idealist) subjective factor which leads Bloch to assign *Lukács* to idealism.

In the main body of the original text, Lukács outlines his theoretical-practical opposition to utopia. Firstly, Lukács regards utopianism as an effect of a contemporary impossibility within social being 'to see society as a whole'[190] – particularly on the part of the workers' movement, which the 'utopian syndrome' infects.[191] The fragmentary form of social life under the utter fetishisation of instrumental rationalisation encages social vision and renders it unable to envisage the whole. A false notion of a perfected whole is thereby projected subjectively. Indeed, the utopian is taken as a hollow and impotent dissatisfaction with the immediately given social structure, 'a straightforward – abstract – desire to alter' that structure, and no more.[192] The hollowness of the utopian content arises from it being unmediated with objective social possibilities. The utopian content remains merely subjective, then, a subjectivism which, as such, is unable 'to read off from history the correct course of action to be followed'.[193] Contrary to Bloch's assessment of Lukács's supposed subject-less notion of totality, for Lukács utopianism is characterised by *too much* subjective factor. Lukács will therefore speak of the need 'to progress *from* utopia *to* reality'.[194] As he writes:

---

187   Lukács 1971, p. xxvii.
188   Lukács 1971, p. xviii.
189   Lukács 1971, p. xv.
190   Lukács 1971, p. 79.
191   Ibid.
192   Lukács 1971, p. 160.
193   Lukács 1971, p. 79.
194   Lukács 1971, p. 387, my emphasis. 'The utopians, it is true, can clearly see the situation that must constitute the point of departure. What makes them utopians is that they see it as a fact or at best as a problem that requires a solution but are unable to grasp the fact that the problem itself contains both the solution and the path leading to it'. (Lukács 1971, p. 296).

If the meaning of history is to be found in the process of history itself and not, as formerly, in a transcendental, mythological or ethical meaning foisted on to *recalcitrant material*, this presupposes a proletariat with a relatively advanced awareness of its own position, i.e. a relatively advanced proletariat, and, therefore, a long preceding period of evolution. The path taken by this evolution leads from utopia to the knowledge of reality; from transcendental goals fixed by the first great leaders of the workers' movement to the clear perception by the Commune of 1871 that the working-class has 'no ideals to realise', but wishes only 'to liberate the elements of the new society'. It is the path leading from the 'class opposed to capitalism' to the class 'for itself'.[195]

Here Lukács betrays a number of underlying assumptions concerning utopianism. Firstly, that the utopian content is always met with *recalcitrant* matter – utopianism is always refractory, contrary, wayward with regards to the total materiality of present social reality. Secondly, and as a consequence of this, that utopian content is inimical to a proper knowledge of social reality, bearing in mind that knowledge, for Lukács, is inclusive of praxis and is thus tied to the question of the right course of action in a given 'now'. Drawing on Marx's correspondence with Ruge in 1843, Lukács will affirm that consciousness lies 'immanent in' rather than 'outside the real process of history'.[196] Lukács takes this position as supplying the appropriate philosophical foundation for dispelling utopianism: the utopians' 'thought', he writes, 'contains this very duality of social process and the consciousness of it. Consciousness approaches society from another world and leads it from the false path it has followed back to the right one'.[197]

Far from engaging with and transforming historical material dialectically, utopianism merely justifies and consecrates the irrationality of that material, since, as with Kantian morality, instead of grasping the social totality and reading off from it a course of action, utopianism is instead said only to ever apply an abstract and formal 'ought' to historical content; the historical content and this 'ought' therefore remain dualistically unmediated with real social life.[198] Lukács therefore associates utopia with a resolution of the irrationality of present social reality merely at the level of the imagination, whether ulti-

---

195   Lukács 1971, p. 22, my emphasis.
196   Lukács 1971, p. 77.
197   Lukács 1971, p. 78.
198   See Bloch in Moir 2020, p. 13. As Bloch describes Lukács's position here: utopianism is therefore said to allow 'the facts to exist and simply transcends them in an arbitrary sub-

mately aesthetic or religious, which as such always leaves practically and materially untouched that irrationality.[199] Utopianism either represents a reluctance
to seek out a transformative subject (a really existing 'We') immanent to present
social being, or else it signals the utter lack of such a subject in the current historical conjuncture, the result of which is imaginary projections which secretly
betray this impotence. Echoes of Voloshinov's criticism of German Expressionism are clearly evident here. In either case, as Kavoulakos writes, here 'the dualism of an a priori utopianism ... takes on the form of a "dialectical" construction
of history that "violates" ... the historical reality, maintaining a "contingent"
relation to it'.[200] To quote Lukács:

> For the ultimate goal is not a 'state of the future' awaiting the proletariat
> somewhere independent of the movement and the path leading up to it.
> ... Nor is it a 'duty', an 'idea' designed to regulate the 'real' process. The
> ultimate goal is rather that *relation to totality* (to the whole of society
> seen as a process), through which every aspect of the struggle acquires its
> revolutionary significance. This relation informs every aspect in its simple
> and sober ordinariness, but only consciousness makes it real and so con-
> fers reality on the day-to-day struggle by manifesting its relation to the
> whole. Thus it elevates mere existence to reality. Do not let us forget either
> that every attempt to rescue the 'ultimate goal' or the 'essence' of the
> proletariat from every impure contact with – capitalist – existence leads
> ultimately to the same remoteness from reality, from 'practical, critical
> activity' and to the same relapse into the utopian dualism of subject and
> object, of theory and practice to which Revisionism has succumbed.[201]

Thus, only a proper understanding of the present totality, and not imagined
distant lands of the future, can gain the revolution traction in the real. As Moir
writes, for Lukács 'it is possible to unambiguously discern what course of action
must be taken by observing the actual situation of the working class in relation to the totality of economic production'.[202] Or, as Bloch himself puts it in

---

jective manner'; it thereby 'can neither really lead nor offer concrete goals or means of
realisation'. (Bloch in Moir 2020, p. 15).
199   See Kavoulakos 2018, pp. 54–5 and Moir 2020, pp. 7–8.
200   Kavoulakos 2018, p. 66. If, then, '*ontological novelty* ... is the animating principle' of Lukács's
social ontology, as Hall (2011, p. 131; see also Kavoulakos 2018, p. 82) suggests, then this
principle is not tied to utopianism, as the possibility and content for the overcoming of
reification 'could be "specified" in advance'. (Hall 2011, p. 135).
201   Lukács 1971, p. 22.
202   Moir 2020, p. 8.

his review of the book, Lukács's 'logic of actual being' goes 'beyond empiricism' in such a way 'that the objects of empiricism are themselves grasped and understood as moments of the totality, that is as *moments of the historically self-transforming society as a whole*'.[203] And so as with Voloshinov, the full purport of the production of an utterance can be said to be grasped in its surrounding *Zeigfeld*, that is, in language's non-verbal situatedness, the totality which surrounds it. But as Bloch suspects, Lukács himself may end up being guilty of developing a restricted notion of the 'whole' through which social being is grasped; he may well himself want an 'impure' proletariat *without* the impurity of their utopian ideals, not to mention the potential political efficaciousness of mobilising the force of utopian ideals which characterises other classes' responses to the utopian content located within capitalist society.

Lukács was preoccupied with utopian yearnings during his earlier aesthetic period, and even in *History and Class Consciousness* Lukács never denies or glosses over the existence of utopian projections, nor does he reject the idea that these projections have an effectivity within the social. He merely perceives this effectivity of utopian content to be far too redundant, retrograde and therefore potentially reactionary, since utopian projections only divert critical attention away from the material possibilities for real transformation afforded by the present totality of social being. Lukács's sharp distanciation from utopianism, on the one hand, as a credible aspect of critical theory, on the other, does not mean, then, that Lukács was blind to the real effectivity in social life that utopianism plays, even if he deems utopian content as lacking revolutionary potential:[204]

> It would be foolish to believe that this criticism and the recognition that a post-utopian attitude to history has become *objectively possible* means that utopianism can be dismissed as a factor in the proletariat's struggle for freedom. This is true only for those stages of class consciousness that have really achieved the unity of theory and practice described by Marx, the real and practical intervention of class consciousness in the course of history and hence the practical understanding of reification. And this did not all happen at a single stroke and in a coherent manner.[205]

---

203   Bloch in Moir 2020, p. 16.
204   See Moir 2020, p. 8.
205   Lukács 1971, p. 78. Cf. 'It would be a utopian illusion to infer that utopianism had been overcome by the revolutionary workers' movement merely because Marx refuted its first primitive manifestation'. (Lukács 1971, p. 296).

It is of note to mention in passing that Lukács locates Expressionism's 'loss of prestige' in a parallel process, in which the 'growing maturity' and 'clarity of the revolutionary consciousness of the masses' led to Expressionism's eventual dissolution.[206] Indeed, for Lukács Expressionism, 'devoid of reality and life', holds no lessons for the masses: 'ordinary people who try to translate these atmospheric echoes of reality back into the language of their own experience, find the task quite beyond them'.[207] Expressionism's language is far too dichotomous to the reality it emerges from, it subjectively draws on another world as its *Zeigfeld*. Of course, for the Marx of the *Brumaire* the point was not to translate *back*, but forward, such that the actual language of life moved into the Front.

In 1923, Bloch had already articulated what he took to be the stumbling block of this Lukácsian reading of utopianism. Lukács's *History and Class Consciousness* had touched on the edges of, but ultimately missed, the importance of utopianism, according to Bloch.[208] Indeed here we have to apply what Bloch calls 'the miserable logic of the Yes-But'.[209] Putting to one side the always underplayed rhetorical nature of the original distinction between utopianism and Marxism,[210] namely the hostility of Marxism to utopianism's so-called 'false transcendence',[211] the drawback with Lukács's position is that it leaves unanswered the question of what precisely the practical, critical theorist is to *do* with this seemingly redundant, though existent, utopian content. As Moir sums up this problem:

> The problem with all this from Bloch's perspective was that the proletariat very obviously *did* have ideals that motivated it and that he believed expressed, in however distorted and partial a way, its manifold desires for a better society. According to Bloch, then, Lukács' focus on the realm of the actual to the detriment of the possible led him to reject the relevance of art, culture, and religion to the task at hand. ... For Bloch, the utopian imagination that points beyond the present reality was just as valuable as sober critique when it came to reading off 'what is to be done' from the totality of history.[212]

---

206   Lukács 1992, p. 52.
207   Lukács 1992, p. 57.
208   See Moir 2020, pp. 4 and 6.
209   Bloch 1991, p. 5.
210   A topic fully treated by Abensour 2016. See also Moir 2020, p. 8.
211   Bloch in Moir 2020, p. 16.
212   Moir 2020, pp. 8–9.

In other words, if utopian content remains even after a theoretical perspective has been developed which strips away this content's illusions, then the Leninist question of what is to be done with this utopian content, which is both existent but deemed totally irrelevant for the struggle, remains in place. Lukács both recognises that utopian content is immanent to, and thus a moment of, social becoming, but severely dismisses its relevance for any project of emancipation.[213] Bloch, however, always sensed the objective factor, or objective correlate, of utopianism, too:

> ... Marx is consciously and intentionally sparing color in depicting the possible future. In this respect he properly parts company with his utopian predecessors, who all too often posited their mere wishes as the actuality of the future, engendered in the mind and produced in the form of utopian 'novels' which had little or no impact on the course of social life. Of course, even this still abstract activity was seldom wholly private and independent of circumambient reality: in general, the successive utopias were not only attached, but in some cases appropriate, to their particular age. Hence, Sir Thomas More was an English 'liberal', Campanella with his 'solar State' corresponded to the contemporary absolutisms of Spain and France, while St. Simon, two hundred years later, offered the magical formula *'l'industrie'*.[214]

As Bloch will write in *The Principle of Hope*: 'without wishes we would be the dead bodies over which the wicked would stride on to victory. This is not a time to be without wishes, and the deprived certainly do not intend to be'.[215] Very much in the same spirit as Voloshinov when thinking through the non-verbal situatedness of the utterance, Lukács is therefore said to have developed a notion of totality *'according to a peculiar agnosticism'*, as Bloch says,

> ... which is only concerned with the transcendent insofar as the concrete dialectical mediation is ripe to manifest this concretely. Calvin brought

---

213   We could therefore argue that a touch of unsublated Kantianism remains in Lukács's position on utopianism: 'In Kant, the tendency prevailed of excluding all content from the subject side, too, to leave only consciousness as such and perhaps not even that, out of simple formalistic purity, relationlessness'. (Bloch in Moir 2020, p. 18). The point being: Lukács wants to adopt a relationless stance vis-à-vis utopian content precisely because he excludes from proletarian consciousness as meaningless and irrelevant that utopian content which is included within it as its own process of becoming.

214   Bloch 2018, p. 170.

215   Bloch 1986, p. 77.

the underworld to consciousness by means of the doctrine of predestination; Lukács, as a theoretician of constitutive praxis, achieves the same thing by means of a quite unique combination of inner-worldly asceticism and Hegel's pure concretional dialectic. The deepest meaning of this heroic, temporary and dialectical agnosticism, however, is undoubtedly timidity before what is hidden, a responsible attitude before what is secretive, a strict need for its limitation, for its undistracted imposition against all apparent concretion or premature abstract constriction.[216]

To be otherwise would require an interruption of a smooth totality. Lukács tries to overcome the supposed dichotomy of utopianism with a renewed account of what Bloch terms 'the problem of nearness', but it is just that this account of nearness and the concreteness it achieves pays the price for ignoring what is hidden and secretive in present social totality.[217] If Lukács was concerned to see the nearness of the lived instant as connected to totality, he nevertheless is said to have missed 'the obscurity of the instant being lived right now', 'a punctiform Now'.[218] As Bloch writes: 'The practice of Lukácsian concretisation ... never fully satisfies the sensitive, endlessly experimental being of history, the richly intertwined deep relationships of the reality process'.[219] Language in its anacoluthic iterations, I argue, is in touch with this intertwined and deep reality process. As Bloch writes:

> But with a certain simplistic tendency to homogenisation, and indeed with an almost exclusively sociological homogenisation of the process, too great a price may have been paid for this concreteness. History is much more, quite apart from all the demands of the *omnia ubique*, a polyrhythmic structure, and not only the social extraction of a still hidden social humanity, but also the artistic, religious, metaphysical production of the secret transcendental human being is a thinking of being, of a *new* depth relationship of being.[220]

The omission of the 'sensitive' and of the 'endlessly experimental being of history', an unwarranted omission of the Lukácsian totality, is, in Bloch's eyes, a cause behind the left's incapacity to stave off fascism in its classical period.

---

216   Bloch in Moir 2020, p. 19.
217   Bloch in Moir 2020, p. 17.
218   Pelletier 2018, p. 37.
219   Bloch in Moir 2020, p. 21.
220   Bloch in Moir 2020, p. 20.

Utopian contents therefore 'still require their own space',[221] and indeed Bloch stakes out a much more elaborate position on this score when he formulates an alternative – though he believed still Marxist – account of the rise of fascism in Germany in the interwar period. Lukács misses how the 'the obscurity of the instant being lived right now'[222] can be put to work for counter-revolutionary ends precisely in and through utopian content. Bloch believed this space ought not to be discarded and left to reaction.

Recent commentators on Lukács's social ontology repeat the Lukácsian line on utopia without considering the above Blochian retort to it. These commentators quite rightly note that Lukács's critique of utopia feeds into his low estimation of Expressionist art which, due to its aesthetically fragmentary character, is unable 'to conceptualize the whole, the totality',[223] by which is meant the *Zeigfeld* as 'the material organisation of society'. Bloch associated Lukács's unappreciative assessment of Expressionism's experimental art with the Marxist Left's general tendency to disavow utopian longing, ceding this content to reactionaries.[224] As an important passage of Marx's runs: 'Criticism has torn up the imaginary flowers from the chain not so that man shall wear the unadorned, bleak chain but so that he will shake off the chain and pluck the living flower'.[225] Bloch's construction of a 'warm side' of critique taps into the spirit of this passage and does so by developing a deeper notion of totality, from which the utterance emerges. This view of utopian projections, which Lukács disavows as unimportant for emancipation, is the reason for Bloch's support of German Expressionism, and Lukács's rejection of the movement as fascist. Premised on the idea that objective material conditions are always recalcitrant to utopian content, Lukács's dismissal of utopianism is one that guides his subsequent negative valuation of Expressionism's aesthetic. Moreover, it is this dismissal of utopianism that allows Lukács to attach to Expressionism the potential for regression which he excavates from within utopian content itself.

A better sense of why Lukács sees utopian content as being dualistically cut off from objective social conditions can be developed by turning to the relation of Expressionism to Russian Formalism. Firstly, Marxism's regrettable neglect

---

221   Ibid.
222   Pelletier 2018, p. 37.
223   See Thompson 2011, pp. 6–7.
224   See Bloch 1991, pp. 7 and 234–53.
225   Marx 1987c, p. 176. Recent commentators on Lukácsian critical social ontology nevertheless faintly grasp the importance of utopia for critical social ontology. This is because, alongside the cold critical account of material conditions, one such commentator broaches in passing the *indispensability* of elaborating 'new ontological social forms' in the struggle for social emancipation (Thompson 2020, p. 454).

of Formalism, as Bennett has noted, derives from the common Marxist repudiation of Formalism as being 'merely Kantian'.[226] At first blush, Formalism
certainly appears to be ill-disposed towards Marxism. The theoretical treat-
ments of literary works that both Formalists and Marxists develop, in the first
instance, seem markedly at odds. This is because while Marxism seeks to grasp
a literary work firstly in its economic, social, political and ideological context
(as Voloshinov does with language), Formalism treats the literary work as an
autonomous entity free from such contexts, analysing the work instead in the
vein of art for art's sake. Moreover, while Marxism seeks to discern the political
effects of literature's ability to eschew or problematise prevailing ideologies,
Formalism intends only to understand the power of literature's ability to defamiliarise in a politically and ideologically unmotivated register. The ability of
literature to defamiliarise is thus grasped purely as an aesthetic capacity, devoid
of clear social demands, and free of answering to a specified conjuncture.[227]

Bennett's *Formalism and Marxism* has, however, critically reassessed this
long-claimed incompatibility of Marxism and Formalism, without fundamentally overturning it however. One of the key points of push-back against the
above thesis concerning the incompatibility of Formalism and Marxism is that,
far from – as the misconception goes – operating in a theoretical register
located in a vacuum free of social context, literariness as defamiliarisation
(*ostrenenie*) can only be understood to be operative through the *relation* between current literary forms and the other, prevailing 'cultural and ideological
forms' of the non-literary.[228] In other words, the device of defamiliarisation
which, for the Formalists, defines the literary proper, 'is essentially a relational
property'.[229] Defamiliarisation therefore relies upon its opposite, the world of
the familiar, to function in its proper scope. No wonder then that Formalism can
count Brecht's approach to theatre among its channels of later influence.[230]
Despite this, the notion of relationality found within Formalism tends to be
one that is empty of a historical grasp of the familiar beyond the familiar
being couched in prevailing *literary styles*. Hence art for art's sake still prevails
because the Formalists, indeed like Saussure, failed to provide a substantial
account of how an 'historical curvature'[231] – that is, 'a firm material base'[232] –

---

226   Bennett 2003, p. 79.
227   See Bennett 2003, pp. 21–2.
228   Bennett 2003, p. 40, see also p. 45.
229   Bennett 2003, p. 54.
230   See Bennett 2003, p. 78. Brecht's epic theatre was influenced by Russian Formalism, the
       Western reception of Russian Formalism only came in 1955 (see Bennett 2003, p. 22).
231   Bennett 2003, p. 49.
232   Bennett 2003, p. 73.

determines changes within a system of language (Saussure), or, if the question be literature in the Formalist sense, there is an overriding failure to construct an account of the transitional changes between dominant forms of literary styles and texts as changes the cause of which reside in anything other than literariness itself. The Formalist's process of defamiliarisation, despite its acknowledgement of historical change, therefore remained abstract insofar as it was only concerned with the literary, rather than its *Zeigfeld*.[233] As an aside, Bloch's notion of totality seems to take more seriously this notion of defamiliarisation as one driven by the not-yet founded humanity mentioned in earlier passages. For Bloch, however, this is firmly tied, is not reducible to, the social, political ideological, and economic forces in train now. This clearly diverges from the Formalists, for whom what motivates the process of defamiliarisation is not 'a something' which arises from historical conditions, and which, if noticed, gives view to the need for, and enables, breaks in literary style; rather it is that motivation towards a 'purely artistic will to break with literary canons' (a kind of hyper-modernism, perhaps), a motivation, then, which lacks a sense of how the old ossifies not simply by dint of being old (by measure of the passing of time), but in relation to 'change in the structure of social, political and ideological relationships'.[234]

Given the closeness of this concept of defamiliarisation with Bloch's utopianism, perhaps it can be said that Bloch at times falls foul of this formalism, specifically with respect to his conception of the utopian breaks in loquacity which, as I have suggested, constitute the anacoluthon, and which, as such, are slipshod in identifying a social force or forces (in conflict) which lie behind such linguistic breaks. If the Formalists demonstrated an 'inability to relate internal mechanisms of change within literature to external forces of propulsion',[235] an incapacity born from their inheritance of Saussure perhaps, so then Bloch too potentially grasps this external force of propulsion abstractly in the form of a present incompleteness which tends towards its own overcoming. No social force is identified behind it. In the anacoluthon essay it is only reality that is said to be breaking up, after all, and little reference to a social force behind the anacoluthic break is speculated on. Bloch therefore can be said to have given no indication of a specific social force that harnesses the novelty of the crises to push forward the contradiction and step into novel language, although it is safe to presume that he had in mind the proletariat, but a proletariat not guided by contemporaneous economic contradiction alone. His essay, then, is

---

233   See Bennett 2003, pp. 45–51.
234   Bennett 2003, p. 51.
235   Bennett 2003, p. 56.

open to the charge that it tends to treat of the anacoluthon in the formalism of an aesthetic reflection, such as we see in Structuralist linguistics, or indeed in Expressionism (the common ground of two otherwise markedly different ways of theorising language). To work out the social, economic and political conditions of the anacoluthic break in the actual life of speech is a task that remains to be fulfilled. Surely only in this way can the utopian content at the centre of a Blochian philosophy of language be properly harnessed to revolutionary ends.

In sum, if the benefit of Bloch's extended notion of relationality is that in comparison to Voloshinov's a deeper sense of totality is sketched out, and so then the objective conditions through which one grasps an utterance are significantly extended with the benefit of a wider political assessment, Voloshinov's clear benefit over the Blochian anacoluthon is, nevertheless, that contrary to Formalism its break in linguistic flow is assigned a more concrete place among the class struggle. Voloshinov had already pre-empted this drawback in Bloch by holding up the German Expressionists' conception of language as engendering the movement's 'utopian radicalism' and 'mystical anarchism',[236] whose 'verbal radicalism' shunned the idea that there is a *realia* standing behind the word'.[237] That said, the restricted notion of totality at work in Voloshinov's theory of the production of an utterance misses that depth of being as connected with utopian content, as intimated in Bloch's utopian philosophy. This is the same restriction on totality which led Lukács to assign to utopian content only regressive tendencies. On the one hand, then, in Bloch, one sees a deeper conception of the utterance's conditions of being; on the other, one witnesses a lack of connecting that depth to more concrete forces in social life. To attempt to resolve this inadequacy, the question of fascism can be broached.

4   Fascism and Language, Then and Now: Postscript

A discussion of language in Bloch's utopian materialism cannot miss a comment on the question of fascism, not least because it indicates one way in which Bloch's philosophy of language can be concretised. In fact, certain tendencies that have emerged from the chapters above have brought us to this point. Indeed, Marx's *Eighteenth Brumaire* text was a spur in the 1920s and '30s for Marxist analyses of fascism.[238] The question of Marxism and language, then, is not the only presence in this text, but rather so too is the question of Marxism

---

236   Voloshinov 2004, p. 242.
237   See Voloshinov 2004, pp. 238–9.
238   Riley 2019, p. xvii.

and fascism – or, to avoid anachronism, the question of the nexus of the state and counter-revolution. Marx's reference to language in the opening stages of that text, a reference that has served to highlight Bloch's contribution to a Marxist philosophy of language, therefore provides a passage through which to transition to a discussion of fascism, allowing for an interrogation of the question of how the fascistic production of utterances can be explained (and countered) in Bloch's philosophy of language.

Bloch himself was a keen analyst of classical fascism. Today the globe is witnessing a re-emergence of, if not fascism, then certainly a new 'world turn to the right'.[239] The re-emergence of the far right as an increasingly potent socio-cultural and political force is, as Enzo Traverso has recently noted, 'one of the most remarkable features of our current historical moment'.[240] However, the odd character of this much-debated resurgence of fascism is that most if not all of the original socio-economic conditions which gave birth to classical fascism do not pertain in the present conjuncture. The *Zeigfeld* which facilitated the classical, interwar fascistic production of utterances no longer holds. That is to say, one witnesses neither a capitalism in a stage of imperialist expansion, nor a clear emergence of global conflict between the core capitalist nation-states; and the current context is not particularly defined by a revolutionary or even strong leftist opposition which finds support in mass mobilisations, as was the case prior to, say, Hitler's rise in Germany.[241] In other words, what Vivian calls the 'linguistic dimensions of fascist phenomena'[242] today must find other objective conditions for their inspiration. This may mean that the very dimension of social life that played front and centre in Bloch's analysis of classical fascism's counter-revolution – namely, culture – is playing an increasingly vital role in the re-emergence of fascism globally.

If the hallmark of Bloch's analysis of fascism's emergence and its appeal to particular classes is defined less by a purely economistic reading, and indeed less by a purely contemporaneous reading (such as Lukács developed), but rather by a philosophical-cultural analysis as is present as a general tendency in the work of Gramsci, then potential criticisms can be levelled against it. As Riley suggests, in Gramsci one encounters a 'Tocqueville of the left'.[243] Gramsci's concept of hegemony inserts a relatively autonomous level between the economy and the superstructure, allowing him to grasp the process by which

---

239   Ibid.
240   Traverso 2019, p. 3.
241   See Riley 2019, pp. xxv–xxx and pp. 12–13. Cf. el-Ojeili 2019, p. 1156 and Poulantzas 2018.
242   Vivian 2021, p. 362.
243   Riley 2019, p. 13.

different classes and class fractions politically tie together into a common project via certain cultural-ideological glues. Centring (utopian) culture and ideology in his analysis of fascism, in like manner Bloch adds a richness to Marxist accounts of the emergence and rule of fascism, but it has its potential pitfalls that can be briefly addressed here. One issues is that Bloch's analysis edges close to a portrayal of fascism as a revolutionary phenomenon at the level of culture or cultural identity. In fascism's quest for a 'new man' this counter-revolution is then joined at the hip with criticisms of communism, since both have been considered comparable in constituting 'a revolution ... of identity'.[244] The suspicion here, then, is that Bloch's ideo-cultural analysis carries the doubled-edged weakness of that broader cultural-ideological 'line of reasoning' in which not only is a 'quite empty' definition of revolution being worked with (and this could also mark Bloch's anacoluthon essay),[245] but its focus simply rehearses '[t]he pillar of the totalitarian model of scholarship' which itself centres on ideology.[246]

This potentially risks Bloch 'being blinded by the language and aesthetics of fascism itself',[247] thereby mistaking fascism for a 'revolutionary' movement which neither radically transformed the socio-economic property relations nor the production forms in existence in its rise to, and hold over, power.[248] This backbone of the totalitarian interpretation of fascism, which has become the purview of a revisionist historiography and which entails lumping together the fascist and communist societies of the twentieth century, is the cultural-ideological or '"ideocratic" model'[249] of interpretation. George L. Mosse's *The Fascist Revolution: Toward a General Theory of Fascism* is emblematic of this current.[250] But perhaps even this 'ideocratic model' itself needs to be stripped back for 'the possible remainder' within it, as Bloch considered was the best approach available for 'irrational' utopian content itself.[251] Just as the utopian content and 'all that involves the imagination' circulating in society was simply delivered over to 'the hands of Nazi swindlers', so too the cultural dimension of fascism and the 'material force' of this dimension should not be given over to revisionism root and branch.[252]

---

244   Riley 2019, pp. xix and xv.
245   Riley 2019, p. xix.
246   Traverso 2019, p. 170.
247   Traverso 2019, p. 119.
248   See Traverso 2019, pp. 116–27, cf. p. 161.
249   Traverso 2019, pp. 170–3.
250   E.g. see Mosse 1999, pp. xv, 8–10, 19, 33, 67, 72 and esp. 88.
251   Bloch 1991, pp. 3–4.
252   Bloch 1998, p. 112.

Indeed, in having developed a heterodox contribution to the Marxist analysis of fascism during the interwar period, the question I would like to ask in closing this book is how Bloch's work in language as it has been developed above helps to us grasp the character of this current growing fascistic conjuncture with respect to the role of language within it, and how it can counter contemporary fascistic productions of language? After all, 'the major enemy of Bloch's thinking and action is fascism'[253] precisely because fascism took seriously that extended notion of totality, or that new depth of being, that Lukács was so adamant should be shunned from the workers' movement and its strategy – a new depth of being that is absent in Voloshinov's work on language, as was shown above. In his exile from Germany Bloch was among a number of thinkers, including Brecht and Karl Kraus, who attempted to gain 'a critical purchase on Nazism through the prism of language', not only, then, to understand fascism, but also to develop an 'adequate anti-fascist language'.[254] What can the utopian-materialist conception of language outlined above do to help this task today?

As el-Ojeili has noted, the 'not-yet' within Bloch's materialism plays an elemental role in his analysis of classical fascism and in the centrality accorded to culture within it. Bloch's analysis is guided by the idea that the future is 'a material force in the world', a force the Nazis were able to direct for their own purposes more successfully than the left.[255] One of the primary ways in which, as a 'material force', the future arises in culture is through language, the future as that proper dimension of the *Zeigfeld* of an utterance. The previous chapters have aimed to speculate on and conceptually furnish how this might be so. The uniqueness of Bloch's analysis of fascism lay, then, in his attempt to grasp the social contradictions of interwar Europe beyond an understanding of the crisis as a synchronous economic crisis of capital accumulation. In doing so, and as Toscano rightly says, Bloch paved the way for an alternative understanding of fascism, one which went beyond the crisis as simply one of the order of the capital–labour antagonism – it had to be understood within a wider *Zeigfeld*, a deeper sense of being, which a certain use of language helped to articulate, and which the fascists were able to exploit. Bloch argued that for Marxists to understand fascism's potency one would also need to constructively and imaginatively confront social contradictions that, while not originating in the capitalist order of the present, nevertheless percolated that order due to the

---

253   Negt 1975, p. 5. The context of Oskar Negt's statement is the question of Bloch's support for Stalinism in his political essays written 1934–39.

254   Dodd, 2018, pp. 72–3.

255   el-Ojeili 2020, p. 15.

unfulfilled desires of times of past that interpolate the present – that dream of a matter that Marx spoke of to Ruge.[256] Bloch's concept of non-synchronicity, or non-contemporaneity, was key to this. And so the logic of the anacoluthon's 'not-following', it being the 'music' of reason (the future of totality in the production of an utterance) captures the very dynamics of Bloch's intervention in attempting to grasp both the nature of fascism and it successes, and how best to confront and overcome its threat.

In the *Heritage of Our Times* (1935), a key text in getting one's bearings with Bloch's analysis of fascism, Bloch writes that it was the fascists with their 'intoxicating deceit'[257] who were able to tap into the transformative potential of the 'material force' of utopian content that circulates social being; a 'material force' of those longings 'for something vaguely different'[258] that Marxists had unwittingly surrendered to reaction, having opted instead to move along the (Lukácsian) line of 'cold stream' critique. In opposition to this line, Bloch advised the following:

> The position of the 'Irratio' within the inadequate capitalist 'Ratio' has been all too abstractly cordoned off, instead of it being examined from case to case and the particular contradiction of this position possibly being concretely occupied. ... The 'Irratio' must not be ridiculed wholesale here, but occupied: and from a position which has a rather more genuine awareness of 'Irratio' than the Nazis and their big business partners.[259]

In other words, not only did classical fascism deploy utopian wishing (that cultural 'seeing around the corner', what is often seen as irrational) for reactionary ends, but, one can say, their use of certain forms of language, irrational as they may have been, helped to this end. In his cultural analysis of fascism Bloch therefore argues that the task is not simply one of ideologically unmasking the utopian longings at play, but culturally re-inheriting their categories. The notion of *Heimat* was a good example of this strategy of refunction. The Marxist

---

256   See Toscano 2017.
257   Bloch 1991, p. 2.
258   Ibid.
259   Ibid. It is also noteworthy to highlight that, in opposition to his more abstract treatment of the anacoluthon, Bloch's original analysis of the non-contemporaneity of earlier utopian longing does not detour into abstract discussion of utopianism, but is instead applied to those classes most susceptible to fascism: the petite bourgeoisie and the peasantry, and not the working class. Bloch calls the former the 'proletarianized but not proletarian strata' (Bloch 1991, pp. 1 and 7).

must seek to motivate 'the possible remainder' of utopian longings once their ideological detritus has been stripped away.[260] This constitutes the warm side of the critique of fascism.[261]

Contemporary fascism's use of the 'material force' of utopian content has been a topic of focus for a number thinkers of today. Traverso himself, who coined the term 'post-fascism', makes some interesting albeit general comments about fascism and utopia.[262] The only other contemporary writers who put the content and form of 'post-fascism' into conversation with Bloch's cultural analysis are Alberto Toscano and Chamsy el-Ojeili.

el-Ojeili's intervention highlights how the neglect of 'post-fascist utopianism'[263] severely limits theoretical conceptions of 'new' or 'post-fascisms'; so much so that in omitting an account of utopia within these analyses only serves to act as a 'barrier to emancipatory social scientific understanding and contestation of post-fascism today'.[264] Thus the general orientation of Bloch's analysis as one concerned with the material force of utopianism remains very much germane for the contemporary conjuncture. And indeed el-Ojeili's account proceeds to determine the ways in which utopianism is present in contemporary fascism itself, even if he only makes a passing mention of 'post-fascist speech'.[265]

Toscano's intervention develops a more critical view concerning the potency of Bloch's analysis to properly capture the unique contours of fascism today. For Toscano, Bloch's cultural analysis is now essentially redundant.[266] While *Heritage of Our Times* constitutes 'one of the most heterodox entries in the interwar philosophical debate on fascism'[267] and while it undeniably acted as a sharp tool for that time, this analysis is now unable to grasp the emergence, content, and form of late, new or 'post-fascism'. 'Severe doubt is cast on this possibility', as Toscano claims, because of 'the evanescence or obliteration of cultural and temporal *difference* from the lived experience of advanced capital-

---

260   Bloch 1991, pp. 3–4.
261   See el-Ojeili 2020, pp. 15–16.
262   Traverso 2019, p. 184. Traverso indicates that the concept of utopia is loosely connected to fascism: 'the radical right and Islamism constitute surrogates for the utopias that have now disappeared' during the course of the twentieth century (Traverso 2019, p. 184, cf. p. 87). 'In fascism the collective imagination found a home, a mirror, an amplifier, and a form of delivery'. (Traverso 2019, p. 109).
263   el-Ojeili 2020, p. 97.
264   el-Ojeili 2019, p. 1157.
265   el-Ojeili 2020, p. 100.
266   See el-Ojeili 2019, pp. 1158–9.
267   Toscano 2017.

ist economies'.[268] The rise of classical fascism found itself in a 'present' defined by non-contemporaneity, as Bloch's analysis had shown, but the 'present' of today's capitalism knows no 'other time' than its own, or at least as a society it is not preoccupied by anything other than its own contemporaneity. Capitalism's incessant adaptation to new historical circumstances from the time of classical fascism to the current conjuncture is, among other things, then, the story of the development of the murder of difference. And with reference to Pasolini's comments on fascism in the 1970s, Toscano will assert that

> ... the total power of contemporary capitalism, to intensively shape and homogenise desires and forms of life, especially under the appearance of difference, choice and freedom, [for Pasolini] meant the destruction of all the signs of historical unevenness, with all their utopian potentials. In the profoundly pessimistic view of Pasolini, and contra Bloch, there were no pasts left to salvage.[269]

Contemporary fascism is thereby defined by 'a *nostalgia for the synchronous, for the contemporary*'.[270] By this Toscano means that the new far-right movements of the world do not desire a past that never was, nor a future that might be – an unfulfilled past that demands a dialectical reawakening, or a future that one can fight for – but rather a present that desires no utopianism as such: 'the nostalgia for Fordist modernity, the utopia of a post-utopian age'.[271] The problem with Toscano's position here, however, is that it echoes Lukács's own notion of an entirely co-present totality which Bloch found so problematic and which came to the fore in the Expressionism debate. One could simply redirect towards Toscano Bloch's counter to Lukács's concept of totality: is it really the case that one can speak today of an homogeneity of desire and a total absence of unevenness and discontinuity? Indeed, in response to Toscano's critical view el-Ojeili himself has already worked to develop a detailed account of how utopian wishes still populate contemporary far right ideologies.[272] Notwithstanding Toscano's reservations, then, the task below, in closing the book, is to begin to understand how Bloch's utopian-materialist account of language helps to grasp and avert fascistic productions of utterances today.

---

268   Ibid.
269   Ibid.
270   Ibid.
271   Ibid.
272   el-Ojeili 2020, pp. 87–93.

It is undeniable that the production of utterances was central to classical fascism in its self-definition and in its attempt to mark out its identity from the otherness which it violently sought to tear away from society.[273] Victor Klemperer's famous study on Nazism and language demonstrated this long ago.[274] And, to be sure, language is unique in the cultural analysis of fascism as the emergence of race science itself 'took its lead from the study of language',[275] a point that perhaps Voloshinov's observation that linguistics has often had a philological concern can be traced back to. But to get a bearing on how utopia and the anacoluthon stand with language in the context of fascism today we can turn to another instance in Bloch's corpus where he explicitly deals with the question of language in the context of a discussion of fascism. What is unique about Bloch's essay 'Ruined Language, Ruined Culture' ('Zerstörte Sprache, zerstörte Kultur') is that, in a discussion of Romantic and analytic concepts of language, it develops an approach to language that adopts the 'both-and ...' pathway that defines the injunction for Kant to burn through Hegel, as discussed in Chapter 1.

In that text, on the one hand, Bloch wants to escape the arid, unimaginative approach to the language speculation of analytical philosophy.[276] The work of these 'Sprachkritiker' (a term first coined by Johan Gottfried Herder)[277] is said to utterly do away with the poetic, musical and mystical (read: creative and imaginative) elements of language, being satisfied instead to treat of language as a mere instrument of knowledge.[278] Moir's account of the key influence of Nietzsche and Expressionism in Bloch's nascent philosophy of language already gives plenty of reasons for why Bloch would want to avoid this type of conception of language. The subjective idealism of this analytical approach to philosophy of language, Bloch says, lies in its positing a gap between language and the world, such that linguistic life bears in itself no ontological thesis. Such an approach to language does not connect utterances to a wider Zeigfeld.

However, Bloch is just as ardently opposed to the 'Sprachmythologie' of the Romantics who endorse a 'metaphysicalisation of language' such that the word is magically congruent with the world's content – on a cosmic scale.[279] As Rancière suggests, in this orientation to the philosophy of language there is an

---

273   See Traverso 2019, pp. 126–7 and 169.
274   Klemperer 2000.
275   Hutton 1999, p. 3.
276   Bloch 1994, p. 383.
277   Surber 2006, p. 5.
278   Bloch 1994, p. 384. Cf. Surber 2006, pp. 5–6.
279   Bloch 1994, p. 387.

'absence of the void or interval' within language, an 'absence of nonsignific-
ation',[280] since the word and its *realia* smoothly combine and are one. Bloch's
view of this approach mirrors what Kavoulakos has noted of Lukács's critique
of early German Romanticism, which, in being said to be merely an aesthetic
overcoming of the subject-object diremption (language as an aesthetic harmony with the world's content), leads only to contemplation and to a non-
practical resolution.[281] In asserting a complete congruence of language and the
world, albeit a world that is complete in itself,[282] the objective idealism of the
Romantics omits the critical gap from which, for Bloch, the Novum emerges.

For Bloch, neither such a Romantic 'worship of language [*Sprachverehrung*]'
nor such a 'contempt of language [*Sprachverachtung*]', which the analytical
philosophers propagate, is feasible.[283] Here, once more, Kant must 'burn'
through Hegel, such that the opening of a disconnection is not between language and world but within the world itself, between its present existence and
what it could become. Language occupies this world, and its congruousness
with the world lies in the non-identity they share within and between themselves.[284] The imaginativeness of language – that it bends around a corner –
is precisely drawn from this diremption that marks the world it occupies. My
contention is that for Bloch this tensioning of language that is born from its
immanence in a discontinuous materiality plays its part in assessing the capacity of language to counter the fascistic production of utterances. But to understand this one first needs to see how the fascistic production of utterances itself
had relied on a Romantic-mythological conception of language.[285]

In another text of Bloch's which deals with the question of language and
fascism, the 1938 short essay, published in *Das Wort* in Moscow, 'Der Nazi und
das Unsägliche', the substance of an effective anti-fascistic production of utterances is the main concern, one that seems to counter the Romantic deployment

---

280   Rancière 2016, p. 226.
281   See Kavoulakos 2018, pp. 54–8.
282   Bloch 1994, pp. 387–8.
283   Bloch 1994, p. 387.
284   In his first volume of *The Philosophy of Symbolic Forms*, Ernst Cassirer writes the follow-
      ing of this mythic notion of language: 'The mythical view of language which everywhere
      precedes the philosophical view of it is always characterized by this indifference of word
      and thing. Here the essence of every thing is contained in its name. Magical powers attach
      directly to the word. He who gains possession of the name and knows how to make use of
      it, has gained power over the object itself; he has made it his own with all its energies. All
      word magic and name magic is based on the assumption that the world of things and the
      world of names for a single undifferentiated chain of causality and hence a single reality'.
      (Cassirer 1980, p. 118).
285   Bloch 1970b, p. 190.

of utterances by the Nazis with an analytic approach to language as simply one of relaying empirical information. The guiding premise of this essay hinges on the supposed inadequacy of language to capture the terrors of the Nazi regime, in fact, there is said to be a tendency of language in this context to fall into cliché in attempting to do so: 'Because the right word cannot be found [*das rechte Wort fehlt*], anti-fascist language is in danger of becoming a cliché'.[286] In this conjuncture the word is not attempting to capture a newness on the horizon that might mark a fulfilment that has nowhere yet walked the earth (the All), but rather instead is trying to capture the circulation of a nothingness, a mundane evil. Language cannot be one with its object of concern here – Hitler's regime – since language has never quite known something like this. There is a non-correspondence between what language must do (describe and condemn the thing), and what it is able to do. There is an anacoluthic break experienced within language. As part of the superstructure, Bloch says, language is historically-laden and only undergoes slow transformation, which renders its capacity to capture the newness of Nazism severely limited.[287] As Dodd writes, for Bloch '[o]ur language resources are not sufficient or not yet sufficient ... for woodlice that have grown enormous'.[288] In a different context Marx's *Brumaire* passage, dealt with in the previous chapter, touches on a similar idea and problem: here the content transcends the phrase, the *Zeigfeld* is incommunicable, beyond words. However, it has already been noted how for Bloch so-called erroneous language can be productive of the new – namely, how language's inability to express the thing itself need not force language into silence but into ungrammatical constructions which help grasp what is new to it in the world. Language can be 'fit and pliant enough to express what in common grammar [in language already become, N.B] ... is incommunicable'.[289] However, despite historical precedents in dealing with great injustice handed down to us by figures like Thomas Müntzer, prior to the qualitatively new Hitler regime even the greatest word can easily become silent. Not every Novum is a good. It is in this light that Bloch rallies against the 'blazing heat of a moralising language [*glühende Sprache*]' in dealing with fascism, and instead he proposes 'descriptive [*beschreibende*]' and 'scientific [*wissenschaftlich*]' language as the best way to expose the Nazi crimes.[290] One precisely defined by a more analytic style of approaching the core essence of language. As Dodd writes:

---

286   Bloch 1970b, p. 185. See Dodd 2018, p. 85.
287   Bloch 1970b, p. 186.
288   Dodd 2018, p. 86.
289   Bloch 1985c, p. 14.
290   Bloch 1970b, p. 190.

... the language of righteous indignation and moral pathos, whilst justified, falls short of the task because it is directed at the metaphysical category of evil ('das Böse'), rather than the profane and mundane category of the bad ('das Schlechte'). Instead, Bloch calls for objective genres, of description, stock-taking and analysis, to be the literary forms of opposition and overcoming. Accounts of personal suffering are powerful testimonies, he notes ...[291]

An aesthetic language of the Expressionist kind will not do, one that relies on an 'ought' of a moral pathos – it ought not to be this way. The descriptive reports from the concentration camps, while not exhausting what is communicable of the Nazi crime, have at least illuminated the contours of what is unspeakable about them.[292] Neither moralising nor satirical language can achieve this, according to Bloch. But here it seems that Bloch is proposing an approach that moves more in the direction of a cold-stream, analytical critique of the events of such crimes, rather than in the direction of a combination of both analytic and Romantic concepts of language, of the kind I have identified above in the 'Ruined Language, Ruined Culture' essay. The key point here, however, is that Bloch's essay concerns the period of time during which the Nazis *had already gained and put to use their power*. It does not concern productions of utterances during the time in which the Nazis had begun to swindle the masses by drawing on the material force of that dream of a thing that Marx had spoken of to Ruge. Such a time as that, during a stage of the rise of fascism, requires an alternative anti-fascist production of language. Such a production of utterances would rely on a metaphysicalisation of language, a reaching to a logical ideal, that contains acknowledgement of a void, of the not-yet. It would be a production of utterances that counters the very same logic of 'not-following' that can be found in fascism's own production of utterances.

---

291   Dodd 2018, p. 87.
292   Bloch 1970b, p. 190.

References

Abel, Mark 2018, 'Is Music a Language? Adorno, Voloshinov and the Language Character of Music', *Historical Materialism*, 26(4), pp. 59–86.

Abensour, Miguel 2016, 'The History of Utopia and the Destiny of its Critique', in S.D. Chrostowska and J.D. Ingram (eds), *Political Uses of Utopia: New Marxists, Anarchist, and Radical Democratic Perspectives*, New York: Columbia University Press, pp. 3–56.

Adorno, Theodor W. 1974, *Noten zur Literatur*, Frankfurt am Main: Suhrkamp.

Adorno, Theodor W. 1992, *Notes to Literature: Volume Two*, ed. R. Tiedemann, translated by S.W. Nicholsen, New York: Columbia University Press.

Adorno, Theodor W. 1993, *Hegel: Three Studies*, translated by S.W. Nicholsen, London: The MIT Press.

Adorno, Theodor W. 2000, *Metaphysics: Concepts and Problems*, ed. R. Tiedemann, translated by E. Jephcott, Cambridge: Polity Press.

Adorno, Theodor W. 2001, *Kant's Critique of Pure Reason*, ed. R. Tiedemann, translated by R. Livingstone, Cambridge: Polity Press.

Adorno, Theodor W. 2005, *Minima Moralia: Reflections on a Damaged Life*, translated by E.F.N. Jephcott, London/New York: Verso.

Adorno, Theodor W. 2008, *Lectures on Negative Dialectics*, translated by R. Livingstone, Cambridge: Polity Press.

Ali, Tariq 2019, 'Foreword', in Karl Marx, *The Political Writings*, London/New York: Verso, pp. xi–xiv.

Alpatov, Vladimir M. 2000, 'What is Marxism in Linguistics?' in C. Brandist and G. Tihanov (eds), *Materializing Bakhtin: The Bakhtin Circle and Social Theory*, Basingstoke: Palgrave Macmillan, pp. 173–93.

Althusser, Louis 2005, *For Marx*, translated by B. Brewster, London/New York: Verso.

Althusser, Louis 2006, *Philosophy of the Encounter: Later Writings, 1978–87*, ed. F. Matheron and O. Corpet, translated by G.M. Goshgarian, London/New York: Verso.

Anderson, Perry 1979, *Considerations on Western Marxism*, London/New York: Verso.

Anon 2013, *A Study Guide for Philip Larkin's 'Aubade'*, Farmington Hills: Gale.

Aristotle 1984a, *The Complete Works of Aristotle, Volume One*, ed. J. Barnes, Princeton: Princeton University Press.

Avanessian, Armen 2016, 'Language Ontology', in A. Avanessian and S. Malik (eds), *Genealogies of Speculation: Materialism and Subjectivity since Structuralism*, London: Bloomsbury Academic, pp. 199–216.

Bachelard, Gaston 1964, *The Psychoanalysis of Fire*, translated by Alan C.M. Ross, London: Routledge & Kegan Paul.

Badiou, Alain 2019, *Wittgenstein's Antiphilosophy*, translated by Bruno Bosteels, London/New York: Verso.

Bakhtin, Mikhail M. 1990 [ca. 1920–23], 'Author and Hero in Aesthetic Activity', translated by V. Liapunov, in M. Holquist and V. Liapunov (eds), *Art and Answerability: Early Philosophical Essays by M.M. Bakhtin*, Austin: University of Texas Press, pp. 4–256.

Bakhtin, Mikhail M. 1994 [1963], 'From M.M. Bakhtin's *Problems of Dostoevsky's Poetics*', translated by C. Emerson, in P. Morris (ed.), *The Bakhtin Reader: Selected Writings of Bakhtin, Medvedev and Voloshinov*, London: Edward Arnold, pp. 89–96.

Balibar, Étienne 2009, 'Eschatology versus Teleology: The Suspended Dialogue between Derrida and Althusser', in P. Cheah and S. Guerlac (eds), *Derrida and the Time of the Political*, Durham, NC: Duke University Press, pp. 57–73.

Balibar, Étienne 2016, 'After Utopia, Imagination?', in S.D. Chrostowska and J.D. Ingram (eds), *Political Uses of Utopia: New Marxists, Anarchist, and Radical Democratic Perspectives*, New York: Columbia University Press, pp. 161–4.

Barad, Karen 2007, *Meeting the Universe Halfway: Quantum Physics and the Entanglements of Matter and Meaning*, Durham, NC: Duke University Press.

Barron, Nathaniel J.P. 2021, 'Ernst Bloch's Ontology of Not-Yet Being: Intuiting the Possibility of Anticipation's Fulfilment', in J. Brassett and J. O'Reilly (eds), *A Creative Philosophy of Anticipation: Futures in the Gaps of the Present*, London: Routledge, pp. 79–97.

Bassett, Caroline 2007, *The Arc and the Machine: Narrative and the New Media*, Manchester: Manchester University Press.

Beasley-Murray, Tim 2007, *Mikhail Bakhtin and Walter Benjamin: Experience and Form*, Basingstoke: Palgrave Macmillan.

Beck, Humberto 2019, *The Moment of Rupture: Historical Consciousness in Interwar German Thought*, Philadelphia: University of Pennsylvania Press.

Beiser, Frederick 2014, *The Genesis of Neo-Kantianism, 1796–1880*, Oxford: Oxford University Press.

Benjamin, Walter 1999a, 'On Language as Such and On the Language of Man', in M. Bullock and M.W. Jennings (eds), *Walter Benjamin: Selected Writings, Volume 1, 1913–1926*, Cambridge, MA: Harvard University Press, pp. 62–74.

Benjamin, Walter 1999b, 'The Task of the Translator', in M. Bullock and M.W. Jennings (eds), *Walter Benjamin: Selected Writings, Volume 1, 1913–1926*, Cambridge, MA: Harvard University Press, pp. 253–63.

Benjamin, Walter 2002, 'Problems in the Sociology of Language: An Overview', in H. Eiland and M.W. Jennings (eds), *Walter Benjamin: Selected Writings, Volume 3, 1935–1938*, Cambridge, MA: Harvard University Press, pp. 68–93.

Bennett, Tony 2003, *Formalism and Marxism*, 2nd edition, London: Routledge.

Bense, Max 1978, 'Ernst Blochs Prosa und die neue Seinsthematik', in B. Schmidt (ed.), *Materialien zu Ernst Blochs 'Prinzip Hoffnung'*, Frankfurt am Main: Suhrkamp, pp. 71–81.

Berardi, Franco 2019, *Futurability: The Age of Impotence and the Horizon of Possibility*, London/New York: Verso.

Blackledge, Paul 2012, *Marxism and Ethics: Freedom, Desire, and Revolution*, Albany, NY: State University of New York Press.

Blechman, Max 2008, ' "Not Yet": Adorno and the Utopia of Conscience', *Cultural Critique*, 70, pp. 177–98.

Bloch, Ernst 1962, *Subjekt-Objekt. Erläuterungen zu Hegel*, Frankfurt am Main: Suhrkamp.

Bloch, Ernst 1965, *Literarische Aufsätze*, Frankfurt am Main: Suhrkamp.

Bloch, Ernst 1969, *Philosophische Aufsätze zur objektiven Phantasie*, Frankfurt am Main: Suhrkamp.

Bloch, Ernst 1970a, *Tübinger Einleitung in die Philosophie*, Frankfurt am Main: Suhrkamp.

Bloch, Ernst 1970b [1938], 'Der Nazi und das Unsägliche', in E. Bloch, *Politische Messungen, Pestzeit, Vormärz*, Frankfurt am Main: Suhrkamp, pp. 185–93.

Bloch, Ernst 1971b, 'Diskussionen über Expressionismus', in H. Mayer (ed.), *Deutsche Literaturkritik. Vom Dritten Reich zur Gegenwart (1933–1968)*, Frankfurt am Main: Fischer Taschenbuch Verlag, pp. 150–60.

Bloch, Ernst 1972, *Das Materialismusproblem, seine Geschichte und Substanz*, Frankfurt am Main: Suhrkamp.

Bloch, Ernst 1975, *Experimentum Mundi, Frage Kategorien des Herausbringens, Praxis*, Frankfurt am Main: Suhrkamp.

Bloch, Ernst 1978, *Tendenz–Latenz–Utopie*, Frankfurt am Main: Suhrkamp.

Bloch, Ernst 1980, *Abschied von der Utopie? Voträge*, ed. H. Gekle, Frankfurt am Main: Suhrkamp.

Bloch, Ernst 1983, 'The Dialectical Method', translated by J. Lamb, in *Man and World*, Vol. 16, pp. 281–313.

Bloch, Ernst 1985a, *Essays on the Philosophy of Music*, translated by P. Palmer, Cambridge: Cambridge University Press.

Bloch, Ernst 1985b, *Ernst Bloch Briefe, 1903–1975, zweiter Band*, ed. K. Bloch et al., Frankfurt am Main: Suhrkamp.

Bloch, Ernst 1985c, *Leipziger Vorlesungen zur Geschichte der Philosophie, 1950–1956. Neuzeitliche Philosophie II, Deutscher Idealismus, Die Philosophie des 19. Jahrhunderts (Band 4)*, ed. Ruth Römer et al., Frankfurt am Main: Suhrkamp.

Bloch, Ernst 1986, *The Principle of Hope*, translated by N. Plaice, S. Plaice, and P. Knight, Cambridge, MA: The MIT Press.

Bloch, Ernst 1988, *The Utopian Function of Art and Literature: Selected Essays*, translated by J. Zipes and F. Mecklenburg, Cambridge, MA: The MIT Press.

Bloch, Ernst 1991 [1934], *Heritage of Our Times*, translated by N. and S. Plaice, Cambridge: Polity Press.

Bloch, Ernst 1992, 'Discussing Expressionism', translated by R. Livingstone, in E. Bloch et al., *Aesthetics and Politics*, London: Verso, pp. 16–27.

Bloch, Ernst 1994, 'Zerstörte Sprache – zerstörte Kultur', in F. Dieckmann and J. Teller (eds), *Viele Kammern im Welthaus. Eine Auswahl aus dem Werk*, Frankfurt am Main: Suhrkamp, pp. 375–96.

Bloch, Ernst 1998, *Literary Essays*, translated by A. Jorden et al., California: Stanford University Press.

Bloch, Ernst 2000a, *The Spirit of Utopia*, translated by A.A. Nassar, California: Stanford University Press.

Bloch, Ernst 2000b, *Logos der Materie, Eine Logik im Werden*, Frankfurt am Main: Suhrkamp.

Bloch, Ernst 2006, *Traces*, translated by A.A. Nassar, California: Stanford University Press.

Bloch, Ernst 2009, *Atheism in Christianity: The Religion of Exodus and the Kingdom*, translated by J.T. Swann, London: Verso.

Bloch, Ernst 2018, *On Karl Marx*, translated by J. Maxwell, London: Verso.

Boella, Laura 2012, 'Spuren', in B. Dietschy, D. Zeilinger, and R.E. Zimmermann (eds), *Bloch-Wörterbuch: Leitbegriffe der Philosophie Ernst Blochs*, Berlin: De Gruyter, pp. 508–13.

Boldyrev, Ivan 2014, *Ernst Bloch and His Contemporaries: Locating Utopian Messianism*, London: Bloomsbury Academic.

Bosteels, Bruno 2019, 'Translators Introduction', in Alain Badiou, *Wittgenstein's Anti-philosophy*, London/New York: Verso, pp. 1–66.

Bowie, Andrew 2003, *Introduction to German Philosophy: From Kant to Habermas*, Cambridge: Polity Press.

Bowles, Michael 2000, 'Kant and the Provocation of Matter', in A. Rehberg and R. Jones (eds), *The Matter of Critique: Readings in Kant's Philosophy*, Manchester: Clinamen Press, pp. 1–18.

Brandist, Craig 2001, 'The Hero at the Bar of Eternity: The Bakhtin Circle's Juridical Theory of the Novel', *Economy and Society*, 30(2), pp. 208–28.

Brandist, Craig 2002a, *The Bakhtin Circle: Philosophy, Culture and Politics*, London/Sterling, VA: Pluto Press.

Brandist, Craig 2002b, 'Two Routes "to Concreteness" in the Work of the Bakhtin Circle', *Journal of the History of Ideas*, 63(3), pp. 521–37.

Brandist, Craig 2004, 'Voloshinov's Dilemma: On the Philosophical Roots of the Dialogic Theory of the Utterance', in C. Brandist, D. Shepherd, and G. Tihanov (eds), *The Bakhtin Circle: In the Master's Absence*, Manchester: Manchester University Press, pp. 97–124.

Brandist, Craig 2009, 'Problems of Sense, Significance, and Validity in the Work of Shpet and the Bakhtin Circle', in G. Tihanov (ed.), *Gustav Shpet's Contribution to Philosophy and Cultural Theory*, West Lafayette, IN: Purdue University Press, pp. 192–206.

Brandist, Craig, and Mika Lähteenmäki 2010, 'Early Soviet Linguistics and Mikhail Bakhtin's Essays on the Novel of the 1930s', in C. Brandist and K. Chown (eds), *Politics and the Theory of Language in the USSR 1917–1938: The Birth of Sociological Linguistics*, London/New York/Delhi: Anthem Press, pp. 69–88.

Brentano, Franz 1975, *On the Several Senses of Being in Aristotle*, translated by R. George, London: University of California Press.

Bruss, Neal H. 2012, 'Appendix II: V.N. Voloshinov and the Structure of Language in Freudianism', in V.N. Vološinov, *Freudianism: A Marxist Critique*, translated by I.R. Titunik, London/New York: Verso, pp. 197–257.

Buber, Martin 1961, 'The Word that is Spoken', translated by M. Friedman, *Modern Age*, 5(4), pp. 353–60.

Bushart, Magadalena 1990, *Der Geist der Gotik und die expressionistische Kunst: Kunstgeschichte und Kunsttheorie 1911–1925*, München: Verlag Silke Schreiber.

Carlucci, Alessandro 2013, *Gramsci and Languages: Unification, Diversity, Hegemony*, Leiden/Boston: Brill.

Cassirer, Ernst 1980, *The Philosophy of Symbolic Forms. Volume 1: Language*, translated by R. Manheim, New Haven, CT: Yale University Press.

Cassirer, Ernst 2015 [1912], 'Hermann Cohen and the Renewal of Kantian Philosophy', translated by L. Patton, in S. Luft (ed.), *The Neo-Kantian Reader*, London: Routledge, pp. 221–35.

Chepurin, Kiril 2015, 'Spirit and Utopia: (German) Idealism as Political Theology', *Crisis and Critique*, 2(1), pp. 327–47.

Claussen, Detlev 2008, *Theodor W. Adorno: One Last Genius*, translated by R. Livingstone, Cambridge, MA: Harvard University Press.

Cohen, G.A. 2000, *If You're an Egalitarian, How Come You're So Rich?* Cambridge, MA: Harvard University Press.

Comay, Rebecca, and Frank Ruda 2018, *The Dash – The Other Side of Absolute Knowing*, Cambridge, MA: The MIT Press.

Côté, Jean-François 2000, 'Bakhtin's Dialogism Reconsidered through Hegel's "Monologism": The Dialectical Foundation of Aesthetics and Ideology in Contemporary Human Sciences', in C. Brandist and G. Tihanov (eds), *Materializing Bakhtin: The Bakhtin Circle and Social Theory*, Basingstoke: Palgrave Macmillan, pp. 20–42.

Davidson, Donald 2001, *Inquiries into Truth and Interpretation*, 2nd edition, Oxford: Oxford University Press.

Derrida, Jacques 2002, *Without Alibi*, translated by P. Kamuf, Stanford: Stanford University Press.

Dewalque, Arnaud et al. 2021, 'Introduction: Mind, Meaning and Reality', in A. De-
     walque et al. (eds), *Philosophy of Language in the Brentano School: Reassessing the*
     Brentanian Legacy, Cham: Palgrave Macmillan, pp. 1–31.

Dodd, Bill J. 2018, *National Socialism and German Discourse: Unquiet Voices*, Cham: Pal-
     grave.

Eco, Umberto 1995, *The Search for the Perfect Language*, translated by J. Fentress,
     Oxford: Blackwell.

el-Ojeili, Chamsy 2019, 'Reflecting on Post-Fascism: Utopia and Fear', *Critical Sociology*,
     45(7–8), pp. 1149–66.

el-Ojeili, Chamsy 2020, *The Utopian Constellation: Future-Oriented Social and Political*
     Thought Today, Cham: Palgrave Macmillan.

Ely, John 1988, 'Ernst Bloch and the Second Contradiction in Capitalism', *Capitalism,*
     Nature Socialism, 1(2), pp. 93–107.

Emden, Christian J. 2005, *Nietzsche on Language, Consciousness, and the Body*, Urbana
     and Chicago, IL: University of Illinois Press.

Engels, Friedrich 1976, 'The Festival of Nations in London', translated by C. Dutt et al.,
     in *Collected Works*, Volume 6, London: Lawrence & Wishart.

Fedorova, Kapitolina 2010, 'Language as a Battlefield – The Rhetoric of Class Struggle in
     Linguistic Debates of the First Five-Year Plan Period: The Case of E.D. Polivanov and
     G.K. Danilov', in C. Brandist and K. Chown (eds), *Politics and the Theory of Language*
     in the USSR 1917–1938: The Birth of Sociological Linguistics, London/New York/Delhi:
     Anthem Press, pp. 89–104.

Feser, Edward 2014, *Scholastic Metaphysics: A Contemporary Introduction*, New Jersey:
     editions scholasticae.

Fischbach, Franck 2016, 'Marx and Utopia', in S.D. Chrostowska and J.D. Ingram (eds),
     Political Uses of Utopia: New Marxists, Anarchist, and Radical Democratic Perspect-
     ives, New York: Columbia University Press, pp. 117–25.

Forster, Michael N. 1998, *Hegel's Idea of a Phenomenology of Spirit*, Chicago: The Uni-
     versity of Chicago Press.

Forster, Michael N. 2011, *German Philosophy of Language: From Schlegel to Hegel and*
     Beyond, Oxford: Oxford University Press.

Freeman, Joel 2006, 'Ernst Bloch and Hugo Ball: Toward an Ontology of the Avant-
     Garde', in D. Jones (ed.), *Dada Culture: Critical Studies on the Avant-Garde*, New York
     and Amsterdam: Rodopi, pp. 225–53.

Freud, Sigmund 1964 [1932–33], *The Standard Edition of the Complete Psychological*
     Works of Sigmund Freud, Volume 20 (1932–36), New Introductory Lectures on Psy-
     cho-analysis and Other Works, translated by J. Strachey, London: The Hogarth Press
     and the Institute of Psycho-analysis.

Freud, Sigmund 2010 [1900], *The Interpretation of Dreams*, translated by J. Strachey,
     New York: Basic Books.

Fryatt, Kit 2012, '"Horny Morning Mood". The Aubade and Alba', in E. Martiny (ed.), *A Companion to Poetic Genre*, Oxford: Blackwell, pp. 200–30.

Gadamer, Hans-Georg 1976, *Hegel's Dialectic: Five Hermeneutical Studies*, translated by P. Christopher Smith, New Haven, CT: Yale University Press.

Geoghegan, Vincent 1996, *Ernst Bloch*, London/New York: Routledge.

Geoghegan, Vincent 2002, '"Let the Dead Bury their Dead": Marx, Derrida and Bloch', *Contemporary Political Theory*, 1, pp. 5–18.

Gluck, Mary 1985, *Georg Lukács and His Generation, 1900–1918*, Cambridge, MA: Harvard University Press.

Gorham, Michael S. 2010, 'Language Ideology and the Evolution of *Kul'tura Iazyka* ("Speech Culture") in Soviet Russia', in C. Brandist and K. Chown (eds), *Politics and the Theory of Language in the USSR 1917–1938: The Birth of Sociological Linguistics*, London/New York/Delhi: Anthem Press, pp. 137–49.

Gray, Piers 2002, 'Totalitarian Logic: Stalin on Linguistics', in C. MacCabe and V. Rothschild (eds), *Stalin on Linguistics and other Essays*, Basingstoke: Palgrave, pp. 164–88.

Gross, David 1972, 'Ernst Bloch: The Dialectics of Hope', in D. Howard and K.E. Klare (eds), *The Unknown Dimension: European Marxism since Lenin*, London: Basic Books Inc., pp. 107–30.

Guyer, Paul 2005, *Kant's System of Nature and Freedom: Selected Essays*, Oxford: Oxford University Press.

Habermas, Jürgen 1970, 'Ernst Bloch – A Marxist Romantic', *Salmagundi*, 10/11, pp. 311–25.

Hamann, Johann Georg 2007, *Writings on Philosophy and Language*, translated and edited by K. Haynes, Cambridge: Cambridge University Press.

Hammer, Espen 2007, 'Habermas and the Kant-Hegel Contrast', in E. Hammer (ed.), *German Idealism: Contemporary Perspective*, London: Routledge, pp. 113–34.

Hartley, Daniel 2016, *The Politics of Style: Towards a Marxist Poetics*, Chicago: Haymarket Books.

Haug, Wolfgang Fritz 2012, 'Marxismus', in B. Dietschy, D. Zeilinger, and R.E. Zimmermann (eds), *Bloch-Wörterbuch: Leitbegriffe der Philosophie Ernst Blochs*, Berlin: De Gruyter, pp. 247–65.

Hegel, Georg Wilhelm Friedrich 1970, *Philosophy of Nature*, translated by A.V. Miller, Oxford: Oxford University Press.

Hegel, Georg 1977a, *The Difference between Fichte's and Schelling's System of Philosophy*, translated by H.S. Harris and W. Cerf, Albany: State University of New York Press.

Hegel, Georg 1977b, *Phenomenology of Spirit*, translated by A.V. Miller, Oxford: Oxford University Press.

Hegel, Georg 1979, *System of Ethical Life (1802/3) and First Philosophy of Spirit (Part III of the System of Speculative Philosophy 1803/4)*, translated and edited by H.S. Harris and T.M. Knox, Albany: State University of New York Press.

Hegel, Georg 1991, *Elements of the Philosophy of Right*, ed. A.W. Wood, translated by H.B. Nisbet, Cambridge: Cambridge University Press.

Hegel, Georg 2010, *The Science of Logic*, translated and edited by G. Di Giovani, Cambridge: Cambridge University Press.

Hegel, Georg 2012, *Vorlesungen über die Philosophie der Natur, Band 21, 1, Nachschriften zu den Kollegien der Jahre 1819/20, 1821/22 und 1823/24*, ed. W. Bonsiepen, Hamburg: Felix Meiner.

Heinrich, Michael 2016, 'The "Capital" After the MEGA: Discontinuities, Interruptions and New Beginnings', *Crisis and Critique*, 3(3), pp. 93–138.

Heller, Monica, and Bonnie McElhinny 2017, *Language, Capitalism, Colonialism: Toward a Critical History*, Ontario/Plymouth: University of Toronto Press.

Hildebrandt, Bernd 2007, 'Kant als Philosoph des Protestantismus', in U. Kern (ed.), *Was ist und Was sein soll: Natur und Freiheit bei Immanuel Kant*, Berlin: Walter de Gruyter, pp. 477–94.

Hillis Miller, Joseph 1990, *Versions of Pygmalion*, Cambridge, MA: Harvard University Press.

Hogh, Philip 2017, *Communication and Expression: Adorno's Philosophy of Language*, translated by A. Hofstätter, London: Rowman & Littlefield International.

Holborow, Marnie 2006, 'Putting the Social Back into Language: Marx, Vološinov and Vygotsky Re-examined', *Studies in Language and Capitalism*, 1, pp. 1–28.

Holquist, Michael 1990, 'Introduction: The Architectonics of Answerability', in M. Holquist and V. Liapunov (eds), *Art and Answerability: Early Philosophical Essays by M.M. Bakhtin*, Austin: University of Texas Press, pp. ix–xlix.

Holz, Hans Heinz 1965, 'Kategorie Möglichkeit und Moduslehre', in S. Unseld (ed.), *Ernst Bloch zu ehren*, Frankfurt am Main: Suhrkamp, pp. 99–120.

Holz, Hans 1975, *Logos Spermatikos: Ernst Blochs Philosophie der unfertigen Welt*, Darmstadt: Herman Luchterhand Verlag.

Honigsheim, Paul 2003, *The Unknown Max Weber*, ed. A. Sica, New Brunswick: Transaction Publishers.

Howard, Dick 2019, *The Marxian Legacy: The Search for the New Left*, 3rd edition, Cham: Palgrave Macmillan.

Hudis, Peter 2012, *Marx's Concept of the Alternative to Capitalism*, Leiden/Boston: Brill.

Hudson, Wayne 1982, *The Marxist Philosophy of Ernst Bloch*, New York: St. Martin's Press.

Hutton, Christopher M. 1999, *Linguistics and the Third Reich: Mother-tongue Fascism, Race and the Science of Language*, London/New York: Routledge.

Ingram, James D. 2016, 'Introduction: Utopia and Politics', in S.D. Chrostowska and J.D. Ingram (eds), *Political Uses of Utopia: New Marxists, Anarchist, and Radical Democratic Perspectives*, New York: Columbia University Press, pp. ix–xxxiv.

Ives, Peter 2004a, *Gramsci's Politics of Language: Engaging the Bakhtin Circle and the Frankfurt School*, Toronto: University of Toronto Press.

Ives, Peter 2004b, *Language and Hegemony in Gramsci*, London: Pluto Press.

Jameson, Fredric 1991, *Postmodernism, Or, The Cultural Logic of Late Capitalism*, Durham, NC: Duke University Press.

Jay, Martin 1984, *Marxism and Totality: Adventures of a Concept from Lukács to Habermas*, California: University of California Press.

Kagan, M.I. 2004 [1922], 'Hermann Cohen (4 July 1842–4 April 1918)', translated by C. Brandist and D. Shepherd, in C. Brandist et al. (eds), *The Bakhtin Circle: In the Master's Absence*, Manchester: Manchester University Press, pp. 193–211.

Kant, Immanuel 2000, *Critique of the Power of Judgment*, translated by P. Guyer and E. Matthews, Cambridge: Cambridge University Press.

Kant, Immanuel 2003, *Critique of Pure Reason*, translated by N.K. Smith, London: Palgrave Macmillan.

Kant, Immanuel 2004, *The Metaphysical Foundations of Natural Science*, translated by M. Friedman, Cambridge: Cambridge University Press.

Karádi, Éva 2010, 'Ernst Bloch and Georg Lukács in Max Weber's Heidelberg', translated by A. Davies, in W.J. Mommsen and J. Osterhammel (eds), *Max Weber and His Contemporaries*, London: Routledge, pp. 499–514.

Kavoulakos, Konstantinos 2018, *Georg Lukács's Philosophy of Praxis: From Neo-Kantianism to Marxism*, London: Bloomsbury Academic.

Kerszberg, Pierre 2000, 'Being as an Idea of Reason: Heidegger's Ontological Reading of Kant', in T. Rockmore (ed.), *Heidegger, German Idealism and Neo-Kantianism*, New York: Humanity Books, pp. 35–61.

Kessler, Achim 2006, *Ernst Blochs Ästhetik: Fragment, Montage, Metapher*, Würzburg: Verlag Königshausen & Neumann.

Klemperer, Victor 2000, *The Language of the Third Reich: LTI – Lingua Tertii Imperii, A Philologist's Notebook*, translated by M. Brady, London: Bloomsbury Academic.

Kolakowski, Leslek 2005, *Main Currents of Marxism: The Founders, The Golden Age, The Breakdown*, translated P.S. Falla, London: W.W. Norton & Company.

Korstvedt, Benjamin M. 2010, *Listening for Utopia in Ernst Bloch's Musical Philosophy*, Cambridge: Cambridge University Press.

Kouvelakis, Stathis 2018, *Philosophy and Revolution: From Kant to Marx*, translated by G.M. Goshgarian, London and New York: Verso.

Kübler, Renate 1975, 'Die Metapher als Argument. Semiotische Bestimmung der Blochschen Sprache', in *Ernst Blochs Wirkung, Ein Arbeitsbuch zum 90. Geburtstag*, Frankfurt am Main: Suhrkamp, pp. 271–83.

Lacan, Jacques 1988 [1975], *The Seminar of Jacques Lacan, Book 1: Freud's Papers on Technique 1953–1954*, ed. J-A. Miller, translated and notes by J. Forrester, Cambridge: Cambridge University Press.

Lacan, Jacques 1991, *The Seminar of Jacques Lacan, Book II: The Ego in Freud's Theory and in the Technique of Psychoanalysis 1954–1955*, ed. J-A. Miller, translated by S. Tomaselli, with notes by J. Forrester, New York/London: W.W. Norton.

Laclau, Ernesto, and Chantal Mouffe 2001, *Hegemony and Socialist Strategy: Towards a Radical Democratic Politics*, 2nd edition, London/New York: Verso.

Laclau, Ernesto 1990, *New Reflections on the Revolution of Our Time*, London/New York: Verso.

Lambrianou, Nickolas 2005, 'Neo-Kantianism and Messianism: Origin and Interruption in Hermann Cohen and Walter Benjamin', in P. Osborne (ed.), *Walter Benjamin: Critical Evaluations in Cultural Theory*, Vol. 1, London/New York: Routledge, pp. 82–103.

Landmann, Michael 1965, 'Ernst Bloch im Gespräch', in S. Unseld (ed.), *Ernst Bloch zu ehren*, Frankfurt am Main: Suhrkamp, pp. 345–71.

Landmann, Michael 1975, 'Talking with Ernst Bloch: Korčula, 1968', *Telos*, 25, pp. 165–85.

Lecercle, Jean-Jacques 2006, *A Marxist Philosophy of Language*, translated by G. Elliott, Leiden/Boston: Brill.

Lecercle, Jean-Jacques 2008, 'Marxism and Language', in J. Bidet and S. Kouvelakis (eds), *Critical Companion to Contemporary Marxism*, Leiden/Boston: Brill, pp. 471–85.

Leibniz, Gottfried Wilhelm 1970, *Philosophical Papers and Letters*, translated by L. Loemker, Dordrecht: Reidel.

Leibniz, Gottfried 1998, *Philosophical Texts*, translated by R.S. Woolhouse and R. Francks, Oxford: Oxford University Press.

Levinas, Emmanuel 2000, *God, Death, and Time*, translated by B. Bergo, California: Stanford University Press.

Liedman, Sven-Eric 2018, *A World to Win: The Life and Works of Karl Marx*, translated by J.N. Skinner, London/New York: Verso.

Lo Piparo, Franco 2010, 'The Linguistic Roots of Gramsci's Non-Marxism', translated and edited by R. Lacorte and P. Ives, *Gramsci, Language, and Translation*, Lanham, MD: Lexington Books, pp. 19–28.

Löwy, Michael, 1979, *Georg Lukács – From Romanticism to Bolshevism*, translated by P. Camiller, London: New Left Books.

Löwy, Michael, 2017, *Redemption and Utopia: Jewish Libertarian Thought in Central Europe*, London/New York: Verso.

Lukács, Georg 1971 [1924], *History and Class Consciousness: Studies in Marxist Dialectics*, translated by R. Livingstone, Cambridge, MA: The MIT Press.

Lukács, Georg 1977, 'Bolshevism as a Moral Problem', translated by J.M. Tar, *Social Research*, 44(3), pp. 416–24.

Lukács, Georg 1992, 'Realism in the Balance', translated by R. Livingstone, in E. Bloch et al., *Aesthetics and Politics*, London: Verso, pp. 28–59.

Luxemburg, Rosa 2004 [1918], 'What Does the Spartacus League Want?', in P. Hudis and K.B. Anderson (eds), *The Rosa Luxemburg Reader*, New York: Monthly Review Press, pp. 349–57.

Mariniello, Silvestra 1994, 'Toward a Materialist Linguistics: Pasolini's Theory of Language', in P. Rumble and B. Testa (eds), *Pier Paolo Pasolini: Contemporary Perspectives*, Toronto: University of Toronto Press, pp. 106–26.

Marx, Karl, and Friedrich Engels 1976a [1932], 'The German Ideology', translated by C. Dutt et al., in *Collected Works*, Volume 5, London: Lawrence & Wishart.

Marx, Karl, 1976b [1848], 'The Manifesto of the Communist Party', translated by C. Dutt et al., in *Collected Works*, Volume 6, London: Lawrence & Wishart.

Marx, Karl, 1976c [1845], 'The Holy Family', translated by R. Dixon and C. Dutt, in *Collected Works*, Volume 4, London: Lawrence & Wishart.

Marx, Karl 1976a [1932], 'Theses on Feuerbach', translated by C. Dutt et al., in *Collected Works*, Volume 5, London: Lawrence & Wishart.

Marx, Karl 1976b, 'The Poverty of Philosophy: Answer to the *Philosophy of Poverty* by M. Proudhon', translated by C. Dutt et al., in *Collected Works*, Volume 6, London: Lawrence & Wishart.

Marx, Karl 1987a [1959], 'The Economic and Philosophical Manuscripts of 1844', translated by C. Dutt et al., in *Collected Works*, Volume 3, London: Lawrence & Wishart.

Marx, Karl 1987b [1844], 'Letters from the *Deutsch-Französische Jahrbücher*', translated by C. Dutt et al., in *Collected Works*, Volume 3, London: Lawrence & Wishart.

Marx, Karl 1987c [1844], 'Contribution to the Critique of Hegel's Philosophy of Law. Introduction', translated by C. Dutt et al., in *Collected Works*, Volume 3, London: Lawrence & Wishart.

Marx, Karl 1988 [1873], 'Political Indifferentism', in *Collected Works*, Volume 23, London: Lawrence & Wishart.

Marx, Karl 1990 [1867], *Capital, A Critique of Political Economy, Volume 1*, translated by B. Fowkes, London: Penguin Books.

Marx, Karl 1993 [1939], *Grundrisse: Foundations of the Critique of Political Economy (Rough Draft)*, translated by M. Nicolaus, London: Penguin/New Left Review.

Marx, Karl 2019 [1970], 'The Eighteenth Brumaire of Louis Bonaparte', in *The Political Writings*, London/New York: Verso, pp. 477–583.

Medvedev, Pavel Nikolaevich 2004, 'Tolstoi's Diary', translated by D. Shepherd, in C. Brandist et al. (eds), *The Bakhtin Circle: In the Master's Absence*, Manchester: Manchester University Press, pp. 188–92.

Mendes-Flohr, Paul R. 1983, '"To Brush History Against the Grain": The Eschatology of the Frankfurt School and Ernst Bloch', *Journal of the American Academy of Religion*, 51(4), pp. 631–50.

Mieszkowski, Jan 2009. 'Who's Afraid of Anacoluthon?' *Modern Language Notes*, 124(3), pp. 648–65.

Mieszkowski, Jan 2019, *Crises of the Sentence*, Chicago: The University of Chicago Press.

Moder, Gregor 2017, 'The Germ of Death: Purposive Causality in Hegel', *Crisis & Critique*, 4(1), pp. 275–91.

Moir, Cat 2013, 'The Education of Hope: On the Dialectical Potential of Speculative Materialism', in S. Žižek and P. Thompson (eds), *The Privatization of Hope: Ernst Bloch and the Future of Utopia*, Durham, NC: Duke University Press, pp. 121–43.

Moir, Cat 2019a, *Ernst Bloch's Speculative Materialism: Ontology, Epistemology, Politics*, Leiden/Boston: Brill.

Moir, Cat 2019b, 'The Birth of Materialism out of the Spirit of Expressionism: Nietzsche and Bloch's Philosophy of Language', *Revue, Internationale de Philosophie*, 3(289), pp. 303–32.

Moir, Cat 2020, 'The Archimedean Point: Consciousness, Praxis, and the Present in Lukács and Bloch', *Thesis Eleven*, 157(1), pp. 3–23.

Moir, Cat, and Johan Siebers 2011, 'Übersetzung als Utopie bei Bloch. Über die Schwierigkeit der Überschreiten', in F. Vidal (ed.), *Bloch-Jahrbuch*, Mössingen-Talheim: Talheimer Verlag, pp. 171–88.

Moltmann, Jürgen 1978, 'Plötzlich, in einem Augenblick, beim Tod der letzten Posaune', in K. Bloch and A. Reif (eds), *'Denken heißt Überschreiten': In memoriam Ernst Bloch, 1885–1977*, Köln: Europäische Verlagsanstalt, pp. 70–7.

Moltmann, Jürgen 2010, *Sun of Righteousness, Arise! God's Future for Humanity and the Earth*, translated by M. Kohl, London: SCM Press.

Morris, Pam 1994, 'Introduction', in P. Morris (ed.), *The Bakhtin Reader: Selected Writings of Bakhtin, Medvedev and Voloshinov*, London: Edward Arnold, pp. 1–24.

Mosse, George L. 1999, *The Fascist Revolution: Toward a General Theory of Fascism*, New York: Howard Fertig.

Most, Glenn W. 2019, 'Anacoluthon: A Sentence by Kafka', *Literary Imagination*, 21(3), pp. 241–55.

Münster, Arno 1982, *Utopie, Messianismus und Apokalypse im Frühwerk von Ernst Bloch*, Frankfurt am Main, Suhrkamp.

Münster, Arno 1986, 'Positive Utopie Versus Negative Dialektik: Geschichtsphilosophie, Ethik, Utopie, Negativität im Denken von Adorno, Lukács und Ernst Bloch', in G. Flego and W. Schmied-Kowarzik (eds), *Ernst Bloch – Utopische Ontologie. Band II des Bloch-Lukács-Symposiums 1985 in Dubrovnik*, Bochum: Germinal Verlag, pp. 71–85.

Münster, Arno 1987, 'Blochs spekulativer Materialismus (Ontologie des Noch-Nicht-Seins) und Materiebegriff in Ernst Blochs marxistischer Philosophie', *Synthesis Philosophica*, 4(2), pp. 571–80.

Natorp, Paul 2015 [1912], 'Kant and the Marburg School', translated by F. Bottenberg, in S. Luft (ed.), *The Neo-Kantian Reader*, London: Routledge, pp. 180–97.

Negt, Oskar 1975, 'Ernst Bloch, the German Philosopher of the October Revolution', translated by J. Zipes, *New German Critique*, 4, pp. 3–16.

Newmark, Kevin 2012, *Irony on Occasion: From Schlegel and Kierkegaard to Derrida and De Man*, New York: Fordham University Press.

Norris, Chris 1989, 'Utopian Deconstruction: Ernst Bloch, Paul de Man and the Politics of Music', in C. Norris (ed.), *Music and the Politics of Culture*, London: Lawrence & Wishart, pp. 305–47.

Pannenberg, Wolfhart 1968, 'The God of Hope', *Cross Currents*, 18(3), pp. 284–95.

Pasolini, Pier Paolo 2005, 'From the Laboratory (Notes *en poète* for a Marxist Linguistics)', translated by B. Lawton and L.K. Barnett, ed. L.K. Barnett, Washington, DC: New Academia Publishing, pp. 50–76.

Peirce, Charles Sanders 1998, *The Essential Peirce: Selected Philosophical Writings, Volume 2, 1893–1913*, Bloomington: Indiana University Press.

Pelletier, Lucien 2018, 'Ernst Bloch's Ontological Realism, Considered from its Sources', in R.E. Zimmermann (ed.), *Ontologische Probleme der Grundlegung nach Schelling und Bloch*, Hamburg: Verlag Dr. Kovač, pp. 29–49.

Poli, Roberto 2006, 'The Ontology of What is Not There', in J. Malinowski and A. Pietruszczak (eds), *Essays in Logic and Ontology*, Amsterdam: Rodopi, pp. 73–80.

Poli, Roberto 2009, 'The Complexity of Anticipation', *Balkan Journal of Philosophy*, 1(1), pp. 19–29.

Poli, Roberto 2010, 'The Many Aspects of Anticipation', *Foresight*, 12(3), pp. 7–17.

Poli, Roberto 2011, 'Steps Towards an Explicit Ontology of the Future', *Journal of Future Studies*, 16(1), pp. 67–78.

Poli, Roberto 2017, *Introduction to Anticipation Studies*, Cham: Springer.

Poli, Roberto 2019, 'Pragmatic Utopias', in R. Poli and M. Valerio (eds), *Anticipation, Agency and Complexity*, Cham: Springer, pp. 1–10.

Ponzio, Augusto 1993, *Signs, Dialogue and Ideology*, translated by S. Petrilli, Amsterdam: John Benjamins Publishing Company.

Poulantzas, Nicos 2014, *State, Power, Socialism*, translated by P. Camiller, introduction by S. Hall, London/New York: Verso.

Poulantzas, Nicos 2018, *Fascism and Dictatorship: The Third International and the Problem of Fascism*, translated by J. White, London/New York: Verso.

Rancière, Jacques 2016, 'The Senses and Uses of Utopia', in S.D. Chrostowska and J.D. Ingram (eds), *Political Uses of Utopia: New Marxists, Anarchist, and Radical Democratic Perspectives*, New York: Columbia University Press, pp. 219–32.

Ratajczak, Miklaj 2018, 'Language and Value: The Philosophy of Language in the Post-Operaist Critique of Contemporary Capitalism', *Language Sciences*, 70, pp. 118–30.

Richter, Gerhard 2000, 'Adorno's Scars, Bloch's Anacoluthon', *German Politics & Society*, 18(4), pp. 93–112.

Rickert, Heinrich 2015 [1934], 'Knowing and Cognizing. Critical Remarks on Theoretical Intuitionism', translated by J. Burmeister, in S. Luft (ed.), *The Neo-Kantian Reader*, London: Routledge, pp. 384–95.

Ricoeur, Paul 2013, *Being, Essence and Substance in Plato and Aristotle: Course Taught at the University of Strasbourg in 1953–1954*, translated by D. Pellauer and J. Starkey, Cambridge: Polity Press.

Riley, Dylan 2019, *The Civic Foundations of Fascism in Europe: Italy, Spain, and Romania, 1870–1945*, London/New York: Verso.

Roberts, John 2006, *Philosophizing the Everyday: Revolutionary Praxis and the Fate of Cultural Theory*, London: Pluto Press.

Roberts, John 2011, *The Necessity of Errors*, London/New York: Verso.

Rose, Gillian 2009, *Hegel Contra Sociology*, London/New York: Verso.

Rose, Gillian 2017, *Judaism and Modernity: Philosophical Essays*, London/New York: Verso.

Rosiello, Luigi 2010, 'Linguistics and Marxism in the Thought of Antonio Gramsci', translated and edited by R. Lacorte and P. Ives, *Gramsci, Language, and Translation*, Lanham, MD: Lexington Books, pp. 29–49.

Rossi-Landi, Ferruccio 1992, *Between Signs and Non-signs*, ed. S. Petrilli, Philadelphia: John Benjamins Publishing Company.

Rowe, M.W. 2011, *Philip Larkin: Art and Self. Five Studies*, Basingstoke: Palgrave.

Saage, Richard 2016, 'Is the Classical Concept of Utopia Ready for the Future?', in S.D. Chrostowska and J.D. Ingram (eds), *Political Uses of Utopia: New Marxists, Anarchist, and Radical Democratic Perspectives*, New York: Columbia University Press, pp. 57–79.

Sanders, W. 2014, 'Anakoluth', in G. Ueding (ed.), *Historische Wörterbuch der Rhetorik*, Berlin: Walter de Gruyter, pp. 485–95.

Sapir, Edward 2014 [1921], *Language: An Introduction to the Study of Speech*, Cambridge: Cambridge University Press.

Saussure, Ferdinand de 2011 [1916], *Course in General Linguistics*, translated by W. Baskin, edited by P. Meisel and H. Saussy, New York: Columbia University Press.

Sayre, Robert, and Michael Löwy 1984, 'Figures of Romantic Anti-Capitalism', *New German Critique*, 32, pp. 42–92.

Schmidt, Alfred 1978a, 'Der letzte Metaphysiker des Marxismus', in K. Bloch and A. Reif (eds), *'Denken heißt Überschreiten': In Memoriam Ernst Bloch, 1885–1977*, Köln: Europäische Verlagsanstalt, pp. 62–6.

Schmidt, Burghart 1978b, 'Zum Werk Ernst Blochs', in K. Bloch and A. Reif (eds), *'Denken heißt Überschreiten': In Memoriam Ernst Bloch, 1885–1977*, Köln: Europäische Verlagsanstalt, pp. 299–307.

Schneider, Volker 2006, 'Das "Daß" als subjektiver Teil des "Noch-Nicht"', *VorSchein*, 25/26, pp. 65–84.

Siebers, Johan 2011, '"Aufenthalt im inerhörten": Bloch's Reading of Hegel (1926–65)', *Oxford German Studies*, 40(1), pp. 62–71.

Siebers, Johan 2012a, 'Novum', in B. Dietschy, D. Zeilinger, and R.E. Zimmermann (eds), *Bloch-Wörterbuch: Leitbegriffe der Philosophie Ernst Blochs*, Berlin: De Gruyter, pp. 412–16.

Siebers, Johan 2012b, 'Front', in B. Dietschy, D. Zeilinger, and R.E. Zimmermann (eds), *Bloch-Wörterbuch: Leitbegriffe der Philosophie Ernst Blochs*, Berlin: De Gruyter, pp. 161–4.

Siebers, Johan 2012c, 'Ultimum', in B. Dietschy, D. Zeilinger, and R.E. Zimmermann (eds), *Bloch-Wörterbuch: Leitbegriffe der Philosophie Ernst Blochs*, Berlin: De Gruyter, pp. 582–9.

Siebers, Johan 2013, 'The Utopian Horizon of Communication: Ernst Bloch's *Traces* and Johann-Peter Hebel's *The Treasure Chest*', in R.D. Sell et al. (eds), *The Ethics of Communication: Genuineness, Directness, Indirectness*, Amsterdam: John Benjamins Publishing Company, pp. 189–212.

Simmel, Georg 2011, *The Philosophy of Money*, translated by T. Bottomore and D. Frisby, London/New York: Routledge.

Simoniti, Jure 2015, 'Hegel's Logic as the Exposition of God from the End of the World', *Filozofija i Društvo*, 26(4), pp. 852–74.

Smith, Daniel Lynwood 2012, *The Rhetoric of Interruption: Speech-Making, Turn-Taking, and Rule-Breaking in Luke-Acts and Ancient Greek Narrative*, Berlin/Boston: De Gruyter.

Smith, Michael G. 2010, 'The Tenacity of Forms: Language, Nation, Stalin', in C. Brandist and K. Chown (eds), *Politics and the Theory of Language in the USSR 1917–1938: The Birth of Sociological Linguistics*, London/New York/Delhi: Anthem Press, pp. 105–22.

Stein, Gertrude 1973, *How to Write*, Barton: Something Else Press.

Steiner, George 1965, 'The Pythagorean Genre', in S. Unseld (ed.), *Ernst Bloch zu ehren*, Frankfurt am Main: Suhrkamp, pp. 327–43.

Steiner, George 1985, *Language and Silence, Essays 1958–1966*, London: Faber & Faber.

Sućeska, Alen 2018, 'A Gramscian Reading of Language in Bakhtin and Voloshinov', *Language Sciences*, 70, pp. 179–92.

Surber, Jere O'Neill 2006, 'Introduction', in J.O. Surber (ed.), *Hegel and Language*, Albany: State University of New York Press, pp. 1–34.

Susman, Margarete 1992, '*Das Nah- und Fernsein des Fremden'. Essays und Briefe*, ed. I. Nordmann, Frankfurt am Main: Jüdischer Verlag.

Taylor, Seth 1990, *Left-Wing Nietzscheans: The Politics of German Expressionism 1910–1920*, Berlin/New York: Walter de Gruyter.

Thompson, Michael J. 2011, 'Introduction: Recovering Lukács's Relevance for the Present', in M.J. Thompson (ed.), *Georg Lukács Reconsidered: Critical Essays in Politics, Philosophy and Aesthetics*, London: Continuum, pp. 1–9.

Thompson, Michael J. 2020, 'Marx, Lukács and the Groundwork of Critical Social Ontology', in M.J. Thompson (ed.), *Georg Lukács and the Possibility of Critical Social Ontology*, Leiden/Boston: Brill, pp. 419–55.

Tihanov, Galin 1998, 'Vološinov, Ideology, and Language: The Birth of Marxist Sociology from the Spirit of *Lebensphilosophie*', *The South Atlantic Quarterly*, 97(3/4), pp. 599–621.

Tihanov, Galin 2000, *The Master and the Slave: Lukács, Bakhtin, and the Ideas of their Time*, Oxford: Oxford University Press.

Toscano, Alberto 2017, 'Notes on Late Fascism', *Historical Materialism*, available at: http://www.historicalmaterialism.org/blog/notes-late-fascism (accessed 14 July 2020).

Traverso, Enzo 2019, *The New Faces of Fascism: Populism and the Far Right*, translated by D. Broder, London/New York: Verso.

Tronti, Mario 2019, *Workers and Capital*, translated by D. Broder, London/New York: Verso.

Vickers, Brian 2002, *In Defence of Rhetoric*, Oxford: Oxford University Press.

Vilmar, Fritz 1965, 'Welt als Laboratorium Salutis: Zur Aufhebung von Transzendenz und Immanenz in der Philosophie Ernst Blochs', in S. Unseld (ed.), *Ernst Bloch zu ehren, Beiträge zu seinem Werk*, Frankfurt am Main: Suhrkamp, pp. 121–34.

Virno, Paolo 2004, *A Grammar of the Multitude: For an Analysis of Contemporary Forms of Life*, translated by I. Bertoletti, J. Cascaito, and A. Casson, South Pasadena: Semiotext(e).

Virno, Paolo 2011, 'Wit and Innovation', in G. Raunig, G. Ray, and U. Wuggenig (eds), *Critique of Creativity: Precarity, Subjectivity and Resistance in 'Creative Industries'*, London: MayFlyBooks, pp. 101–5.

Virno, Paolo 2015, *When the Word Becomes Flesh: Language and Human Nature*, translated by G. Mecchia, South Pasadena: Semiotext(e).

Virno, Paolo 2018, *An Essay on Negation: Towards A Linguistic Anthropology*, translated by L. Chiesa, Kolkata: Seagull Books.

Vivian, Bradford 2021, 'The Incitement: An Account of Language, Power, and Fascism', *Rhetoric Society Quarterly*, 51(5), pp. 361–76.

Voloshinov, Valentin Nikolaevich 1973, *Marxism and the Philosophy of Language*, translated by L. Matejka and I.R. Titunik, New York: Seminar Press.

Voloshinov, Valentin 2004, 'Report on Work as a Postgraduate Student, 1927/28', translated by C. Brandist and D. Shepherd, in C. Brandist et al. (eds), *The Bakhtin Circle: In the Master's Absence*, Manchester: Manchester University Press, pp. 226–50.

Voloshinov, Valentin 2012, *Freudianism: A Marxist Critique*, translated by I.R. Titunik, London/New York: Verso.

Walker, Gavin 2019, '*The Eighteenth Brumaire of Louis Bonaparte* (1852)', in J. Diamanti, A. Pendakis, and I. Szeman (eds), *The Bloomsbury Companion to Marx*, London: Bloomsbury Academic, pp. 33–40.

Wallace, William 1977, *Elements of Philosophy: A Compendium for Philosophers and Theologians*, Eugene: Wipf & Stock.

Webb, Darren 2002, 'Here Content Transcends Phrase: The Eighteenth Brumaire as the Key to Understanding Marx's Critique of Utopian Socialism', in M. Cowling and J. Martin (eds), *Marx's Eighteenth Brumaire: (Post)modern Interpretations*, London: Pluto Press, pp. 243–57.

Weber, Andreas, and Francisco J. Varela 2002, 'Life After Kant: Natural Purposes and the Autopoietic Foundations of Biological Individuality', *Phenomenology and the Cognitive Sciences*, 1, pp. 97–125.

White, Alan 2014, *Towards a Philosophical Theory of Everything: Contributions to the Structural-Systematic Philosophy*, London: Bloomsbury Academic.

Willey, Thomas E. 1978, *Back to Kant: The Revival of Kantianism in German Social and Historical Thought, 1860–1914*, Detroit: Wayne State University Press.

Williams, Raymond 1977, *Marxism and Literature*, Oxford: Oxford University Press.

Williams, Raymond 2005, *Culture and Materialism*, London/New York: Verso.

Witschel, Günter 1978, *Ernst Bloch, Literatur und Sprache: Theorie und Leistung*, Bonn: Bouvier Verlag.

Wittgenstein, Ludwig 1974, *Tractatus Logico-Philosophicus*, translated by D.F. Pears and B.F. McGuinness, London/New York: Routledge.

Zeilinger, Doris 2012, 'Tendenz', in B. Dietschy, D. Zeilinger, and R.E. Zimmermann (eds), *Bloch-Wörterbuch: Leitbegriffe der Philosophie Ernst Blochs*, Berlin: De Gruyter, pp. 555–67.

Zimmermann, Rainer E. 2001, *Subjekt und Existenz: Zur Systematik Blochscher Philosophie*, Berlin: Philo Verlag.

Zimmermann, Rainer E. 2014, *Nothingness as Ground and Nothing but Ground: Schelling's Philosophy of Nature Revisited*, Berlin: xenomoi.

Žižek, Slavoj 2013, 'Preface: Bloch's Ontology of Not-Yet-Being', in S. Žižek and P. Thompson (eds), *The Privatization of Hope: Ernst Bloch and the Future of Utopia*, Durham, NC: Duke University Press, pp. xv–x.

Zudeick, Peter 1987, *Der Hintern des Teufels; Ernst Bloch, Leben und Werk*, Bühl-Moos: Elster Verlag.

Index

www.ingramcontent.com/pod-product-compliance
Lightning Source LLC
Chambersburg PA
CBHW061737120626
46550CB00005B/1813